WALK

LOS ANGELES

Few people

know how to take a walk.

The qualifications...

are endurance, plain clothes,

old shoes, an eye

for nature, good humor,

vast curiosity,

good speech, good silence

and nothing too much.

—RALPH WALDO EMERSON

WALK

LOS ANGELES

Adventures on the Urban Edge

JOHN McKINNEY

Olympus Press
SANTA BARBARA, CALIFORNIA

Cover design and illustrations, book design and layout by Deja Hsu
Editor: Cheri Rae
Cartography: Susan Kuromiya

Acknowledgements:

For their cooperation, field- and fact-checking, the author wishes to thank the rangers and administrators of Angeles National Forest and Santa Monica Mountains National Recreation Area. Also a thanks to the Los Angeles City and County parks departments, as well as to the Santa Monica Mountains District office of the California Department of Parks and Recreation. A special thanks goes to the Santa Monica Mountains Conservancy; its hardworking employees have had a positive effect on almost half the walks in this guide! Particularly enthusiastic during the preparation of this book was Ruth Kilday, Executive Director of the Mountains Conservancy Foundation. Thanks also to the many Sierra Club members who shared the trail with me, and to friends and family members who joined me in my field research. My most heartfelt thank you goes to Olympus Press editor Cheri Rae for her encouragement and deft editorial hand.

Portions of this manuscript have appeared in the author's hiking column in the *Los Angeles Times*.

Photo Credits:

Angeles National Forest: 213; Brand Library: 93; California State Libary: 88, 165, 184, 187, 217, 228; David Crane, *Los Angeles Daily News*: 103; Duarte Parks and Recreation Department: 200; Tom Gamache: 284, 294; Linda Hardie-Scott: 295; Hollywood Chamber of Commerce: 55; Leslie Holtzman: 320; Bob Howells: 251; Los Angeles City Recreation and Parks Department: 69; Los Angeles County Visitors and Convention Bureau: 33; San Fernando Valley Historical Society: 129; Santa Clarita Valley Historical Society: 115; Santa Monica Mountains Conservancy: 56, 118, 124, 127, 132, 134, 231, 257; Marc Tulane: 253; University of Southern California Library: 269; David Werk: 73, 76, 193, 272; All other photos by John McKinney. Historic postcards from Adventures in Postcards, Sunland, California.

Library of Congress Cataloging-in-Publication Data
McKinney, John
Walk Los Angeles: Adventures on the Urban Edge / John McKinney
p. cm.
Includes index.
ISBN 0-934161-08-9 : $12.95
1. Hiking—California—Los Angeles Metropolitan Area—Guidebooks.
2. Los Angeles Metropolitan Area—Guidebooks. I. Title.
GV199.42.C22L656 1992
917.94'93—dc20   92-14887
CIP

Published by Olympus Press
P.O. Box 2397 Santa Barbara, CA 93120 (805) 965-7200

Table of Contents

Chapter VIII

✳ San Gabriel Mountains 161

Chapter IX

✳ Coast 219

Introduction

Walking on Edge

I STOOD, AT THE EDGE OF THE CITY, WATCHING IT BURN. Mayday, 1992. Los Angeles was ablaze, up in arms and up in smoke, whole city blocks set afire by people angry enough to burn down their own neighborhoods and the neighborhoods nearby.

From my view atop Mt. Hollywood in Griffith Park I could see fires consuming Koreatown, Hollywood and South Central L.A.

Hundreds of times have I walked up one of the mountains above the metropolis and contemplated the city. Sometimes it's the summit view that inspires me, sometimes it's the walk itself, but always I've returned to the bottom of the big basin with a slightly different perspective on Los Angeles.

It's my job, as *Los Angeles Times* hiking columnist, to encourage readers to follow in my footsteps— to climb the aerie heights, to walk to the edge of the city and view L.A. quietly, slowly, from a pretty place.

This day was not the first day I'd walked up a mountain above the metropolis and watched a fire; however, on every other occasion the fire I'd witnessed was a *wild*fire. I never felt particularly bad about the fires that seared the slopes of the Santa Monica Mountains, the San Gabriel Mountains or the Hollywood Hills. A brushfire removes dead wood, relieves floral overcrowding, gives healthy plants room to grow. Chaparral, the hardy heather that blankets the foothills, has not only evolved to live with fire; it actually requires it for good health. "Nature's way of cleaning house," naturalists say.

The first spring after a fire brings a profusion of wildflowers—popppies, lupine and white violet and azure clouds of ceanothus blossoms. A testimonial it is to nature's power of regeneration after disaster.

But the fire that I was watching was not a natural occurence in a natural world, it was a wholly manmade creation in a wholly artificial world. Apocalyptic, it seemed to me. Sinners in the hands of an angry God. Maybe what I was watching wasn't the end of civilization, but it was damn close—civilization's farthest edge, its meanest edge.

I stared into the flames for a very long time, wondering how a city that had long sold itself as an Eden could so much resemble The Inferno.

Truly, I am way out of my depth as a sociologist to explain the breakdown of the city's social systems—the racial polarity, economic disenfranchisement, crime and violence. I shall leave it to better minds than mine to produce the sort of political-aesthetic-economic treatise that can move governments to action.

And I might be just a little bit out of my depth, (scientifically speaking anyway), as an ecologist to explain how the city's once healthy ecosystems—clean air, clean water, green space—became befouled. Or why.

What little enlightenment I can offer comes from having walked the land we call L.A., from studying it in its many moods. I am interested, fascinated, by the less-explored, wild side of Los Angeles. It seems to me we already spend too much time building Los Angeles County and not enough time knowing it.

The edges between the natural and built environments ingrigue me as a writer. What absorbs me are the edges, the margins between the natural world and what political commentators call "America's first Third World City."

I've resided in many parts of this city: Hoover Boulevard by U.S.C., Topanga Canyon, Whittier, Downey, Glendale, Venice, East L.A. and West L.A., Santa Clarita and Santa Monica. I've lived in neighborhoods where the people were as bland as the whitewashed walls of their neat stucco homes, and in neighborhoods where the sights and sounds reflected the full cultural diversity of L.A. Wherever I have lived—and where I haven't lived—I've walked, trying to get to know the land, the faces on the land.

I've walked some of the world's other great cities, too: New York, London, Rome, and a dozen more. And I've walked a couple cities far, far more divided than Los Angeles: Berlin before the wall came down; Nicosia, Cyprus, where the so-called green line divides the capital city into Greek and Turkish sectors. I know what barbed wire and barricades bring.

Always, it's been my experience that the best way to explore a city—even a divided one—is on foot. It's the best way to explore the countryside too, as I've discovered while hiking in three dozen states, a dozen foreign countries. You get the most from nature, and the best of human nature, when you journey afoot.

Still, no matter where or how far I roam, I keep coming back to walk L.A., a native son who can't stay away.

The edges of this city have always fascinated me, always beckoned me to explore: the edges hidden from view, the edges between populous valleys and lonesome mountains, the edge between the shore and the sundown sea, the edges between neighborhoods and between neighbors of different colors.

Especially fascinating to me—a nature writer—are nature's edges. By edges I mean the rag-tag remnants of the natural world that surround the metropolis. Edges are places that don't quite fit, anomalies of metropolitan life.

Ecologists say many of the most interesting and dynamic habitats are on the edges: places where the forest meets a meadowland, where the land meets the sea, where the city meets the country.

Here plants and animals confront conditions that give rise to increased variety. Studies of Southern California bird populations reveal that species are more abundant in places where the chaparral meets the pine forest than in chaparral-only or forest-only environments. Various plants and animals that might be rare in one community or the other may flourish on the edge between them.

Similarly, life is abundant in the intertidal zone, the edge between land and sea. The ocean is wet and the land is dry, but the line separating them is never the same from one minute to the next. When the tide is high, the sandy bottom and tidepools provide nourishment for fish; when the tide is low, birds claim the zone and eat intertidal residents.

These areas of transition between ecological communities are called ecotones: their existence depends on two differing environments, yet they also create a world unto themselves.

States George Clarke in his classic text, Elements of Ecology: "As a rule the ecotone contains more species and often a denser population than either of the neighboring communities, and this is generally known as The Principle of Edges."

At nature's edge, there is variety, but with this variety comes tension. The hardy, sun-drenched chaparral plants approaching the pine forest must cope with the shade preferred by—and created by—the forest. Soil composition and nutrients where one community thrives might not benefit the other. A wildfire that sweeps such an edge will benefit the chaparral community but may destroy the pine forest community for a century, or forever.

On the edge of the city, what city planners in the peculiar jargon of their trade call "the urban-rural interface," there is also variety and tension. In particular, alien, that is to say, non-native trees and shrubs battle native species for land and light. Since almost anything can—and does—grow under the Southland sun, many a plant escapes the garden and grows wild, often displacing native members of the chaparral and coastal scrub community.

At the edges of Los Angeles, it is not merely differing plant communities that conflict; differing people conflict. The ecotones of human life—places where various cultures and ethnicities meet—are also enriched with variety but filled with tension.

From time immemorial, it's been the lot of neighboring peoples to make contact with trade, although fighting has all too often been the result instead. In today's multi-cultural metropolis, various ethnic and economic groups have learned, after a fashion, to get along with each other, although there is still often tension.

And violence, mayhem, madness.

People feel on the edge. Pastor Cecil L. Murray of the First AME Church, home of Los Angeles' oldest black congregation, said after the riots. "The people have been fed sour grapes and their teeth are set on edge."

To which I would add, some of the sour grapes are a result of letting nature die on the vine, of allowing neighborhoods to become concrete jungles without trees and pathways.

City leaders have called for the "greening" of disadvantaged areas; by green they mean the color of money, which should be spent, they say, rebuilding burned-out and riot-torn areas and increasing economic opporunities. Certainly greenbacks are needed to revive these areas, but I'd also suggest adding another kind of green to the city: some green space in the form of parks and pathways.

It's no coincidence that the most civil disturbance took place in the most environmentally disturbed parts of the city, in the most park-poor and pedestrian unfriendly areas. We've watched far too many experiments with crowded rats and impossible mazes not to know better: unnatural behavior occurs in un-natural environments.

As we restore the city, we must restore the land. You can prune and shape a tree, but it won't thrive if its roots are rotten. Somehow, in all this talk of Los Angeles as first world or third world, we forgot about the green world.

Green streets are not mean streets. Places where people walk—city plazas or mountain parks—are common ground, an environment where we can come together. The more green the ground, the gentler, the more fruitful, our coming together is likely to be.

Making the urban scene more green requires work on a

number of levels. It means just saying "No" to developments high on precipitous slopes and in the bottom of pristine canyons. It means adding some parks and leaving some open spaces in the older, more developed parts of the metropolis. It means restoring the Los Angeles River to some semblance of a natural waterway, with a greenway alongside of it, to link, literally and symbolically, the diverse neighborhoods of the city.

I hope that in some small way this book—and the walks it inspires—contributes to the regeneration of the land, the rebirth of the city. Like the tenacious chaparral that rises from the ashes stronger and more beautiful than ever before, may Los Angeles flower once again.

The View
From Sandstone Peak

WHEN I WAS 11, IT WAS THE HIGHEST PEAK IN THE world. It was place where eagles soared, mountain lions lurked, Chumash Indian spirits dwelled. Remote it was, and regal. The great shoulders of the mountain were perfumed with sage. A crown of red rock touched the heavens. Often the peak was enshrouded in fog, activating a tenderfoot scout's already over-active imagination. It was a big mountain and more than a little scary. During my first trip to the top I shivered in my brand-new hiking boots.

Sandstone Peak, high point of the Santa Monica Mountains, was an awesome height to me and to the other Boy Scouts of Troop 441, particularly from our campsite vantage point located far below. It was an awesome ascent from the Circle X Scout Ranch to the summit, a trek through miles of chaparral. We dodged poison oak, forded a creek, clambered over big boulders. Most awesome of all was the view from the summit. We could see the whole world: Old Baldy and the Los Angeles Basin, the Channel Islands and the San Fernando Valley, the Santa Monica Mountains themselves from end to end, and much more geography that our scoutmaster patiently helped us match to our map.

It was a cruel disappointment to me to learn that Sandstone Peak (elevation 3,111 feet) was not the highest peak in the world, or even in Southern California, and that I couldn't see the whole world, or even all of the Southland from the summit. By the time I was an experienced 14-year-old hiker and an Eagle Scout, I had climbed 9,399-foot Mt. Baden-Powell, the San Gabriel Mountains peak named for the Scouts founder, 11,499-foot Mt. San Gorgonio, highest peak in Southern California, and many more two-mile high mountains.

As the years passed, my memory of the the mysterious peak hidden in the fog, and the long trail to the top of Sandstone faded away. Only the view stayed with me, a 1960s view of a Southern California that had no limits, of a land big enough, empty enough to accomodate every dream.

It was this view, from Scout days, that I carried with me one spring day to the top of Sandstone Peak. I wanted to compare my boyhood view with a view of today. I wanted to see how my part of the planet had changed.

As I headed for the hills, I managed to make myself feel a little guilty. I told myself that if if I really was a a dedicated eco-journalist I would be at my desk studying the just released report by the Los Angeles Environmental Quality Board, entitled "The State of the City's Environment Primer." (But frankly, studying the city's environment from the top of Sandstone Peak sounded like much more fun.)

The peak was part of the Scout's Circle X Ranch until 1988; now the ranch and peak belong to the Santa Monica National Recreation Area and is patrolled by the National Park Service. At the beginning of the trail is a parking area the size of an aircraft carrier and some signs, but to my relief, nothing else has changed. As I hike up Mishe Mokwa Trail, the soft colors of the high chaparral—black sage, golden yarrow, red shank, wooly blue curls—bring back memories as surely as faded Kodachrome slides.

My spirits lift as I continue up the trail. Unlike so many mountain scenes from my boyhood memory that have been destroyed by the hand of man, this one has remained intact. I pass a striking red volcanic formation, we scouts called Balanced Rock and a pyramid-like rock we called Egyptian Rock. The oak-shaded path brings me to the old trail camp and the old outhouse ("the historic four-holer") and to another aptly named rock formation—Split Rock. We Scouts long had a tradition of hiking through the narrow split in the rock. I drop my pack and honor the tradition.

I push on to Sandstone Peak. As I scramble up the rocks to the summit, I spot a blue flag. To my delight, floating in the Pacific breeze at the very top of Sandstone Peak is an Earth Day flag—a portrait of planet earth as seen from outer space etched on a blue banner.

My view of the earth isn't quite the cosmic one on the flag, but it's mighty impressive. To the east is snow-capped Mt. Baldy towering over Los Angeles. I can see the sandy sweep of Santa Monica Bay, Palos Verdes Peninsula, Catalina Island. And I can see the San Fernando Valley, the Los Padres

National Forest back of Ojai, the Channel Islands, and of course the mountains.

The Santa Monica Mountains.

My mountains.

I was born on the other side of the Santa Monica Mountains, just outside Griffith Park; in a quite literal way, these mountains are home for me. For many years, I lived in Santa Monica and looked up from the beach at the mountains that beckoned from nearby. I've lived in the most urban section of the Santa Monica Mountains—the Hollywood Hills—and in in one of the most rural parts—Topanga Canyon.

Maybe you can go home again if your home is a mountain range. Not even the awesome proximity of Los Angeles and its hundred satellite cities has succeeded in leveling the home mountains.

A fella's home mountains are where he goes on his first overnight trip with the scouts, where he learns to drive a car with a clutch, the isolated make out spot where he kisses his first girl, and later in life as a meditation site for the great issues of his day.

A lot of people have an interest in my home. The Santa Monica Mountains is the only mountain range in the U.S. that bisects a major metropolitan area. Portions of the mountains are a near wilderness within an hour's drive of six million people, and stretch all the way from Griffith Park in the heart of

Los Angeles to Pt. Mugu 50 miles away. A lot of developers say the slopes and canyons are ideal for subdivisions, which could be connected by a trans-mountains freeway.

And a lot of government agencies say they're committed to protecting my mountains—the Los Angeles County Parks Department, the California Department of Parks and Recreation, The Santa Monica Mountains Conservancy and even the National Park Service which says the home mountains are ecologically important because they're an example of Mediterranean terrain, the only such terrain in the nation in their care.

When I first looked over these mountains from Sandstone Peak, the mountains had no governmental guardians. The view west of the rugged hills and grassy valleys was that of the Broome Ranch and the Danielson Ranch; not Pt. Mugu State Park. And the view east was of private property not the Santa Monica Mountains National Recreation Area, which was not set aside by Congress until 1978.

Progress, change, in these mountains hasn't all been for the worse.

From Sandstone Peak, I can see Santa Monica Bay, from RAT (Right at Torrance) Beach to Malibu Beach. Somehow the beach meant more when you had to travel from the 'burbs to the beach. I've always imagined myself half beach boy, half mountain man, so it's always given me a charge to look down from a mountain at the home shore.

My shore.

The bay view, from this mountaintop anyway, has changed little from my youth. The pollution of the bay, the unfortunate sewage discharges, both accidental and deliberate, are not visible from afar. I rejoice that I do not look down at Malibu Nuclear Power Plant, once proposed for landslide-prone and seismically active Corral Canyon. And I rejoice that I do not see State Highway 60, the Malibu Freeway that was proposed in the 1960s.

One structure—"the plumber's nightmare" that was unsightly 25 years ago and is visible today- is the mammoth Hyperion Waste Treatment Plant. It's '50s design to the max, massive and heavy with miles of pipe; it would look right at home with a parking lot full of chrome-teethed Buick Roadmasters and Cadillac Coupe de Villes.

Below Sandstone Peak is County Line Beach. It hasn't changed a bit. Oh, the surfboards are lots smaller and the radios lots bigger than their '60s counterparts, but the vibes, good vibes, and the waves, good waves, are still the same.

From Sandstone Peak I can see the San Fernando Valley.

My valley.

It's changed a lot since 1769, when Father Juan Crespi of the Portola expedition named the Valley De Valle Santa Catalina de Bononia de los Encinos. And it's changed a lot since the '60s when my family joined the rest of Southern California on the road. Every Sunday after church my parents packed up the family station wagon and journeyed out beyond the last citrus groves to visit what seemed like every new subdivision. I can still remember the perfect model homes with their odd combination of smells: the real estate agent's after-shave, sawdust and new shag carpet, fertilizer and freshly poured asphalt and concrete. We traveled to the four corners of the valley—Agoura Hills and Granada Hills, Sherman Oaks and Thousand Oaks, and dozens of new 'burbs in between.

Today, the view of the Valley from Sandstone Peak is of a 24-mile long, 12-mile wide rectangle that has been completely urbanized, suburbanized. The view is of an almost endless suburb, of green lawns, glistening swimming pools imported trees and shurbs, parking lots and shopping malls, a strange combination of tidiness and unseemliness.

Twenty-five years ago when I looked down on the San Fernando Valley—and neighboring Simi and Conjeo Valleys—the suburban tracts were the islands on the land. How green was my valley then! Now the green spaces resemble a scattered archipelago that's fast disappearing beneath a tidal wave of development. One island visible from Sandstone Peak is Cheeseboro Canyon, just saved from development.

From Sandstone Peak I can also see real islands.

My islands.

As seen from Sandstone Peak, the Channel Islands—Anacapa, Santa Cruz, Santa Rosa and San Miguel—are a series of blue-tinged mountains floating on the horizon, out there in the Pacific where I want to be, 14 to 60 miles away. Once in a great while I can see Santa Barbara Island, way out to sea.

There's much more—both paradisiacal and polluted—to see from Sandstone Peak. I contemplate the orange cloud of mustard gas that hangs over downtown Los Angeles; it's the worst air in the nation. I look over the Basin and think how we residents curse the bowl-shaped topography encircling us and hold the Basin responsible for our stinging eyes and scratchy throats. (This, of course, is misplaced criticism, like holding the shape of the bottle responsible for the quality of the wine.) I have a condor's-eye-view of the Ojai backcountry, where biologists are attempting to reintroduce zoo-bred birds to their rocky kingdom. I look down on the Oxnard Plain and question the wisdom of converting some of our most fertile farmland into suburban housing.

I sure like the view from Sandstone Peak, but I guess if I lived in, say, Pasadena, I might climb Mt. Lowe, Mt. Lukens or Mt. Wilson in the front range of the San Gabriel Mountains to get a view of the world near my home. Elsewhere, I might climb Signal Hill for a look at the South Bay, Mt. Hollywood for a look at downtown, Mt. Bliss to view the San Gabriel Valley.

But Sandstone Peak is my place to view the home mountains, home shore, home valley, home islands.

The Earth Day flag flutters over Sandstone Peak, over the whole earth.

Your earth.

My earth.

Maybe I should rush home and finish reading the "State of the City's Environment Primer" and study the report's 94 ways we can improve metropolitan life. And I really should get to those three long articles about the greenhouse effect and those books about the rain forest piled on my desk. Or maybe I'll just stay atop Sandstone Peak a while longer, reconciling the present with the past, predicting the future from the present-day panorama at my feet.

When you're 11, you think every peak is the highest in the world. You think you can see the whole world from a place like Sandstone Peak.

Maybe you still can.

How To Use This Book

FIRST DECIDE WHERE YOU WANT TO WALK. MT. Washington? Mt. Baldy? Downtown? San Gabriel Valley? Palos Verdes? Pick a walk in your geographical area of interest. Next, turn to the corresponding walk description in the main body of the book.

Unsure of what to expect in the Santa Monica, San Gabriel or Verdugo Mountains? Read the chapter introductions.

More than one hundred walks are described in this guide. Add the options and you can design a hundred more walks.

Beneath the name of the trail is a capsule summary, or Highlights of the walk.

Following the Highlights, is the Distance from the trailhead to one or more destinations.

Mileage, expressed in round trip figures, follows each destination. The walks in this guide range from one to twelve miles. Gain or loss in elevation follows the mileage. In matching a walk to your ability, you'll want to consider both mileage and elevation as well as condition of the trail, terrain and season. Hot, exposed chaparral or miles of boulder-hopping can make a short walk seem long.

You may wish to use the following guideline: A walk suitable for beginners and children would be less than 5 miles with an elevation gain of less than 700-800 feet. A moderate walk is considered a walk in the 5 to 10 mile range, with less than a 2,000-foot elevation gain. You should be reasonably fit for these. Preteens sometimes find the going difficult. Walks over 10 miles, and those with more than a 2,000-foot gain are for experienced walkers in top form.

Season is the next item to consider. Although Los Angeles is one of the few places in the country that offers four-season hiking, some climactic restrictions must be heeded. You can walk all of the trails in this guide all year with just a few exceptions: Snow closes the trails to Mt. Islip, Mt. Baldy and sometimes Mt. Wilson. High water can close canyon walks in the San Gabriel Mountains and elsewhere. Particularly prone to flooding are Big Tujunga Canyon and Eaton Canyon.

Closure for fire season is the chief restriction in certain

state park and national forest areas. Length of closure (or whether an area closes at all) varies from jurisdiction to jurisdiction, depending on the year's rainfall. At one time some sections of national forest closed automatically on July 1 and did not open up again until after the first heavy rain of winter. Now, however, forest closure is more infrequent and on the front range of the San Gabriel Mountains, where the walks in this guide take place, it is a rare occurrence.

Directions take you from the nearest major highway to trailhead parking. For trails having two desirable trailheads, directions to each are given. A few trails can be walked one way, with the possibility of a car shuttle. Suggested car shuttle points are noted.

You may notice a slight L.A. bias to the directions (no doubt prompted by my years as *Los Angeles Times* hiking columnist). For the sake of clarity and orientation, I've chosen downtown L.A. as a reference point. It seems to me, L.A. is as good a place to leave from as any. My apologies to Downey, Duarte, Pomona.

An introduction to each walk describes what you'll see: plants, animals, panoramic views. You'll also learn about the geologic and human history of the region.

After the highlights, distance, directions and introduction, you'll read a description of The Walk. Important junctions and major sights are pointed out, but I've left you to discover the multitude of little things that make a walk an adventure.

WALKING

Choose the pace that's best for you. Rest once an hour for a few minutes. To keep your momentum and to avoid stiffness, several shorter rest periods are better than one long one. Set a steady pace, one you can keep up all day. Wear a watch, not because you have an appointment with a waterfall and you have to be punctual, but because a watch gives you some idea of pace and helps you get back to the trailhead before dark.

Walking uphill takes energy. Walking 2 miles an hour up a 10 percent grade requires as much energy as hiking 4 miles an hour on level trail.

Climbing can be especially difficult at high altitude. Altitude sickness affects some walkers at about 8,000 feet. (Only a few walks in this guide are above this elevation.) Altitude can cause discomfort—shortness of breath, headache and nausea above 5,000 feet.

Walking alone or with company is strictly a matter of personal preference. Having two or three in your party is a definite advantage if something goes wrong; someone can go for help. Walking with a group is a good idea for first-time walkers. Most inexperienced walkers are uncomfortable going solo.

Sometimes, after a few walks, a craving for solitude develops—by which time you should be able to take care of yourself on the trail. There's a lot to be said for solitary hiking, as the writings of Thoreau, Whitman and Muir reveal.

Alas, travelers on the urban edge are not always immune from big-city attitudes, stresses and crimes. While most of parks and preserves visited in this guide are far safer than city streets, walkers—particularly women walkers—must be aware that unsavory characters are not unknown on the trail. Your "street smarts" coupled with your trail sense are two keys to avoiding trouble.

Know that park and national forest authorities are committed to protecting the public. Many of the "rangers" you see on patrol are California peace officers—meaning they have the authority to write citations, make arrests, etc., just like their city cop counterparts. Call on them if you feel at all uncomfortable about anyone/anything; they're dedicated to not only protecting the land, but public safety as well.

Equipping for a Walk

M OST WALKS REQUIRE LITTLE MORE EQUIPMENT than comfortable shoes, yet walkers often overburden themselves with nonessentials. The idea with equipment is to take only what you need. You want to get so comfortable with your equipment that you don't think about it; what little you need is on your back and what you don't need is far away.

Footwear: Walking begins and ends with the feet. You've no

doubt seen walkers wearing everything from old sneakers to World War II combat boots. For decades, lug-soled boots were considered mandatory, but if you're carrying a day pack over easy terrain you don't need a heavy pair of boots. Running, city-walking or cross-training shoes can serve to get you started. But if you do much walking over rough terrain, a good pair of boots is necessary and well worth the money. A lightweight pair with a sturdy sole will do nicely. Don't buy more boot than you need. Blisters can ruin any walk, so be sure to break-in your shoes before you hit the trail.

A number of fine walking shoes and running shoe/hiking boot combinations on the market will give you miles of comfortable walking.

Clothing: You already own most of what you need.

A T-shirt with a cotton shirt that buttons gives you lots of temperature regulating possibilities. Add a wool shirt and a windbreaker with a hood and you'll be protected against sudden changes in temperatures.

Shorts are useful much of the year in Southern California. Test your shorts to make sure they're not too tight. Step up on a chair and if they pull around the groin, butt or thigh, they're too tight.

For cooler days or walking through brush, a sturdy pair of long pants is necessary.

Hats prevent the brain from frying and protect from heat loss when it is cold.

Sunglasses are a big help when walking over snow or on hot, exposed slopes. Make sure you buy a pair that provides UV protection.

Rainwear: An inexpensive water-resistant jacket is okay unless you walk through brush. Some of the new breathable, high-tech fabric laminates are superb, but expensive.

Food: On a day walk, weight is no problem, so you can pack whatever you wish. Remember to pack out what you pack in. The day you walk is not the day to diet. There's a lot of calorie burning on a walk and quite an energy cost. You'll need all your strength, particularly on steep grades. Gorp, or trail mix, with fruit, nuts, raisins, and M&M's is good high-octane fuel. A sandwich, fruit and cookies make a good lunch. A continental spread featuring sourdough bread, a fine cheese and a splash of chablis is also nice. Avoid a big lunch. Exertion after a big lunch sets up a competition between your stomach and your legs and your legs lose, leading to weakness and indigestion.

Water: It's still possible to drink from some local creeks and springs without ill effect, but I highly recommend against drinking any untreated water. Many walkers assume water is pure and 48 hours later have a queasy feeling that tells them that their assumption was wrong. Water may harbor the organism *Giardia Lamblia*, one of the causes of "traveler's diarrhea." Treat any backcountry drinking water with purification tablets and/or a filter.

First Aid Kit: A standard kit supplement with an ace bandage in the event of walker's knee or a sprained ankle. Take moleskin for blisters. Insect repellant won't stop mosquitos from buzzing around but it will inhibit their biting. Bring asprin or a pain reliever in case of a headache. Sunscreen, with the proper protection factor for your individual skin tone, is important in our sunny climate. A pocket knife, a compass, a flashlight round out what the Sierra Club hike leaders like to call "The Ten Essentials."

Day Pack: A day pack is a soft frameless pack that attaches to your shoulders and sometimes includes a hip band or waist belt for support. A good one will last a lifetime. Those thin cotton or nylon bike bags or book bags won't hold up well. Shoulder pads are a nice feature in a day pack. You'll only be carrying five or ten pounds, but the pads are comfortable on a long walk. Get one with a tough covered zipper. Double-O rings slip and aren't the greatest shoulder strap adjusters. Get tabler buckles; they don't slip and they adjust quickly.

Fanny packs have their fans among walkers. Buy a good one with ample padding and storage. Look for rugged, covered zippers and easy access to pouches. Be sure the pack you choose allows you to comfortably carry water bottles.

PRECAUTIONS

We still react in instinctive ways when we feel threatened by some aspect of the natural world. Don't let the few biters, stingers, and hazards mentioned below make you apprehensive about heading for the hills.

Blisters: There's nothing worse than walking on feet that burn like hot coals. To avoid blisters, make sure your boots fit properly. Keep pulling up your socks and see to it that they don't bunch up. Act quickly if you feel a blister develop. Cut a hole in moleskin a little larger than your red spot and stick it in place with the blister poking through the hole. The idea is to surround it so the boot can't get at it. (If you covered it you could irritate it further and you'd have to peel the tape off the blister. Ouch!) Some walkers put a double layer of tissue paper over the blister and tape the tissue in place with surgical tape. If you get a full grown blister, pop it with a clean needle inserted under the edge and apply antiseptic, then put moleskin over the area.

Poison Oak: This infamous plant grows abundantly throughout Southern California mountains up to an elevation of 5,000 feet. It's a sneaky devil. It may lurk under other shrubs or take the form of a vine and climb up an oak tree. The leaves are one to four inches long and glossy, as if waxed.

All parts of the plant at all times of the year contain poisonous sap that can severely blister skin and mucous membranes. Its sap is most toxic during spring and summer. In fall, poison oak is particularly conspicuous; its leaves turn to flaming crimson or orange. However, its color change is more a response to heat and dryness than season; its "fall color" can occur anytime in Southern California. Leaves on some plants can be turning  yellow or red while plants in most spots are putting out green leaves. In winter, poison oak is naked, its stalks blending into the dull hue of the forest.

Contrary to popular belief, you can't catch it from someone else's rash, nor from oozing blisters, but petting an animal or handling clothing that carries it can make you a victim.

There are many remedies. Perhaps most common is the regular application of calamine lotion or cortisone cream. If you're particularly sensitive to poison oak, always wash down thoroughly immediately after a walk with cold water and a basic soap such as laundry detergent. Launder your hiking clothing separately as soon as possible. A dip in the ocean can help; a few tablespoons of baking soda added to a tub of lukewarm water calms the itchies as well. You organic types will probably want to pick some mugwort, an effective panacea. Its fresh juice applied directly to the pained area relieves itching.

Rattlesnakes: Like typical Southern Californians, rattlesnakes take to the trail to enjoy the sunshine, so keep an eye out. Despite the common fear of rattlers, few people see them and rarely is anyone bitten. An estimated 300 yearly snake envenomations occur in the Southland. Only a small percentage of these bites cause serious injury.

If you've been bitten, remain calm. Check to be sure you've actually been envenomated. Look for swelling around the wound within five minutes. If it doesn't swell, you've probably escaped and may not require hospital treatment. If swelling and other symptoms occur—numbness around the lips or hairline, a metallic taste in the mouth or twitching facial muscles, it got you and you need immediate treatment.

Getting to a hospital emergency room is more important than any other first aid. Keep the site of the wound as immobilized as possible and relax. Cutting and suction treatments are now medically out of vogue and advised only as a last resort if you're absolutely sure you can't get to a hospital within four hours.

Bees: More fatalities occur from allergic reaction to insect stings than from rattlesnake bites. People allergic to bee stings can get a desensitization shot and a specially equipped bee kit from an allergist.

Ticks: They're 1/4 to 1/2 inch long and about the same color as the ground, so they're hard to see. Ticks are usually picked up by brushing against low vegetation. When hiking in a tick area it's best to sit on rocks rather than fallen logs. Check your skin and clothing occasionally. You and your loved one can groom each other like monkeys at the zoo. If one is attached to the skin, it should be lifted off with a slow gentle pull. Before bathing, look for ticks on the body, particularly in the hair and pubic region.

Lyme Disease, while rare in California, is the most common tick-carried disease. Symptoms usually include a red, ring-like rash on the skin where the tick attaches itself. The rash is often accompanied by flu-like symptoms of headaches, chills and fever, fatigue and aching muscles. If the disease goes untreated, second-stage symptoms are meningitis and abnormal heartbeat; third-stage symptoms (months or years later) can include arthritis. A blood test can determine if a person is infected. Antibiotics are a very effective treatment.

Smog: Consult your daily newspaper for the smog forecast or call the South Coast Air Quality Management District at 1-800-242-4022. You don't want to be walking on days and in areas when air quality is considered unhealthful; that is to say, when there are more than a .12 parts per million (ppm) concentration of ozone in the atmosphere, which is equal to 100 on the Pollutant Standard Index, or PSI. Good air quality is 0-50; moderate air quality 51-100; 101-200 unhealthful; 201-275 very unhealthful; over 275 hazardous.

GETTING LOST AND FOUND

No one expects to get lost on the urban edge. "After all," say novices, "the mountains aren't big and icy like the High Sierra and we're only out for the day and..."

Even the experienced adventurer can get lost. Getting lost is usually the result of taking a "short cut" off an established trail. Danger is magnified if a walker ventures out alone or fails to tell anyone locale and return time.

Try to avoid getting lost in the first place. Know your physical condition and don't overtax yourself. Check your boots and clothing. Be prepared for bad weather. Inquire about trail conditions. Allow plenty of time for your walk and allow even more for your return to the trailhead.

When you're on the trail, keep your eyes open. If you're hiking so fast that all you see is your boots, you're not attentive to passing terrain—its charms or its layout. STOP once in a while. Sniff wildflowers, splash your face in a spring. LISTEN. Maybe the trail is paralleling a stream. Listen to the sound of mountain water. On your left? On your right? Look up at that fire lookout on the nearby ridge. Are you heading toward it or away from it? LOOK AROUND. That's the best insurance against getting lost.

So you're really lost? Stay calm. Don't worry about food. It takes weeks to starve to death. Besides, you've got that candy bar in your day pack. You have a water bottle. And you have a jacket in case of rain. You're in no immediate danger, so don't run around in circles.

LOOK AROUND some more. Is there any familiar landmark in sight? Have you been gaining elevation or losing it? Where has the sun been shining? On your right cheek? Your back? Retrace your steps, if you can. Look for other footprints. If you're totally disoriented, keep walking laterally. Don't go deeper into the brush or woods. Go up slope to get a good view, but don't trek aimlessly here and there.

If it's near dark, get ready to spend the night. Don't try to find your way out in the dark. Don't worry. If you left your itinerary, your rescuers will begin looking for you in the morning. Try to stay warm by huddling against a tree or wrapping yourself in branches, pine needles or leaves. The universal distress signal is three visible or audible signals—three shouts or whistles, three shiny objects placed on a bare summit. Don't start a fire! You could start a major conflagration.

Relax and think of your next walk. Think of the most beautiful place you know. You'll make it, don't worry.

MAPS

Finding the trailhead—and staying on the trail—is far easier if you're in possession of a good map. Maps are invaluable aids to trip planning and provide relatively painless, hands-on geography lessons.

The Automobile Club of Southern California has several maps useful to the walker. Particularly useful is Los Angeles County and Vicinity. The richly-detailed Thomas Brothers maps will also help you get around Los Angeles County. Use care when you select a map off the rack. Many of the maps sold to tourists are okay for civic sightseeing, but they don't show our adventures on the urban edge.

A good collection would include the following Auto Club maps: San Fernando Valley Area, Central and Western Area, Los Angeles County and Vicinity, San Gabriel Valley, and Southern Area (Long Beach). Add to these city maps: Angeles National Forest (U.S. Forest Service Map)and Trails of the Santa Monica Mountains (Olympus Press).

If you're hiking in a state park, map/brochures are (sometimes) available at park visitor centers. A complete state park planner, is the Olympus Press *California State Parks Guide*.

Some walkers have a love affair with topographic maps; the think those blue rivers, green woods and labyrinthine contour lines are...well, artistic. Topos show terrain in great detail (probably far more detail than you'll require for any walk in this guide) and can help prevent getting lost. If, for example, you know absolutely there's a road on mile to the west that runs north and south, it can be quite a comfort. Topos show trails, elevations, waterways, brush cover and improvements.

COURTESY

• Leave your electronic music machines at home.

• Dogs, depending on the personality of the individual pooch, can be a disruption to walkers and native wildlife. Be warned, many state and county parks, as well as national forest wilderness areas, don't allow dogs, either on or off a leash.

• No smoking on trails

• Resist the urge to collect flowers, rocks or animals. It disrupts nature's balance and lessens the wilderness experience for future walkers.

• Litter detracts from even the most beautiful backcountry setting. If you packed it in, you can pack it out.

• You have a moral obligation to help a walker in need. Give whatever first aid or comfort you can, and then hurry for help.

• Remember, walkers yield to horses, and mountain bikes are *supposed* to yield to walkers. However don't insist on your right-of-way when confronted with a speeding cyclist.

• Don't cut switchbacks.

Chapter I

Downtown

Quote to remember: *"In a semi-arid region, the city was established next to the only stretch of the Los Angeles River where water flowed year-round. Now more than 90 percent of the region's water supply is imported and the Los Angeles River is used for training bus drivers. The only practical reasons for the location of downtown are the freeway system and inertia."*

CHARLES LOCKWOOD AND CHRISTOPHER B. LEINBERGER,
The Atlantic Monthly, 1988

Downtown

AFTER THE MOST RECENT CONSTRUCTION BOOM, downtown Los Angeles has finally gained a big-city skyline—as well as more cars and commerce than ever before. Still, the urban adventurer will find a number of green spaces and quiet places near the city center.

Geography: Paris was founded on the Seine, London on the Thames, Los Angeles on the Los Angeles River, though the city has long turned its back on this now inglorious-looking concrete viaduct.

Most of the city's 451 square miles spreads across the basin from the mountains to the ocean. Downtown itself lies midway between the mountains and the sea.

Natural Attractions: If you take a walk on the wild side of downtown, you'll realize how much Los Angeles needs open space. New York City has some eighteen percent of its land area in parks; San Francisco has fourteen percent (not counting the Golden Gate National Recreation Area), but Los Angeles has only four percent.

Still, there are some surprisingly green spaces within the Los Angeles city limits, and it's all the more precious because of its scarcity. It's space you never imagined when stuck in rush hour traffic on the Harbor Freeway. On a clear day, downtown's new skyline is a dramatic sight from atop the nearby highpoints—the Elysian Park hills, the Montecito Hills, Mount Washington.

The city's waterways—the Arroyo Seco and the Los Angeles River—could very well become natural attractions if conservationists have their way. Greenbelts, complete with jogging and nature trails have been proposed along the Los Angeles River, which could be restored to its once native splendor.

History: Los Angeles, long regarded as one of the newer American cities, or as an outgrowth of the movie industry and quick buck real estate promoters, is actually as old as America itself; it was founded during the Revolutionary War.

The city's benign climate has always encouraged residents to enjoy outdoor life. During the last century, the struggle to preserve parkland parallels the history of the city itself. Obviously, with the city's paucity of parkland, conservationists lost more battles than they won near downtown; nevertheless some gems remain. Among them are Elysian Park, one of the city's oldest, and Debs Park in the rarely-climbed Montecito Hills.

Administration: The city and county parks departments each have their green territory near downtown. A number of private and public conservation agencies are working to restore the Los Angeles River, despite the efforts of some developers and politicians who would like to pave the whole river and turn it into a freeway.

There's more to Los Angeles than meets the commuter's eye.

Elysian Park
Portola Trail

Highlights: *Elysian Park, close to downtown Los Angeles, is a 575-acre retreat from urban Angst. Although the park has been cut by many roads, it's possible to follow trails that will immerse you in greenery and leave the roar of traffic far behind.*

Distance: 5-miles round trip, with 200 feet of elevation gain.

Directions: From downtown Los Angeles, head north on North Broadway through Chinatown. Turn left on Park Row Drive and park along the road. The trail begins at the historical landmark commemorating Portola's campsite.

ALTHOUGH IT'S NEAR THE CENTRAL CITY, ELYSIAN Park is usually uncrowded. It has a remote feeling—possibly because access is a bit confusing. Elysian Park appears to be everywhere and nowhere at the same time. You can see the park while motoring along the Golden State and Pasadena Freeways, and you pass through it on the way to Dodger Stadium; to commuters and Dodger fans, it's a familiar sight. But when you explore the park on foot, it somehow seems as if it's in the middle of nowhere.

Elysian Park's hilly acreage is an undeveloped remnant of the original 17,172-acre Spanish land grant from which Pueblo de Los Angeles grew. Part of the park, along with Pershing Square, are among the lands set aside for public use at the founding of Los Angeles in 1781.

More than 10 miles of hiking trails and dirt fire roads lead through some surprisingly wild terrain.

Portola Trail takes you through shady glens, over grass carpets and past rare palms. You can picnic under imported rubber trees or native oaks and enjoy the views of the Big Basin offered by the park's promontories.

Contemplate civic scenery from Elysian greenery.

The trail and the historical marker at the trailhead honor explorer Don Gaspar de Portola who, with Father Juan Crespi, led the first overland expedition to California.

On Aug. 2, 1769, Capt. Portola's party camped on the banks of the Los Angeles River near what would soon become Pueblo de Los Angeles. Three months later, Portola overshot his intended destination of Monterey and made a great discovery—San Francisco Bay.

Head uphill on wide Portola Trail, which soon crosses Park Row Drive. You'll pass among oak and eucalyptus trees, top a grassy knoll, then descend to Park Row Drive, which you'll follow over a bridge that spans the Pasadena Freeway.

Beyond the freeway bridge is a junction with a dirt fire road on your right. The next mile of travel is through the most tranquil part of the park. Portola Trail winds through a zany mixture of trees that you would find only in Southern California—

eucalyptus, walnut, oak, pine and palm.

Your path crosses East Park Drive and continues on a narrow hillside path. Periodically, you will emerge from the greenery and look down at the metropolis in miniature: freight yards, Glendale, Interstate 5. Beware of a small amount of poison oak that crowds the trail in a couple of places.

As the trail descends toward Stadium Way, the cacophony of urban life is gradually overwhelmed by bird music. Mockingbirds, jays, red-tailed hawks, bush tits, Audubon's warblers, red-shafted flickers, house finches and many more birds have been spotted in Elysian Park. The great wealth of trees here attracts many birds. In 1940, the California Audubon Society dedicated the park as a bird sanctuary.

You'll enjoy views of Dodger Stadium, which occupies Chavez Ravine in the southwest corner of the park. During pueblo days, indigents were buried in a "potter's field" in the ravine; it was a quarantine area during Nineteenth Century smallpox epidemics. The name belongs to Julian Chavez, city councilman circa 1850 and the original owner of the canyon.

Portola Trail reaches a junction with Elysian Park Drive and Stadium Way. On the west side of Stadium Way is a wide grassy area for picnicking. Within easy walking distance are other park attractions: Palm Hill, the fountain and stream of Grace S. Simons Lodge, the Arboretum and Elysian Fields.

Those wishing to extend their walk will pick up a bridle trail from the grassy knoll of Palm Hill and climb south for views of Dodger Stadium and the Los Angeles skyline.

A Short Hop Through Frogtown
Los Angeles River Trail

Highlights: *Semi-natural stretch of L.A. River. Dream of a river restored as you walk through Frogtown.*

Distance: From Riverside Drive, where it nears the river at the Pasadena/Golden State Freeway overpass, to Fletcher Drive is 2 1/2 miles one way. Continuing from Fletcher Drive to Los Feliz adds another 1 1/4 miles but along this stretch of river, fences and locked gates impede progress; this part of the river, as it flows through Atwater, is posted No Trespassing.

Directions: Join this river walk from Riverside Drive, either at its south end where Riverside passes beneath the Harbor and Golden State Freeways, opposite Elysian Park, or at its north end on Fletcher Drive just west of Riverside.

DIFFICULT AS IT IS FOR ANGELENOS TO BELIEVE, THE Los Angeles was once a great river—or at least a real one. Certainly it was a real river in 1781 when a weary group of colonists who had traveled a thousand miles from Sonora Mexico settled on the river's west bank and built El Pueblo de Nuestra Sonora las Reina de Los Angeles.

In recent years the river has captured headlines as a result of a proposal to utilize the riverbed as a freeway. While some see the wide, sterile concrete river bottom as 8-lanes of highway awaiting signs and lane lines, Friends of the L.A. River, as well as conservationists and urban planners, see a river restored with a greenway and lots of open space, that would link, both symbolically and ecologically, the diverse neighborhoods of the metropolis.

The Los Angeles has always been a river of dreams and schemes. In 1799, shortly after the founding of the San Fernando Mission, the padres dammed the river, helping themselves to the water. They incurred the wrath of the pueblo citizens who filed suit against the mission, thus beginning what has been for Southern California two hundred years of water politics. The pueblo people, in turn, built a waterwheel, powered by the river flow that spilled water into the canal; townspeople were then able to irrigate land high above the river banks.

For more than a hundred years, the Los Angeles River was the sole source of water for the city that grew up around it. The river in the best of times could support a population of 250,000 and the first decade of this century was not the best of

Lewis MacAdam, founder Friends of the Los Angeles River.

times. The city's population was rapidly expanding and a prolonged drought was shrinking the water supply. What happened next is well known: The Los Angeles Department of Water and Power tapped the snowmelt of the High Sierra and sent it to the city via the Owens Valley Aqueduct.

Less well known is what became of the Los Angeles River. After the great aqueduct and other water projects were built, city engineers relied less and less on the river, which was seen as a kind of quaint relic. During the 1920s it flowed through Bandini (Van Nuys), Home Gardens (South Gate), Hynes (Paramount) and Davidson City (Carson).

Surprisingly, in this land of little rain, it was not the need to capture more water but the need to dispose of it that led local politicians and the Army Corps of Engineers to cement the river channel. Most of the river's 49-mile-length was encased in concrete after the great flood of 1938.

Some six miles of riverbed were spared a cement topping, primarily because the significant springs that exist underground would break up the cement. Three semi-natural areas of the river remain today: between Burbank and Balboa Boulevards in the Sepulveda Basin; between Griffith Park and

"Frogtown" just north of downtown; between Willow Street and the Pacific Ocean in Long Beach.

Frogtown received its name for the abundance of frogs that lived along the riverbanks here. Alas, California's native red-legged frog, for whom this part of town is named, are faring poorly these days, in part because of a loss of breeding ground and because of a hostile takeover of turf by a carnivorous bullfrog from Africa.

The river passes behind a poor, but prideful, neighborhood, which currently makes pretty good use of the river path: joggers, mothers pushing baby carriages, kids on bikes, walkers and cycling commuters.

Begin walking the river path behind some houses. Behind you, near where the Pasadena and Golden State freeways cross, there's a distinct line of demarcation separating the semi-natural part of the river from the completely concreted portion.

Judging by the number of fences pulled down at the end of the cul-de-sacs bordering the river path, a lot of people like to use the walkway. You view backyards and chicken coops on your left, the river below, the freightyards on the opposite bank. The river may not be Amazonian in size, but its big enough to provide a lot of "white noise" to drown out the sounds of auto traffic and of the trains on the opposite bank.

The river path meanders from east to west, passing an industrial area, then passing under the Glendale Freeway. The path climbs the embankment and ascends to Fletcher Drive.

Intrepid walkers, disdaining gates, fences and warning signs, will follow the river road through the Atwater District to Los Feliz Blvd. and the end of the semi-natural part of the L.A. River. Other walkers will use Atwater side streets on the west bank of the river to make their way to Los Feliz. Still others might decide enough is enough and return the way they came, or via Riverside Drive.

Mount Washington
Jack Smith Trail

Highlights: *Follow the historic path of a streetcar line to the old Mt. Washington Hotel, now headquarters for the Self-Realization Fellowship. Wander the mountain's bucolic lanes, visit that long-standing institution—the Southwest Museum.*

Distance: 4 miles round trip with a 400-foot elevation gain.

Directions: Exit the Pasadena Freeway on Avenue 43, head west to Figueroa Blvd and turn right. Turn left onto Avenue 45, then make another left onto Marmion Way and park. Begin this walk at the flight of stairs that ascend west from the west side of Marmion Way, just north of Avenue 43.

SOMETIMES CALLED "THE POOR MAN'S BEL AIR," MT. Washington manages to be both in the city and off the beaten track at the same time. Most motorists speeding north on the Pasadena Freeway have no clue to the charms of the hill to the left of the freeway, or to the northeast of Dodger Stadium.

Mt. Washington was subdivided by realtor Robert Marsh and electrical products manufacturer Arthur St. Claire Perry, who built a two-car Angels Flight-like incline railway to carry passengers up the mountain. The developers hoped that people riding the railway would be inspired to buy lots and homes on the hill.

The ploy worked. As the March 7, 1909 *Los Angeles Times* enthused about Mt. Washington: "Now right here in our own Los Angeles, the man of even moderate wealth may build his home on a charming, sun-kissed eminence that commands a vista of snow-capped mountains, several cities and the blue ocean—not surpassed on either hemisphere."

Located at the top of the railway was the Mt. Washington Hotel, completed in 1908. Visiting socialites, as well as sports and entertainment celebrities, were attracted to the hotel.

After World War I, the hotel and railway fell upon hard times. The hotel served as a convalescent hospital for wounded soldiers, then closed in 1916. Citing unsafe operating conditions, the Board of Public Utilities closed down the railway three years later.

In 1925, Paramahansa Yogananda, a monk of the ancient Swami Order, acquired the hotel and converted it into an international headquarters for his Self-Realization Fellowship. The handsomely landscaped grounds have long been a quiet place to meditate for both members and the visiting public.

Mt. Washington today is a socially and ethnically diverse community whose residents cherish the hill's semi-rural flavor. With the help of city and county government, as well as the Santa Monica Mountains Conservancy, residents recently united to preserve Rainbow Canyon, a ravine filled with native California walnut trees.

A walk up Mt. Washington offers great clear-day views of the city. This jaunt is named for long-time *Los Angeles Times* columnist Jack Smith who has often written about the peculiarities of the mountain he calls home.

Also located on Mt. Washington is the Southwest Museum, one of the most complete collections of native Californian artifacts, including basketry, tools and other evidence of cultures that one flourished in the Southland and throughout the Southwest.

From Marmion Way, march up the stairs to Canyon Vista Drive. You'll be walking in the tracks (torn up in 1919) of the Mt. Washington railway. Two cars, the Florence and the Virginia, were pulled by a cable running under wooden planking. The conductor would ride up on one car and collect the fare then, when the two cars met, would jump across to the other and collect monies for the descent.

After a stiff, half-mile climb, Canyon Vista merges with Mt. Washington Drive. You bear right, continuing your ascent via a white fence-lined walkway on the left side of the road. After a couple of curves along Mt. Washington's namesake drive, you'll reach San Rafael Avenue and turn right.

You're now walking close to the crest of Mt. Washington (elevation 940 feet). You'll see the huge iron gates of the Self-Realization Fellowship. Stroll the serene grounds and contemplate the city at your feet.

41

Meditation completed, continue along San Rafael Avenue past the Mt. Washington School and turn left onto Sea View Lane. Until the 1930s, the lane was a dirt road known as Central Terrace; after winter rains, its adobe surface was infamous for trapping autos. After a quarter-mile, you'll reach pavement's end and begin a U-shaped traverse around one of Mt. Washington's more rustic knolls. On clear days, the dirt portion of Sea View Lane lives up to its name, offering vistas of Santa Monica Bay, Palos Verdes Peninsula and Catalina Island.

After a quarter-mile, Sea View Lane resumes as a paved road and returns you to San Rafael Avenue. Bear left, then right onto Moon Avenue. Now you begin your descent along roads that wander like lost children. Moon leads to Crane Drive, which descends to Museum Drive. Bear left and descend another half-mile to the entrance to the Southwest Museum. After touring Casa de Adobe, continue on Museum Drive to its junction with Marmion Way, where you began this walk.

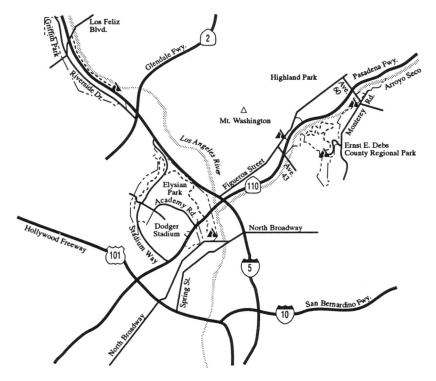

Arroyo Seco Park-ways
Arroyo Seco Trail

Highlights: *A chain of parks along the lower stretch of the famous Arroyo Seco; this is an area rich in human, architectural and automotive history.*

Distance: From Heritage Square to Avenue 60 is 4 miles round trip; through Arroyo Park to the border of Pasadena is 8 miles round trip.

Directions: From the Pasadena Freeway (formerly the Arroyo Seco Parkway!) exit on Avenue 43. Head south on the residential street east of the Freeway—Homer Street—and drive to its end at Heritage Square. Park along Homer or in the dirt lot bordering the arroyo just outside the gates to Heritage Square.

CONSTRUCTION OF A SUPERHIGHWAY BETWEEN LOS Angeles and Pasadena was a dream that began with the motoring age. Arroyo Seco Parkway, the nation's first freeway, opened to traffic the day before the 1941 Tournament of Roses.

But before Arroyo Seco became a parkway, it became a park. A sand and gravel company was digging up the channel bed near Avenue 43 and an aroused public demanded that Los Angeles buy the riverbed and convert it to a park. This was done between 1927 and 1930, though Highland Park, Lincoln Heights and Mt. Washington residents were severely taxed for Arroyo Seco Park.

The Chamber of Commerce and City Council next decided a "parkway" leading through the land, now in public ownership. would be a wonderful asset to the growing city. Depression-era WPA workers helped build the first stretch of road, about six miles long, which extended from Pasadena to Avenue 22 in Los Angeles. The financial cost? The then-remarkable sum of a million dollars a mile. Motorists came from all over the Southland just to drive back and forth on the parkway, free of stop signs and stop lights.

The environmental cost of the parkway? Few citizens back then were asking such questions. Looking back now, it's clear

Detail: Heritage Square

Arroyo Seco Parkway not only made automotive history, but environmental history as well: the Arroyo Seco was the first instance of parkland lost to or cut up by a flood control channel and a freeway.

Today, much of the green around the arroyo is picnic grounds and ball fields. In various corners of the green-belt, the walker will discover an archery range and a driving range, golf courses and stables, bike trails and bridle trails. Those with an interest in architecture will enjoy glimpses of Craftsman-style brown-shingled bunga-lows near the arroyo: Isolated jewels are found in the Highland Park area, a treasure trove of the period is found north of Colorado Boulevard in Pasadena.

Walkers with an architectural interest will also enjoy the start of this walk at Heritage Square which includes also a number of significant structures of Victorian Southern California. Palms Depot, a Southern Pacific Railroad stop relo-cated here from the community of Palms; Octagon House; the Lincoln Avenue Methodist Church; a carriage barn; the Ford House and Hale House are among the historic houses and buildings located in the square. The Square is open on week-ends, and guided tours are given on Sundays.

El Alisal, the Lummis Home and Garden, is also located near the beginning of this walk at 200 East Avenue 43. The house was built by writer Charles Lummis, founder of "Arroyo Culture," and promoter of all things Southwest and Southern Californian. Built of concrete and arroyo stone, the house has Pueblo Indian, Spanish and Craftsman architectural features.

From Heritage Square, walk along Homer Street to Avenue 43 and turn left. Visit the Lummis House now, or continue your walk by turning right on Mosher Avenue and following it a block to its end at the ball fields and picnic ground of the Montecito Heights Recreation Center.

Join the signed bike path that leads down into the arroyo. Across the arroyo—and the freeway—from you is Sycamore Grove. During the 1920s and 1930s, this was one of the favorite picnic grounds of the various state societies. Thousands of former residents—mostly of Midwest states—would gather annually for speeches, sports and picnics.

The path stays by the arroyo, curving slowly eastward around the Montecito Hills, the undeveloped portion of which is within the borders of Ernest E. Debs Regional County Park. The bike path emerges from the arroyo briefly in Arroyo Seco Park, then heads back down to the channel again and enters South Pasadena. Just short of the par 3 Arroyo Seco Golf Course, you'll abandon the arroyo for a bridle path that climbs a brushy slope along the eastern edge of the course, passes a driving range, then crosses under the freeway and leads to Arroyo Seco Park. Another bridle path leads alongside the park road, Stoney Lane, crosses San Pasqual, then heads behind a stables and above the arroyo.

(If you want to extend your walk along Pasadena's portion of the Arroyo Seco and ramble to the Rose Bowl, see the Arroyo Seco walk in the San Gabriel Valley chapter of this book.)

A pathway along the parkway.

City Views from Debs Park
Montecito Hills Trail

Highlights: *Sunset-watching from the viewpoint near the park's lake. The park and its paths see few visitors.*

Distance: 2-mile loop through park with a 300-foot elevation gain.

Directions: From the Pasadena Freeway (110) in Highland Park, exit on Marisol Avenue and head right (west). (Marisol Avenue separates Debs Park on your right from Arroyo Seco Park on your left.) When you reach Monterey Road, turn right and proceed 3/4 mile to the park entrance. Turn right into the park and follow the park road 1/2 mile past picnic sites to its end at a parking lot.

MANY URBAN RESIDENTS VIEW THIS PARK FROM their homes in Lincoln Heights and from the heights of Mt. Washington, as well as from Highland Park and South Pasadena. Thousands of motorists whiz by it on the Pasadena Freeway. And yet this park, glimpsed daily by so many, remains unknown to most city dwellers.

Debs is the name of this overlooked county park in the heart of the metropolis. It offers the urban mountaineer a great place for some exercise and terrific clear-day city views.

Debs Park was not named for the Socialist labor leader and presidential candidate Eugene V. Debs, but for Ernest E. Debs, a former Los Angeles County Supervisor. Governmentally speaking, the park is something of an orphan. It's Los Angeles city land, but in 1967 the city gave it to the county on a 25-year lease. The county contracts with a private firm for the park's maintenance and has not been gung-ho about developing the park with a lot of facilities.

Ernest E. Debs Regional County Park, as it's officially known, occupies a small range of hills called the Montecito Hills. The 300-acre park is on the east side of the Pasadena Freeway, more or less opposite Mount Washington. Subdivision maps of the last century showed the Montecito Hills divided into lots, but developers apparently opted for the more buildable neighboring areas of Mt. Washington and El Sereno.

The park includes a family picnic area with barbecue facilities, and plenty of lawn for play, but the greater part of the park is brush-covered hillsides. Trails and fire roads loop through the park.

Join the asphalt fire road at the north side of the parking lot. The road leads steeply north up a hillside to the park's high point. Views from the road include downtown, Elysian Park, and Mt. Washington. The front range of the San Gabriel Mountains, including Mt. Baldy, as well as much of the San Gabriel Valley is also part of a clear-day panorama.

Just left of the road is the park's small man-made lake. Continue on the road, which soon passes a huge graffiti-covered shade shelter. You'll pass a junction with a dirt fire road on your left, then approach a turnaround at road's end. Join a dirt fire road on your right and follow it along the ridgetop. Next pick up a trail (marked with a blue arrow on an oak), which at first descends through some eucalyptus trees toward Monterey Road. The trail soon swings north and drops to a fire road, which offers views of the Arroyo Seco, Pasadena Freeway and Pasadena as it turns west. Another good view of the arroyo is offered at a viewpoint on the westernmost curve of the fire road. That striped stretch of asphalt you see below you, the one closest to the hillside, is an old soapbox derby track.

Stay on the fire road which brings you back up to the park's paved road near the shade shelter. Or join a steep, but distinct, shortcut trail that does likewise. If you're hiking at day's end, the park lake is the place to watch the sun set over the metropolis.

Baldwin Hills
Baldwin Hills Trail

Highlights: *While the Baldwin Hills are only 500 feet high, they offer dramatic, unobstructed views of the basin: the Santa Monica Mountains, the whole sweep of Santa Monica Bay, the San Gabriel Mountains and much of the metropolis.*

Distance: 3-mile loop through Kenneth Hahn State Recreation Area with a 300-foot elevation gain

Directions: From the Santa Monica Freeway (10) in Los Angeles, exit on La Cienega Boulevard and drive south a few miles to Kenneth Hahn State Recreation Area. Park in the lot signed "Olympic Forest."

FROM A DISTANCE, THE BALDWIN HILLS APPEAR TO have little attraction for the walker. Oil wells work the hills, whose slopes have been scarred by roads and bulldozers. But the oil is petering out, the hillsides are being ecologically rehabilitated, and a park is in the making.

Located in the west/central part of Los Angeles, Kenneth Hahn State Recreation Area—named for the long-time Los Angeles County Supervisor—is a park developed and operated by Los Angeles County. It takes in hills and canyons between La Brea and La Cienega Boulevards. Few Southern Californians seem to know about Baldwin Hills, but the clean, well-kept, developed part of the park is no secret to nearby residents, who enjoy weekend picnics and barbecues on the expansive lawns. Anglers cast for catfish in the park's pond, which is stocked every couple of weeks.

A highlight for hikers of all ages and abilities is a path that leads through the park's Olympic Forest. The forest includes at least one tree for each of the 140 nations that participated in the 1984 Olympic Games.

From the interpretive displays posted at the edge of the parking lot, take the path into the Olympic Forest. The "forest" is divided into a half-dozen habitats, including desert, tropical and temperate environments. Contemplate the paper mulberry from Tonga, the carob from Cyprus, the date palm from Egypt. The forest is yet another proof of the oft-repeated adage that "anything can and does grow in Southern California."

After your around-the-world tree tour, ascend a path leading toward some rather forlorn palms. Here at a manmade oasis, you'll find a waterfall cascading into a little grotto. From the palm oasis, you'll continue your ascent on trail and dirt road to a picnic ramada perched on the hilltop. Near the ramada is a pine grove planted by "Top Teens of America, Inc."

The view from the summit includes the Wilshire corridor, Century City, Westwood and the Hollywood sign. You'll spot sailboats tacking this way and that as they head out to sea from Marina del Rey. And you'll get an air traffic controller's view of the amazing number of jets zooming in and out of LAX.

A dirt road crosses the hilltop plateau and passes two more picnic ramadas. Enjoy the striking views of Palos Verdes

When the smoggy curtain lifts, all of L.A. is at your feet.

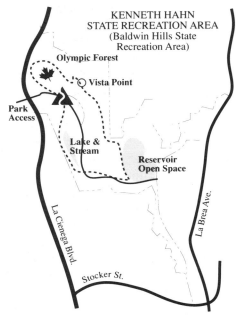

KENNETH HAHN
STATE RECREATION AREA
(Baldwin Hills State
Recreation Area)

Olympic Forest

Vista Point

Park
Access

Lake &
Stream

Reservoir
Open Space

La Cienega Blvd.

La Brea Ave.

Stocker St.

Peninsula and Catalina Island. The road, then a footpath, follows a fence beside some high-tension power lines.

Rabbits and quail are frequently sighted in the hills, which are covered with California sagebrush, black mustard, coyote bush and prickly pear cactus. The native plant community—coastal sage scrub—has been greatly altered by the hand of man, so much so that botanists describe Baldwin Hills flora as being in a condition called "disclimax." Introduced "weeds" such as castor bean, milk thistle and tree tobacco have invaded the canyon bottoms. The hills host a number of domestic plants gone wild, including agave, hottentot fig, nasturium and lantana.

The trail passes near the old Baldwin Hills Dam, which failed a quarter-century ago. Overlooking the empty reservoir back of the dam is an observation tower, which resembles a castle from the Middle Ages. Fennel, chamise and dandelions have pushed through the cracked cement bottom of the reservoir. The county has plans to convert the reservoir into parking and picnic areas.

Near the dam, you'll meet a road coming up from the developed part of the park. Join a paved path, which parallels this road, and descend a landscaped hillside to the main park picnic area. Improvise a route past the pond, bubbling brook and picnic grounds back to Olympic Forest and the trailhead.

Chapter II

MULHOLLAND DAM, HOLLYWOOD RESERVOIR, HOLLYWOOD, CALIFORNIA

Hollywood Hills

Quote to remember: "Then there are the hillsides, laced with meandering public paths and stairways tunneling through profusons of wild vegetation and presenting, from raw crests and melanges of balconies, breathtaking views of Hollywood and the city beyond."

—SAM HALL KAPLAN, *L.A. Follies*

Hollywood Hills

ONE SOCIAL CRITIC COMPLAINED THAT THE HOLLY-wood hills are "as unreal as flats of stage scenery, stage pieces." Actually, the quiet chaparral hills—famous throughout the world because of the Hollywood sign—are a quiet retreat from the glitz and grime and unreality of the metropolis below. The urban mountaineer will prefer the trail to the Hollywood sign over the Walk of Fame along Hollywood Boulevard.

Geography: The Hollywood Hills are the eastern end of the Santa Monica Mountains and share a similar ecology to the range's taller and wilder peaks to the west. The differences between the two ends of the range have more to do with human settlement than natural history; the Hollywood Hills are by far the most developed part of the mountains.

The hills separate the San Fernando Valley from Hollywood, Beverly Hills and parts of Los Angeles. They present a dramatic picture from afar, not because of their height which varies from 800 to 1,600 feet, but because the steep canyons of the hills makes them look particularly rugged.

Natural Attractions: During the holiday season, the rich green crown of the toyon bush is aglow with a mass of red berries. Toyon—also known variously at Christmas berry or California holly—is the most festive of flora. It's believed that masses of this native shrub growing on the hills above Hollywood gave the community its name.

Plant communities in the Hollywood Hills include chaparral, coastal sage scrub and oak/sycamore woodland. From the trail, your window on the world is similar to the huge picture windows of the residents who make their homes in the hills—a combination of rustic slopes and the city beyond.

History: Anthropological evidence suggests that the Chumash occupied the Santa Monica Mountains as far east as Topanga Canyon and the land we now call the Hollywood Hills was occupied by Shoshonean-speaking people. The most eastern part of the hills was occupied by the Gabrielinos.

Difficult as it is to imagine now, during Spanish and Mexican times, the hills were considered of little value. Ranchos were located down in the valley and property lines extended rather vaguely into higher terrain. Cahuenga Pass was the only noteworthy spot in the Hollywood Hills because it was along the principal stage route between northern and southern California.

Until the turn of the century, the population of Hollywood was only about 500; deer often ventured down to Hollywood Boulevard in the early morning and evening hours. When the moviemakers came, Hollywood's flatlands and hills were settled. "The most beautiful suburb in America," some said of Hollywood. Hollywood is no longer a filmmaking center and has more than its share of urban problems, but the hills still have an attraction. Many of the hillside residences, resting on stilts and constructed on the tiniest of terraced pads, are truly amazing to behold.

Administration: The Santa Monica Mountains Conservancy has been successful at protecting small parcels of the Hollywood Hills. The Hollywood Reservoir is part of the domain of the Los Angeles Department of Water and Power.

Cahuenga Pass, circa 1897.

Hiking to the Hollywood Sign
Mt. Lee Trail

Highlights: *A visit to the world renown Hollywood sign; views north of San Fernando Valley, to the south to Tinseltown.*

Distance: 3 miles round trip with 500-foot elevation gain.

Directions: In Hollywood, from the corner of Franklin Avenue and Beachwood Drive (Beachwood is one short block east of Gower), turn north and proceed up Beachwood into the Hollywood Hills. After 1.7 miles, you'll spot Hollyridge Drive on your right. Park in a safe and courteous manner along Beachwood Drive near its intersection with Hollyridge. (You can also park along Hollyridge, but it's rather narrow. The unsigned trail to Mt. Lee begins 50 yards up Hollyridge Drive from Beachwood Drive. The wide trail is on your left.

TO MAKE SURE EVERYONE KNEW ABOUT THE NEW Beachwood Canyon real estate development, the developers, including *Los Angeles Times* publisher Harry Chandler, ordered a huge wooden sign built atop Mt. Lee. HOLLYWOODLAND read the sign.

The Beachwood Canyon residences were advertised as "above the traffic, congestion, smoke, fog, and poisonous gas fumes of the lowlands." Looking back now, it's hard to believe Angelenos were worried about pollution in the early 1920s.

Never kept in the best repair, letters—particularly the "H" frequently blew down. In 1923, a depressed actress leaped from the sign. During a 1949 gale, the sign lost its LAND. Finally, in 1978, celebrities—among them Alice Cooper, Hugh Hefner and Gene Autry—pledged $27,777.77 a letter to restore the HOLLYWOOD sign, sans LAND, to its former glory.

Besides the sign, 1,640-foot Mt. Lee has another claim to fame: L.A.'s first television signals were broadcast from the peak in the 1940s.

The intrepid walker can also trek a rough trail to nearby Cahuenga Peak, at 1,820 feet the king of the Hollywood Hills. As the story goes, the Shoshone tribe had a village called Kawi located on the banks of the Los Angeles River near present

54

day Universal City. Some have speculated that Cahuenga, which names a pass, a peak and nowadays a boulevard, originated from the village Kawi, combined with the Indian word for village "nga;" that is, "Kawi-nga."

From Hollyridge Drive, the trail follows a ridge just east of the stables. Your views of the Hollywood sign begin almost immediately. Off to the right, looking very sci-fi from this angle, is the dome of the Griffith Park Observatory.

You'll ignore the bridle path on your left coming up from the stables, and continue your ascent to an unsigned junction with Mulholland Trail. A right would lead into Griffith Park and intersect Mt. Hollywood Drive, but you turn left on the fire road and wind west to an intersection with Mt. Lee Drive.

As you ascend paved Mt. Lee Drive, you'll enjoy excellent clear-day views of Forest Lawn, beautiful downtown Burbank, and the Valley beyond.

(Just short of the summit, as the trail makes a sharp left bend, look for a rough, narrow trail leading westward. Cahuenga Peak Trail climbs steeply a quarter-mile to the summit. After more good views, the trail heads along the ridge, then swithcbacks down to Wonderview Drive.)

You can't stand right on top of Mt. Lee because a locked gate keeps you out. (There's a civil defense communication facility on the summit.) But you can—and will—enjoy the views from your perch above the Hollywood sign. Resist the urge to climb over the fence in order to have your picture taken next to the sign; it's strictly illegal.

Hollywood Reservoir
Lake Hollywood Trail

Highlights: *Nestled in the Hollywood Hills, this lovely lake is one of the quietest and most secluded bodies of water in the city. The pathway around the lake is a favorite exercise circuit for stressed-out film industry folks.*

Distance: 4 miles around the lake

Directions: From the Hollywood Freeway (101) in Los Angeles (Universal City area) exit on Barham Boulevard and head north a short ways to Lake Hollywood Drive. Turn right and do your best to stay on the Drive as it winds east through a residential area, then turns south toward the reservoir. Park along the Drive near the gate to the reservoir. The path is open from 6:30-10 a.m. and 2-7:30 p.m. daily, and 6:30 a.m.-7:30 p.m. weekends. During winter, the reservoir sometimes opens later and closes earlier.

I F YOU EXPERIENCE A *DÉJÀ VU* WHILE WALKING AROUND the reservoir, don't be surprised. Scenes in *Chinatown*, the 1974 movie that showed the slimy side of Los Angeles water and power struggles, were shot around the lake. In

L.A.'s water never looked so good.

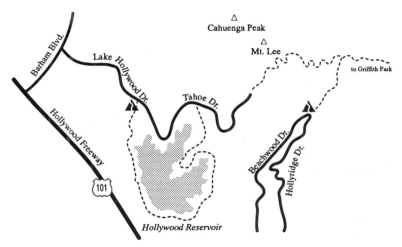

another 1974 film, *Earthquake*, the reservoir dam fictionally collapsed and flooded the city below.

Hollywood Reservoir was built in 1925 by city water commissioner William Mulholland as part of the city's gigantic waterworks program designed to secure, ship, and store water for the rapidly expanding population of Los Angeles. Compared to some of the city's other, more utilitarian-looking reservoirs, Hollywood gets an "A" for aesthetics.

Less concerned with aesthetics than with evaporation, pollution and possible sabotage, the Los Angeles Department of Water and Power periodically makes noises about covering the tops of L.A.'s reservoirs, and invariably is confronted by outraged citizens who prefer their lakes remain topless. The Department went so far as to close the Hollywood Reservoir to walkers during America's 1991 war with Iraq.

The pine-shaded service road soon isolates you from the noise of the city; unfortunately a chain link fence and high vegetation precludes more than an occasional glimpse of the lake. The effect is rather like that of moving through a green tunnel.

Lake views are dramatic, however, when you cross over to the other side of the reservoir via the top of Mulholland Dam. The view includes the Hollywood sign, reflections on the lake above and the metropolis below.

The reservoir service road doesn't completely make a circle, so you'll have to follow Lake Hollywood Drive back around to your starting point.

Runyan Canyon Park
Runyan Canyon Trail

Highlights: *No Man's Canyon was the earliest name given to the deep arroyo that nature sculpted in the Hollywood Hills. A century-and-a-half ago, it was the wild domain of birds, rabbits, coyotes and lizards. Amazingly, it still is.*

Distance: 3-mile loop, 500-foot elevation gain

Directions: From the Hollywood Freeway in Hollywood, exit on Highland Avenue and head south past the Hollywood Bowl to Franklin Avenue. Turn west on Franklin to Fuller. Turn right and proceed a short distance on Fuller to road's end at The Pines entrance gate to Runyan Park.

RUNYAN CANYON PARK IN THE HEART OF THE Hollywood Hills is a wildlife preserve and quite a contrast from the wild life associated with nearby Hollywood and Sunset Boulevards.

The remarkable story of how the canyon was preserved—a tale of Greek, Irish and Iranian immigrants, movie stars and millionaires—could be the subject of a miniseries.

"Greek George" Caralambo was the first to receive title to the canyon in 1867. The canyon was part of a land grant awarded Greek George for his service as leader of the Army Camel Corps.

Coal magnate Carmen Runyon bought the canyon in 1919 and built a hunting lodge. But it has been mostly Runyan Canyon ever since, usually spelled with an "a", not an "o."

Actor/singer John McCormick, just after his appearance in the hit movie *Song of My Heart*, purchased Runyan Canyon in 1929. He build a mansion called San Patrizio, after St. Patrick, and began extensive landscaping projects in the canyon. Wallace Beery, John Barrymore and Basil Rathbone were frequent guests.

In 1942, McCormick sold his property to millionaire Huntington Hartford, who renamed the estate "The Pines." Hartford had ambitious plans. He commissioned Frank Lloyd Wright and Wright's son Lloyd to draw up plans for a futuristic resort hotel perched on the canyon walls overlooking the city.

Plans included four saucer-shaped buildings, a giant circular pool, art gallery theater and sculpture garden.

While Hartford definitely left his mark on the cultural life of Southern California, he was unable to build the Huntington Hartford Play Resort, despite 15 years of effort. Local hotel owners eyed the project with jealousy and Hartford was never able to secure the necessary city permits.

In 1964, Kahlua importer Jules Berman purchased Runyan Canyon, razed San Patrizio mansion and the guest house to avoid paying taxes on improved property, and tried to develop a subdivision of luxury houses. Local homeowner groups fought Berman's development plans, as well as those of a later canyon owner—Iranian exile Mana Vasir, who purchased the canyon in 1979.

Finally in 1984, the city of Los Angeles, with funding provided by the Santa Monica Mountains Conservancy, purchased Runyan Canyon and it was proclaimed a city park.

Today, the Friends of Runyan Canyon, a volunteer group, works to keep the canyon clean, as well as interpret the area's rich architectural and natural history. The Friends hope to generate funds for a visitors center and ranger station.

For the walker, Runyan Canyon Park offers a great after-work leg-stretcher. Anyone interested in Hollywood's faded glory will enjoy exploring the ruins of the old McCormick estate. Clear-day vistas from the canyon overlooks encompass Hollywood, downtown and many a civic landmark.

From the wrought-iron gate enscribed "The Pines," enter Runyon Canyon Park. You'll soon encounter the ruins of the great estate San Patrizio.

Angle left at the first opportunity and join the asphalt road ascending north along the west canyon wall (This walk is a clockwise tour of Runyan Canyon.) Runyan Canyon Road (closed to vehicles) climbs through a chaparral community of chamise, ceanothus, buckwheat and sage. Castor bean, tree tobacco, sugar bush, toyon and golden yarrow are also part of this community.

Nearing the head of Runyan Canyon, the road intersects a dirt road that leads down the east wall of the canyon. (Paved

Runyan Canyon Road continues north to a park entrance—or exit as the case may be—at Mulholland Drive.) Near the intersection is a viewpoint offering great clear-day vistas of the Griffith Park Observatory, the Hollywood sign and the front range of the San Gabriel Mountains.

Bear right on the narrow dirt road and descend along the steeply pitched east wall of the canyon. The trail gets quite steep (use caution) as it descends to Inspiration Point and the ruins of the Lloyd Wright-designed pool house, occupied by Errol Flynn in 1957-58.

From here you get good views of the rooftop pools of Hollywood hotels, the pagoda of Mann's Chinese Theater, Century City and Wilshire high-rises, and much more. Your path turns up-canyon for a short distance, passes a tennis court overgrown with vines, and reached the canyon bottom. Leave the road at a huge cactus and wander the canyon bottom trail under pines, palms and eucalyptus, to the stone and cement ruins of several structures.

Returning to the dirt road, head down-canyon past more ruins to the trailhead.

Hollywood Hills: Before "the Industry" came to town.

To the Treepeople's Domain

Dearing Mountain Trail

Highlights: *Wilacre Park and Fryman Overlook, Coldwater Canyon Park and Franklin Canyon Ranch—these four recreation areas comprise Cross Mountain Park. Individually and collectively, they contribute some much-needed breathing room to the San Fernando Valley side of the Hollywood Hills.*

Distance: Wilacre Park to Coldwater Canyon Park is 2 1/2 miles round trip with 500-foot elevation gain; to Fryman Overlook is 6 miles round trip with 700-foot elevation gain.

Directions: From the Ventura Freeway (101) in Studio City, exit on Laurel Canyon Boulevard and drive south 1 1/2 miles to Fryman Canyon Road. Turn right and park immediately. The unsigned trail begins at a yellow vehicle gate.

B ETTY P. DEARING TRAIL—OR DEARING MOUNTAIN trail as it's usually called—connects Fryman Overlook with both Coldwater Canyon Park and Wilacre Park. The trail honors a determined conservationist for her efforts to create a trail across the Santa Monica Mountains from Los Angeles to the sea.

The trail begins in the wilds of Studio City in Wilacre Park, the former estate of silent movie cowboy Will Acres. The land was saved from the bulldozer by environmentalists and the Santa Monica Mountains Conservancy in 1982. From the park's high points, great clear-day vistas of the San Fernando Valley await the urban mountaineer.

The trail continues to Fryman Overlook on Mulholland Drive, where the aforementioned valley vistas are even more terrific. From the overlook, you can follow a footpath and a suburban street back to Wilacre Park.

Between the panoramic viewpoints is Coldwater Canyon Park, headquarters of the TreePeople. The group's well-publicized tree-planting campaign has contributed a great deal to the greening of Los Angeles. You can learn about the Treepeople's work by visiting their exhibits, landscaping display, nursery and headquarters. And you can learn about the trees themselves by taking Magic Forest Nature Trail, which winds through the preserve. Benches and drinking water welcome the weary hiker.

Along Dearing Mountain Trail, you'll observe two man-made alterations of the landscape. One alteration is botanical; many exotic trees and shrubs grow on the steep slopes of Coldwater and Fryman canyons. TreePeople Headquarters was once Fire Station 108, built by the Los Angeles Fire Department in 1923. During the years the firemen were in residence, eucalyptus, pine and many other kinds of nonnative trees were planted in the area.

Another alteration is the terracing of hillsides to create pads for the construction of homes. Building on steep slopes is, of course, prevalent in canyons all around Southern California, but in the Coldwater-Laurel Canyon area it has reached ridiculous heights. The hiker looks up at some truly astonishing residences—homes on stilts, homes built stairstep-like down preciptious canyon walls, homes that seem certain to slide down to Ventura Boulevard after the first good rain.

Ascend the asphalt road past bay laurel and towering toyon, walnut trees and assorted planted pines. The road retires to dirt and soon proffers terrific clear-day vistas of the San Fernando Valley.

At a wide spot in the road, a bit more than a mile from the trailhead, you'll intersect Coldwater Canyon Park's Magic Forest Trail. You may continue on Dearing Mountain Trail, still a dirt road at this point. If you want a little break, detour right on the park's nature trail. Ascend one of the handsome stone staircases, built by the WPA in the 1930s, to the domain of the TreePeople. After learning about the group's tree-planting efforts, rejoin Dearing Mountain Trail.

A half-mile descent on the trail brings you past the backside of some homes, a yellow vehicle gate, and down to Iredell Street. Walk 50 yards on the street and rejoin Dearing Mountain Trail at another yellow gate. After a hundred yards the trail junctions. Stay left and begin a short, but very steep ascent of a terraced slope. The trail then descends to the head of a ravine that's watered by a seasonal creek and shaded by

View from Fryman Overlook.

towering eucalyptus. Frogs provide musical accompaniment to the path, which traverses the canyon wall, then dips again to the bottom of another ravine. The trail ascends moderately up the chaparral-covered south wall of Fryman Canyon to Mulholland Drive and Fryman Overlook. From the overlook, much of the San Fernando Valley is at your feet. Beyond the valley, smog-free views also take in the Verdugo, Santa Susana and San Gabriel mountain ranges.

Fryman Overlook displays two commemorative plaques. One praises Mulholland Drive. Betty P. Dearing (1917-1977) is honored for her efforts to "create a nature walk from Los Angeles to the sea."

Return a short distance on Dearing Mountain Trail to a junction; instead of descending the way you came, keep straight and follow the sage- and toyon-lined path as it heads east below Mulholland Drive. The trail turns north then east again and soon junctions. Take the left fork and descend steeply down a mustard-cloaked hillside to a dirt fire road. Turn left on the fire road, which after a hundred yards continues as a cement path and descends to a yellow gate at the corner of Dona Maria Drive and Fryman Road. Follow Fryman Road 3/4-mile to the trailhead at Wilacre Park.

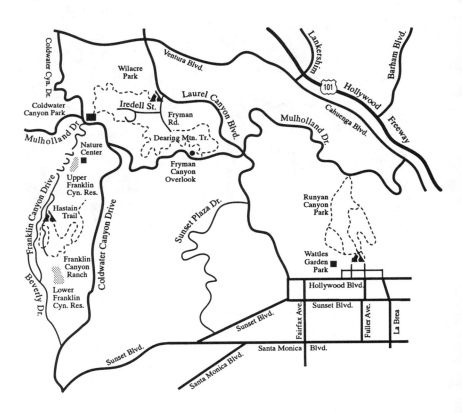

Franklin Canyon
Hastain Loop Trail

Highlights: *Despite frequent invasions of Hollywood film crews, Franklin Canyon on most days offers hikers, bird-watchers and nature lovers a tranquil retreat. The canyon is protected by Franklin Canyon Ranch, a national park service preserve perched atop the hills above Beverly Hills.*

Distance: A canyon tour from Franklin Canyon Visitor Center is 2 1/2 miles round trip with a 400-foot elevation gain.

Distance: From the westside of Los Angeles, proceed through the intersection of Beverly Drive and Coldwater Canyon Drive and follow Beverly Drive north for 1.2 miles. Turn right onto Franklin Canyon Drive and continue 0.8 mile to Lake Drive. Make a sharp right for 0.7 mile to the outdoor classroom headquarters, Franklin Canyon Ranch House. Park along Lake Drive.

From the San Fernando Valley: Exit the Ventura Freeway (101) on Coldwater Canyon Drive. Head south past Ventura Boulevard to the top of Coldwater Canyon Drive and Mulholland Drive. Cross Mulholland and proceed south on Franklin Canyon Drive. After a mile, the pavement ends. Continue 0.8 mile on a dirt road past Upper Franklin Reservoir to a junction and bear left onto Lake Drive. Parking is available on Lake Drive near the outdoor classroom headquarters.

FRANKLIN CANYON AND ITS VISITORS BENEFIT ENORMOUSLY from interpretive efforts provided by the William O. Douglas Outdoor Classroom (WODOC), named for the Supreme Court justice and environmentalist whose eloquence on behalf of America's wildlands will long be remembered. WODOC offers a hike/nature experience for almost everyone. Each year, docents conduct thousands of schoolchildren through the canyon. Leading through the canyon are special trails for senior citizens, the disabled and the blind. Aerobic walks, moonlight hikes, bird walks and map-and-compass walks are offered regularly.

The upper part of the canyon centers around Upper Franklin

View from
Hastain Trail
overlook.

Reservoir, which was constructed in 1910, then improved and expanded in the 1930s. After the 1971 earthquake, the earthen dam was declared unsafe, so the reservoir is no longer part of the Southland's far-reaching waterworks system. Today the reservoir—now more lyrically referred to as Franklin Lake—is home to bass, catfish, ducks and coots. The nine-acre lake is an important stop-over for migratory birds. More than 90 different species of birds have been sighted in the canyon.

Hastain Trail explores the lower part of Franklin Canyon. It ascends the eastern ridge of the canyon and offers fine views of both the San Fernando Valley and the westside of Los Angeles.

You can pick up a trail map at the visitor center/outdoor classroom headquarters.

From the Visitor Center, you may walk up Lake Drive to the start of Hastain Trail or cross Lake Drive to the Canyon Trail, which winds beneath live oaks and sycamores and through a chaparral community on the west slope of the canyon. A rightward fork of Canyon Trail returns you to Lake Drive, which you'll follow a short distance to a fire road (Hastain Trail).

A bit more than a mile's walk brings the hiker to an overlook where there's a good view of Beverly Hills and the Wilshire corridor. (The fire road—Hastain Trail—continues climbing to good views of Upper Franklin Canyon and the San Fernando Valley.) Turn right onto the distinct trail that descends to the nature center/outdoor classroom headquarters. Walk back up Lake Road to your car.

Chapter III

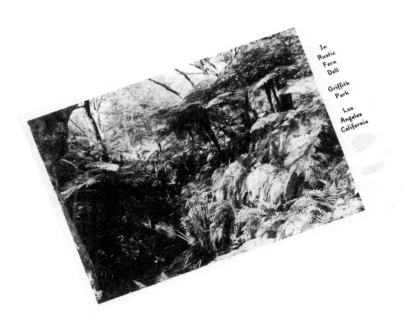

In
Rustic
Fern
Dell

Griffith
Park

Los
Angeles
California

Griffith Park

Quote to remember: *"A rock is a rock, a tree is a tree. Shoot it in Griffith Park."*

—Oft-repeated dictum of cost-conscious movie producers, credited to Abe Stearn.

Griffith Park

THERE REALLY ARE TWO GRIFFITH PARKS. ONE IS THE familiar urban park with its landscaped shrubbery, golf courses, picnic areas, train museum, observatory and zoo. The other is a wild park—mountain country—with 53 miles of trail to explore.

Geography: The 4,107-acre park forms the eastern terminus of the Santa Monica Mountains and offers the hiker a taste of the range's cliffs and crags. The mountains—often called the Hollywood Hills on this eastern end—include the park's famed high point 1,625-foot Mt. Hollywood.

The park is surrounded on three sides by freeways: the Hollywood Freeway on the west, the Ventura Freeway on the north, the Golden State Freeway on the east. A more natural boundary (though not much more natural) is the Los Angeles River, which borders the park east and north.

Natural Attractions: Two-thirds of the park, the nation's largest municipal park (attracting an estimated 10 million visitors annually), is rugged, undeveloped mountain country.

The park shares a common flora and fauna with the rest of the Santa Monica Mountains to the west. Most hillsides are covered with chaparral—chamise, ceanothus, toyon and buckwheat. Poppies, bush lupine, and the occasional wild purple onion splash color around the park.

Canyon bottoms are shaded with oak and sycamore. Planted pines and eucalyptus groves are scattered on hill and dale. More than a hundred tree species grow in the park; this diversity contributes to a variety of birdlife which numbers over a hundred species as well.

The park has a few botanical surprises including ferns in Fern Canyon and a grove of redwoods in Ferndell. Two lovingly tended gardens—Amir's and Dante's View—are hilltop oases that delight plant-lovers.

History: Colonel Griffith Jenkins Griffith, a Welshman who made fortunes in gold mining and Los Angeles real estate astonished the city when he presented it with 3,000 acres in 1896. Many in Los Angeles, however, resented his philanthropy, suggesting Griffith's gift was a ruse to dodge taxes.

Colonel Griffith J. Griffith

In 1903 Griffith lost even more of the citizenry's respect when he stood trial for the attempted murder of his wife. Convicted, he served two years in San Quentin Prison, and came back to Los Angeles, still trying to prove his civic spirit. He offered the city $100,000 for an observatory, but the city refused. Only after Griffith's death in 1919 did the city take the Colonel's money, in order to build the observatory and Greek Theater.

Eventually the city built golf courses, picnic grounds and a zoo. During the Depression, thousands of workers built the park's road and trail system.

Griffith Park's rugged terrain has long been a favorite and convenient location for filmmakers. The city, apparently less inspired by the park's scenery, for years permitted Toyon Canyon to be used as a dumpsite.

Administration: The nation's largest municipal park is under the protection of the city's Recreation and Parks Department.

Beacon Hill
Via Fern Canyon Trail, Upper Beacon Trail, Coolidge Trail and Lower Beacon Trail

Highlights: *Among Griffith Park's surprises is Beacon Hill, which offers grand views of the metropolis today, and a nostalgic look back at the early days of flight.*

Distance: 4-mile loop around Griffith Park's Beacon Hill; 600-foot elevation gain

Directions: From the Golden State Freeway (I-5) just north of downtown Los Angeles, exit on Los Feliz Boulevard and head west a short ways to Griffith Park's Crystal Springs Drive. Turn right and continue to a junction with the park's ranger station on your right (where you can stop for a map and trail information). From this junction, turn left on the road leading to the park's merry-go-round. Park in the lower lot below the merry-go-round.

L ONG BEFORE LOS ANGELES INTERNATIONAL AIRPORT was constructed, Glendale's Grand Central Airport was the Southland's main terminal. During the teens and twenties, bankers, businessmen, politicians and Hollywood stars (commercial air travel was not for the masses in those days) boarded planes on the runways next to San Fernando Road. Flying to the East Coast was a several day, multi-stop journey.

Atop Beacon Hill was a beacon, illuminated at night to warn approaching aircraft of the high Hollywood Hills near the airport. The beacon is long gone, but you can still get a pilot's-eye-view of Los Angeles from the summit of Beacon Hill.

This 4-mile workout could be a delightful way to unwind for downtown workers. Take off a wee bit early from work, or take advantage of the longer summer daylight hours and head for the Griffith Park hills. From atop Beacon Hill, you can survey your commute route—the Pasadena, Golden State and Ventura Freeways. The tranquil trail around the hills is a nice way to wait out rush hour.

Hike up the short asphalt road below the parking lot. The first trail on your left that you'll spot, signed "No Bicycles Allowed" will be your return route from Beacon Hill. Ignore a second trail on your left, the Fern Canyon Nature Trail (a wonderful side trail but not part of this hike) and walk 40 yards along the bridle trail to a 3-way junction at a large eucalyptus tree.

Bear left on unsigned Fern Canyon Trail and ascend the wide path into the brushy hills. Clouds of ceanothus accent the sandstone cliffs. You'll soon cross an old stone bridge and climb through a mixture of pine, oak and eucalyptus, which frame clear-day views of the San Gabriel Mountains.

As you climb, you get a good view of Fern Canyon with the city's suburbs beyond and below. It's a woodsy journey, with the wind blowing through an assortment of pines and the chattering birds offering relief from the din of the city.

At a 5-way trail junction, you'll take the left-most trail and ascend a short distance along a brushy ridge to the top of Beacon Hill. Nowadays it takes some imagination to realize how Los Angeles must have looked to the pilot of 1920: No freeways, no dramatic skyline. Not much there, there, then.

Today, you'll get great clear-day vistas of downtown, Elysian Park, Silverlake Reservoir, freeways and freightyards, and the big bold "G" etched into the hill above Glendale. You'll also get a grand view of the Los Angeles River, once a real river before being channelized for flood control. Contemplate the conservationists' notion of creating an urban greenbelt and restoring the river to something like its natural state, something like the pilots of old saw when they swooped in for a landing at Grand Central Airport.

Retrace your steps back to the 5-way junction and stay left. Follow unsigned Coolidge Trail on a pleasant 1-mile descent. Stay left at a fork (the right fork leads down to Coolidge Picnic Area and the train and pony rides) and continue along unsigned Lower Beacon Trail, which parallels Griffith Park Drive. You'll descend toward the noisy Golden State Freeway, and toward the park's ball fields, before the path deposits you back at the trailhead, just opposite the merry-go-round parking area.

Top of the Park: Mt. Hollywood

Mount Hollywood Trail

Highlights: The trail to Mount Hollywood offers a fine tour of the wild side of the park, and delightful clear-day views of the Big Basin.

Distance: Griffith Park merry-go-round to Mount Hollywood is 6 miles round trip with an 800-foot elevation gain; to the Observatory makes 9 miles round trip

Directions: Griffith Park, with its central location, is accessible by numerous freeways and surface streets. One good way to reach the trailhead to Mount Hollywood is via the Los Feliz Boulevard entrance, turning onto Griffith Park Drive. Follow the signs to the merry-go-round and park in the lot off Griffith Park Drive. The trail begins across the Drive from the parking lot.

THIS IS A NICE OUTING IN WINTER, WHEN THE RICH green crown of the toyon bush is aglow with a mass of red berries. At a time when most members of the chaparral communities have donned their gray apparel, the toyon—known variously as Christmas berry or California holly—is the most festive of flora.

Botanically speaking, the 6-to-25-foot high evergreen shrub is in no sense a holly, but its timely appearance is a delight to the holiday hiker, and something to point to when friends from colder climes claim that "there's nothing Christmas-y about Southern California."

You can reach Mt. Hollywood the long way, as described in the walk below, or go the more popular easy way—3 miles round trip from the Observatory parking lot.

Three trails embark from the road opposite the parking lot. The lowermost trail leaves for Five Points, the hike's first destination; the middle path is the Fern Canyon Nature Trail, a pleasant and educational experience; but the uppermost trail, marked "Bridle Trail" is the departure point for Mount Hollywood. This trail almost immediately forks, and you'll veer left. The trail climbs high above lush Fern Canyon and

Dante's view

offers fine views of the San Fernando Valley. Soon you'll arrive at Five Points, a place where five trails converge.

From Five Points, take the trail to your right (southwest). You'll cross Vista del Valle Drive, continuing your ascent as the sparkling Observatory comes into view. The trail grows more rugged as it nears Dante's View.

How did Dante's View get its name? Some hikers, climbing to Dante's during a smog alert, look out over the smoky metropolis and conclude that the viewpoint must have been named for the 14th-Century Florentine Dante Alighieri and his version of the Inferno. The more romantic, no doubt inspired by a clearer day, hypothesize that some jilted young man wandered about these hills to this promontory in a search similar to Dante's quest for his fair, lost Beatrice. Actually, Dante's View was named for 20th-Century artist-writer Dante Orgolini. Orgolini, an immigrant of Italian descent, was a mural painter during the Depression. In his later years, he put his artistic energies into planting a two-acre retreat of pine, palm and

The Observatory

pepper trees high on the south-facing slope of Mount Hollywood. A water fountain and picnic tables await the hiker at the top.

From Dante's, continue the short distance to the top of Mount Hollywood. By now you've figured out that Mount Hollywood is not the mountain crowned by the historic Hollywood sign; you can, however, see the sign quite well as you near the summit of Mount Hollywood (elevation 1,625 feet). Wonderful sunsets can be observed from the peak, and on clear days, the entire Basin is spread out before you from the San Gabriel Mountains to the Pacific Ocean. Sometimes Mounts San Gorgonio, Baldy and San Jacinto can be seen. Return to the trailhead the same way, or continue on to the Observatory.

The stretch from Mount Hollywood to the Planetarium is the most popular hike in the park, and you have several routes to choose from. One way is to retrace your steps to Dante's View and continue along this path to the Observatory parking lot. Several other trails branch off from this one and also lead to the Observatory.

Ferndell, Mount Hollywood
Ferndell Trail

Highlights: *This day hike visits two of the park's most interesting sights. First, the trail climbs to Griffith Observatory, where you can tour a little museum and catch the planetarium show. More ambitious hikers can continue to the top of Mount Hollywood, highest peak in the park, for great views of the metropolis.*

Atop Mount Hollywood

Distance: Ferndell Canyon to Griffith Observatory is 2 1/2 miles round trip with 500-foot gain; to Mount Hollywood is 5 miles round trip with 1,000-foot gain

Directions: This day hike begins at the south end of Griffith Park off Los Feliz Boulevard. One way to go: Exit the Hollywood Freeway (101) on Sunset Boulevard and head east to Western Avenue. Turn left and follow Western north until it jogs right onto Los Feliz Boulevard. Turn left on Ferndell Drive and park alongside the drive. If parking is scarce, continue up the road a little farther to Ferndell Picnic Area.

I N WELL-NAMED FERNDELL, A BROOK BUBBLES through a woodsy, fern-lined glen. The brook waters a grove of coast redwood that thrives in the bottom of the dell. The redwoods complement the native sycamore and alder, which shade this oasis in the heart of the Hollywood Hills.

Hopefully, your sense of surprise upon discovering ferns and redwoods won't be lessened when you discover that human engineering, not Mother Nature, is responsible for the life-giving brook that waters Ferndell. Recycled water from Griffith Observatory's cooling system is released from the top of the hill and sent merrily on its way down to the dell.

Still, the urban mountaineer can be grateful for the brook, which attracts numerous birds including brown towhees, robins and jays. Around sunrise and sunset, Griffith Park's deer often descend from the hills for a drink.

Join the path to the east of Ferndell Drive. Large sycamores shade the trail which ascends alongside the moss-covered banks of a brook, past tiny waterfalls, to Ferndell Picnic Area. The picnic ground has plenty of tables and is a great place for a post-hike lunch stop.

As you walk toward the redwoods and past the picnic area, stay to the right, east, side of the brook.

(Two other trails that ascend from Ferndell should be noted. One trail follows the left, west, bank of Ferndell Brook. A second trail, which departs from the end of the picnic area where Western Canyon Road makes a wide left turn, climbs to an intersection with the trail that connects Mount Hollywood with the Observatory; this path is a good, optional return route.)

Your trail, officially known as Lower West Observatory Trail, lingers for a time alongside the east bank of Ferndell Brook, then begins to climb out of the dell. Gaps in the eucalyptus and chaparral allow good views of the Hollywood sign above and the city below. Three-fourths of a mile from Ferndell is an unsigned three-way junction. You'll bear right, continue a quarter-mile to another junction and bear left, then ascend another quarter-mile to the Observatory.

From the Observatory, enjoy clear-day views of Hollywood and its hills, Century City, the Wilshire corridor and downtown, as well as the beach cities to the south and west.

Those hikers bound for Mount Hollywood should walk to the north end of the Observatory parking lot, where a handsome trail sign points the way to Mount Hollywood. The path soon begins ascending a tree-shaded ridge. After a quarter-mile's travel, you'll cross a ridge that's above the Mount Hollywood Drive tunnel. Here you'll pass a junction with a trail leading left down Western Canyon to Ferndell. (This is the optional return route mentioned above.)

Continuing your ascent, you'll climb west, then east. After ascending a long westward switchback, you'll reach a junction and fork left, heading north then west around the shoulder of Mount Hollywood. You'll pass Captain's Roost, a eucalyptus-shaded rest stop, then take the first right turn up the fire road to the top of Mount Hollywood. Wonderful sunsets can be observed from the 1,625-foot peak, and on clear days the entire basin is spread out before you from the San Gabriel Mountains to the Pacific Ocean.

To return via a different route: Leave the peak and join the first fire road leading right. Soon you'll pass Dante's View, a two-acre retreat of pine, palm and pepper trees high on the south-facing slope of Mount Hollywood. From Dante's, you descend to the trail that brought you up from the Observatory.

Batman's Lair in Brush Canyon

Brush Canyon Trail

Highlights: *Brush Canyon Trail offers a short stroll to Batman's Cave and a moderate workout to many of Griffith Park's most popular destinations—Captain's Roost, Dante's View and Mt. Hollywood.*

Distance: From Canyon Drive to Bat Cave is 1/2 mile round trip; to Mt. Hollywood is 4 1/2 miles round trip with 800-foot gain.

Directions: From Franklin Avenue, on the southern boundary of Griffith Park, turn north on Bronson Avenue or Canyon Drive (the streets soon join and continue as Canyon). Follow Canyon Drive a winding mile through the hills into Griffith Park. You an park alongside the road near a picnic area or in a small parking lot by the trailhead at road's end.

T O THE BAT CAVE, ROBIN." WITH THAT CRY, BATMAN and Robin of television fame hopped into the Batmobile and sped off to their hideaway. The dynamic duo's underground lair was not, as you might guess, a movie set built on a studio back lot, but a real cave in the southwest corner of Griffith Park.

Batman was not the only television show to make use of the area known as the Bronson Caves. About every Western from *Gunsmoke* to *Bonanza* used the caves as a hide-out for desperadoes. *Star Trek*, *Mission Impossible* and many more shows filmed here.

Long before moviemakers discovered the caves, the rocky walls of the canyon were quarried by the Los Angeles Stone Co. During the early years of this century, the crushed rock from the quarry formed the railbed for the Pacific Electric Transit System. In later years, the crushed stone from the quarry was used to pave such thoroughfares as Sunset and Wilshire Bouelvards.

Brush Canyon Trail is much less traveled than other routes to Mt. Hollywood and offers the same great clear-day views of the metropolis.

Those heading directly for the Bat Cave will look to the right (east) side of Canyon Drive for a red wall, a white pipe gate and a Griffith Park locater sign that reads "49." You'll join a fire road and heads south a short distance to the Bronson Caves. Heed the "No Climbing" signs on the steep canyon walls above the caves.

Those hikers bound bound for Mt. Hollywood will join the unsigned fire road (Brush Canyon Trail) at the end of Canyon Drive. The lower stretch of this trail is popular with local dogs and dog walkers.

The trail passes some handsome sycamores that line the canyon bottom. In autumn, the sycamores, cloaked in yellow, brown and rust-colored leaves, provide a welcome burst of color.

Once the trail begins climbing northeast and leaves the trees behind, Brush Canyon begins to live up to its name. The brush includes the usual chaparral plants plus fennel and toyon (California holly).

A mile's walk from the trailhead brings you to an unsigned junction with Mulholland Trail. Head right, and ascend to a turnout alongside Mt. Hollywood Drive. Turn left, walk a short distance along Mt. Hollywood Drive and rejoin Mulholland Trail on your right.

After a short ascent up Mt. Bell, Mulholland Trail will continue east around the mountain, but you'll bear right on a narrower trail. From graffiti-splattered Water Tower No. 52, you'll join a narrow footpath and descend first moderately, then steeply, to a junction with Mt. Hollywood.

Junctions with various fire roads let you head toward Dante's View or Captain's Roost, but Mt. Hollywood-bound hikers will head straight for the picnic tables atop the peak and take in the famed views.

Most hikers will want to return the same way. The very experienced, armed with a good park map, can use Mt. Hollywood Trail and the extremely steep and washed-out trail dropping southwest off Mt. Hollywood Drive to make a loop trip back down to the caves and Canyon Drive.

Toyon Canyon, Mt. Bell
Mineral Wells, Toyon,
Mt. Hollywood, Eckert Trails

Highlights: *Amir's Garden offers a tranquil retreat while Mt. Bell, located in almost the exact geographic center of Griffith Park, offers good views of Hollywood, the Hollywood Hills and the San Fernando Valley.*

Distance: 5 mile loop with 800-foot elevation gain.

Directions: From the valley side of the park, take the Ventura Freeway (134) and exit on Forest Lawn Drive in Burbank. Follow it into the park, turn right on Griffith Park Drive and continue to Mineral Wells Picnic Area.

From the south side of the park on Los Feliz Boulevard, turn north on Griffith Park Drive and follow it just past Harding Golf Course clubhouse and driving range to Mineral Wells Picnic Area.

Park in the picnic area and look for a three-way trail junction at the extreme lower end of the picnic ground, close to where the road splits to go around the picnic area.

OVER THE YEARS, TOYON HAS MEANT DIFFERENT things to different people. To the native Americans who once roamed these hills, the sweet toyon berries, boiled or toasted, were a treat. Spanish Californians crushed them into a drink. It's believed that masses of this California native shrub (also called California holly), growing on the hills above Hollywood gave the community its name.

To some modern-day conservationists, however, toyon has more unhappy meaning; to their horror, the city of Los Angeles for years dumped garbage in Griffith Park's Toyon Canyon.

Today Toyon is no longer a canyon, but a mountain of earth-covered trash awaiting landscaping. You've got to see it to believe it. And you will see it on your walk through the center of the park. Fortunately, this loop hike is much more than a dumpsite-seeing tour!

Amir's Garden, a tranquil retreat located just a half- mile from the trailhead, is one lovely spot en route. Iranian immigrant Amir Dialameh planted the two-acre oasis that now bears his name. Another hike highlight is 1,582-foot Mt. Bell, just a smidgin smaller than 1,625-foot Mt. Hollywood, highest peak in Griffith Park.

In some ways, the loop around Mt. Bell is a typical Griffith Park hike: You'll get some views that please and some that won't, you'll enjoy the good trails and be annoyed at the lack of trail signs. Keep alert on this hike; there are lots of trail junctions and changes of direction.

At the unsigned junction of three bridle trails, you'll see that both the trail on your left and the one on your right (Mineral Wells Trail) parallel Griffith Park Drive. The trail on your left (heading southeast) will be your return route.

Join the middle trail and ascend moderately to steeply a half-mile to Amir's Garden. You'll leave behind (some of) the din of the Ventura and Golden State Freeways and find an eclectic collection of pine and pepper trees, asparagus fern and spider plant, as well as a host of succulents.

After catching your breath, leave behind Amir's and climb again for another half-mile to a junction near water tank 112. To your right, you'll spot what remains of Toyon Canyon. Make your vow to recycle, then bear left at the junction onto Mt. Hollywood Trail and continue your ascent.

The trail crosses paved Vista Del Valle Drive and soon comes to another junction. A right (west) turn will take you around Mt. Bell. In a hundred yards or so you'll spot a number of "goat trails" which enable the agile to scramble up to the top of Mt. Bell. Great views of the Hollywood sign and the San Fernando Valley are the hiker's clear-day reward.

To complete the loop, however, you'll bear left at the above-mentioned junction, then soon make another left onto Eckert Trail which leads back down to Vista Valle Drive. Walk down the paved drive a hundred yards or so and rejoin the dirt trail on your left.

You'll begin a long looping descent. Below are the park's golf courses and the Los Angeles Zoo. The trail passes by the site of the old zoo, then parallels Griffith Park Drive a mile and returns you to Mineral Wells Picnic Area and the trailhead.

Chapter IV

Verdugo Rancho, Glendale, California.

Verdugo Mountains

Quote to remember: "*The Verdugo Mountains area
serves as an island refuge, providing what remains of a link
between plant and animal populations
found in the Santa Monica and San Gabriel Mountains.*"

—ENGLAND AND HALE, Environmental Consultants.

Verdugo Mountains

THE VERDUGOS ARE A MOUNTAIN ISLAND IN THE midst of metropolitan Los Angeles. Although the 13-mile-long, 3 1/2-mile wide range is surrounded by millions of people, the cities of Burbank, Glendale, La Canada-Flintridge, Los Angeles, Pasadena and four freeways, few walkers have discovered it.

Geography: The Verdugo Mountains bound the L.A. Basin on the southwest. Trending northwest to southeast, the mountains separate the San Fernando Valley on the western margin from La Crescenta Valley to the north and the San Gabriel Valley to the east.

The mountains are composed of highly fractured metamorphic rocks. High point is 3,077-foot Verdugo Peak. A sister range to the Verdugos—the San Rafael Hills—bound the basin on the southwest. The hills are similar in composition to the Verdugos, but lower (Flint Peak is tops at 1,889 feet) and more extensively weathered and eroded.

Uplift of the Verdugo Mountains occurred during the Pleistocene period, a half-million or more years ago. The Verdugo Mountains/San Rafael Hills are a large block detached from the San Gabriel Mountains by thrust-faulting.

Natural Attractions: Because the crest of the range is so steep, the upper parts of the Verdugos have been isolated from human impact. Remanants of the grassland that once covered the San Fernando Valley grow on the western and southwestern slopes of the Verdugos. Spring wildflowers include lupine, forget-me-not, phacelia and California poppy.

The coastal scrub community, including varieties of sage and buckwheat. also contributes a floral display in spring. Spectacular displays of goldenbush are a Verdugo Mountains highlight.

On higher slopes, the chaparral community predominates, while in the canyon bottoms—particularly Henderson, Engleheard, and branches of La Tuna—is riparian woodland. This woodland, characterized by sycamore, alder and willow,

84

is relatively rare in the Verdugos and is critical habitat for wildlife.

Rare and endangered plant species and animal life have a haven in the Verdugos. The unique tiger lily is a botanical surprise. The legless lizard, red-shouldered hawk and California dog-face butterfly (California's official state insect) have been spotted in the Verdugos.

History: The name of the mountains derives from one of the oldest Spanish land grants in California, Rancho de Los Verdugos. Jose Maria Verdugo was the owner of this 36,000-acre spread, granted him by the Mexican governor of California in 1798.

The official name of Verdugo's land was Rancho San Rafael. Over time, the large western portion of the range was called the Verdugo Mountains and the southeast section known as the San Rafael Hills.

**Master trailbuilder
Ron Webster**

Verdugo's rancho is famed for being the site of the 1847 Cahuenga Treaty, signed at Cahuenga Pass, where Spanish Californians surrendered to invading American forces. The "Oak of Peace" in Verdugo Canyon is a state historical marker.

Ownership of the Verdugos changed hands many times. Mainly the larger, lower parts of the range's dozen canyons were settled, while the precipitous upper ramparts were left untouched. During the 1930s, the Civilian Conservation Corps cleared fire breaks and built fire roads in the mountains.

During modern times, thanks to the efforts of SWAP (Small Wilderness Area Preservation) the cities of Burbank and Glendale, and the Santa Monica Mountains Conservancy, several mountain parks were established. Conservation efforts continue on all sides of the range.

Across the Verdugo Mountains
Verdugo Fire Road (Backbone Road)

Highlights: *The entire length of the Verdugo Mountains; clear-day views all over the Southland.*

Distance: 13 miles one-way; 1,900-foot elevation gain

Directions: From the Golden State Freeway (5) in Burbank, exit on Hollywood Way. Head north to Penrose Street (one block south of La Tuna Canyon Road) and proceed to Village Avenue. Turn right and follow it to road's end at the trailhead.

To reach this long walk's end point, exit the Glendale Freeway (2) on Mountain Street. Head west a short distance to Verdugo Road, turn right, then fork left onto Canada Boulevard. Turn left on Colina Drive. Follow the Drive, onto Sunshine Drive, to the trailhead—Los Flores Fire Road.

THIRTEEN-MILE LONG VERDUGO FIRE ROAD, SOMEtimes called Backbone Road, travels almost the whole length of the Verdugos. Like its much ballyhooed cousin, the Backbone Trail in the Santa Monica Mountains, it traverses the spine of the range and offers grand mountain and city views. However, unlike Backbone Trail, Backbone Road in the Verdugos is complete, and its relatively short length (13 miles as opposed to 65 in the Santa Monicas) makes

L.A. Conservation Corps workers and the tools of their trade.

it possible to hike the whole trail in one day.

At their northwest corner, the Verdugos often look similar to the San Gabriel Mountains; in fact, geologically speaking, the Verdugos are a splinter block of this range. As one travels east to the midsection of the Verdugos, it's the San Fernando Valley, sprawling below that predominates. At the southeastern edge of the range, the hills seem annexed to Los Angeles.

The west-east walk described below is more difficult than traversing the mountains from east to west. By all means, feel free to hike the Verdugos from either direction.

From Erdmore Place the road wastes no time ascending. After a mile, you'll note the trail coming up from Village Avenue (this is one of the few trails—as opposed to fire roads in the Verdugos and it offers another way to begin your cross-mountains journey.).

The road ascends to the head of Cabrini Canyon, passes a junction with Wildwood Fire Road and three miles along passes the junction with Stough Canyon Fire Road coming up from the south. You're above 2,000 feet in elevation now, and you'll stay this high, or higher, for quite a few more miles.

Rising sharply to the east is Verdugo Peak and its radio towers, and Fire Wardens Grove; it's two more miles of ridge walking to the welcome shade of the Grove. Continuing east on Verdugo Fire Road, you'll pass the second highest peak in the Verdugos, an unnamed 3,120-foot-antennae-topped summit. You pass a junction with Hostetter Fire Road, which drops north off the ridge, then pass mighty Verdugo Peak. The road drops a bit, rises again, then drops for good, passing Whiting Woods Fire Road and reaching the "Hub" of the Verdugos, where roads come up from Brand Park and Sunset Canyon.

Take a seat on the only bench for miles around, then continue down Verdugo Fire Road, passing a junction with Beaudry North Fire Road, ascending a half-mile to a viewful peaklet crowned by candy-striped radio towers, then descending again past the junction with Beaudry South Fire Road. Now you drop sharply off the west end of the range on Las Flores Fire Road, descending two zigzagging miles to the fire road's junction with Sunshine Drive.

La Tuna Canyon
La Tuna Canyon Trail

Highlights: *La Tuna Canyon Trail visits some quiet oak- and sycamore-lined canyons and ascends to the range's principal feature—and its main attraction for hikers— its ridgetop, which extends the length of the range. The ridgetop offers grand clear-day views of the San Fernando Valley, San Gabriel Mountains and downtown Los Angeles.*

CCC workers built roads and trails in the Verdugos during the Great Depression.

Distance: From La Tuna Canyon Road to Horny Toad Ridge is 6 miles round trip with 1,000-foot elevation gain; to Fire Wardens Grove is a 9 miles round trip with 1,700-foot gain; returning via Hostetter Fire Road is 10 1/2 miles round trip.

Directions: From the Foothill Freeway (210) in Tujunga (between the communities of La Crescenta and Sunland), exit on La Tuna Canyon Road. As you head west, look sharply left, and you'll spot what looks like a frontage road paralleling the freeway. This road, closed to vehicular traffic, is the road you'll be descending from the ridgetop if you elect the longer loop option of this hike.

One mile from the freeway exit, you'll spot a turnout on the south side of the road with a Santa Monica Mountains Conservancy sign. (A short trail leads to a grotto and a seasonal waterfall.) Continue another 3/10 of a mile to a second turnout on your left and park.

L A TUNA CANYON TRAIL, CONSTRUCTED IN THE SPRING of 1989, is the first foot trail built in modern times to explore the Verdugo Mountains. The trail was built by the Los Angeles Conservation Corps, under the leadership of Ron Webster. The Santa Monica Mountains Conservancy, a state conservation agency, provided funds for the project.

Hikers who have hiked a lot of trails will be delighted with the look and feel of La Tuna Canyon Trail. The hand-built trail follows the lay of the land and is not at all obtrusive.

The unsigned trail descends into the mouth of a narrow canyon, then promptly ascends the canyon wall to a little wooden overlook. The path switchbacks out of the canyon, tops Horny Toad Ridge, then descends holly-leaved cherry-covered slopes into a second, unnamed canyon. (Not only are the charms of the Verdugos undiscovered, they're also unnamed.) Reaching the bottom of the canyon, the trail visits an oak- and sycamore-shaded glen. Beneath the trees are ferns, tangled vines and plenty of of poison oak.

At the canyon bottom, the trail joins a very steep, crumbling dirt road. Below the road are a couple of old pickup trucks; one guesses their owners drove them down the steep grade, but couldn't get them back out of the canyon. The road climbs at a 25 percent grade for a half-mile, then joins Horny Toad Ridge, so-named by the trail builders for the abundance of spiky-looking, brown, tan, and cream-colored horned toad lizards found here. Another half-mile's ascent along the ridge brings you to a junction with Verdugo Fire Road. Looking sharply to the east, you can see the hike's next destination—the radio towers and pine plantation near Verdugo Peak.

Turn left (east) on Verdugo Fire Road, sometimes called

"Backbone Road," and begin a moderate ascent. Enjoy the great ridgetop views of the San Fernando Valley. Near the top of the range, you'll reach Fire Wardens Grove, planted by the Los Angeles County Department of Forestry more than a half-century ago. The department's Fire Wardens patrolled the Verdugos until 1953 when the agency was combined with the Los Angeles County Fire Department. The mixed stand of conifers planted by the Fire Wardens offers some welcome shade.

From the ridge just above Fire Wardens Grove, enjoy great views, particularly to the south, of Griffith Park, the Santa Monica Mountains and downtown Los Angeles On a clear day, even the Palos Verdes Peninsula, Los Angeles Harbor and Catalina Island are visible from this vantage point.

From Fire Wardens Grove, continue east on the ridge road, and you'll soon pass the second-highest peak in the Verdugos, a 3,120-foot-antennae-topped (again we have a shortage of names here) peak. Continue toward Verdugo Peak, and you'll soon reach a junction; Verdugo Fire Road continues along the top of the range, then descends to Glendale, but you turn left and begin descending on unsigned Hostetter Fire Road toward La Tuna Canyon. As you descend the north slopes of the Verdugos, and look north, particularly prominent is Mount Lukens—bristling with antennae—the highest peak within the city limits of Los Angeles. You'll also get a good look at the Glendale Freeway and narrow Verdugo Valley, which separates the mountains from its smaller sister range, the San Rafael.

A bit more than a mile's descent from the top brings you to a water tank, and two miles along to an apiary. The Foothill Freeway comes into view, the road turns to asphalt, and you'll travel the frontage road one-half mile to La Tuna Canyon Road. Here you'll head west (use caution when walking on the road shoulder) 1.3 miles back to the trailhead.

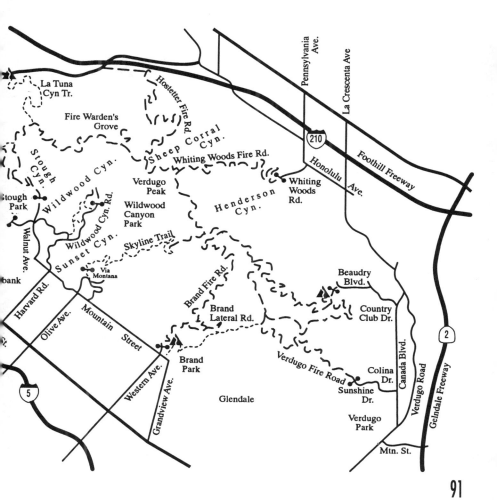

Glendale's Brand Park
Brand Trail

Highlights: *Brand Park, shaped a little like Italy, preserves a portion of the Verdugo Mountains back of Glendale. You'll enjoy great city views from Verdugo Overlook.*

Distance: From Brand Park to Verdugo Overlook is 6 1/2 miles round trip with a 1,300-foot elevation gain.

Directions: From the Golden State Freeway (I-5) in Glendale, exit on Western Avenue and head northeast on the palm-lined avenue 1 1/2 miles to Brand Libary.

"H AVE YOU BEEN TO GLENDALE?" THIS WAS THE question posed in full-page advertisements that ran every Sunday in Los Angeles newspapers during the early years of this century. The man placing these ads was civic booster/real estate tycoon Leslie C. Brand, often referred to as "The Father of Glendale."

Born in St. Louis, Brand moved to the Southland in 1898 and did quite well in the insurance business, becoming president of Guarantee Title and Trust Company of Los Angeles. By 1902, he owned one thousand acres in the Verdugo Mountains.

At the base of the mountains Brand built El Mirador, a 5,000-square-foot mansion. Brand had visited the East Indian Pavillion built for the 1893 Columbia World Exposition in Chicago and was so impressed by the architecture that he decided to have something similar designed for himself. El Mirador, with its elegant white exterior, horseshoe arches and bulbous domes is a unique example of Saracenic architecture—a mixture of Spanish, Moorish and Indian styles.

Brand died in 1925, his widow in 1945, after which, by the terms of his will, Brand's property was deeded to the city of Glendale for use as a park. El Mirador is now Brand Library.

Brand Trail is a fire road that offers a moderately steep ascent from El Mirador, through Brand Park to the ridgeline of the Verdugos. Fine valley views are yours from an overlook, where a strategically placed bench offers a rest for tired walkers. From Verdugo Overlook, the intrepid can easily extend their hike by joining one of several fire roads that travel the rooftop of the Verdugos.

Near the parking area is an ivy-covered slope where abandoned Brand Nature Trail awaits rejuvenation. You'll take the asphalt road to the left of the library that leads past the "Doctor's House," an 1880s Victorian home in the Queen Anne style that was occupied by a series of four doctors. Citizens saved this historical treasure from the wrecking ball and moved it to its present site.

A bit past a pipe gate that closes the road to vehicle traffic you'll encounter Canary Island pines, palm trees and other tropical vegetation gone wild. These trees and various tropical

Leslie Brand, Glendale's founding father.

shrubs are what's left of Brand's estate grounds, once a fairyland of waterfalls, fountains and exotic flora.

A half-dozen roads crisscross this area. Stay on the main, widest one. A mile from the trailhead you'll pass a less attractive scene—a small sanitary landfill.

Beyond the landfill, the road, now dirt, returns to a more natural setting. You pass a sycamore-lined canyon and reach a signed junction. Keep left on "Brand" and don't stray onto "Brand Lat."

Those parts of the hills where tilted rock outcroppings don't predominate are covered with the chaparral and coastal sage communities. Lemonade berry, toyon, ceanothus, sage, buckwheat, manzanita and tree tobacco are among the more common flora.

Two miles of ascent brings you to an oak tree, which offers the only shade en route. Keep climbing another long mile to the overlook.

A clear-day view takes in much of the San Fernando Valley and part of the Los Angeles Basin, including downtown. You can see the southeast end of the Santa Monica Montains, the Hollywood Hills and Griffith Park.

It sure is busy down there. Planes fly by, cars stream by on the Golden State Freeway. Surprisingly, you can even hear and see trains: the main north-south tracks of the Southern Pacific Railroad pass below.

From the overlook, you can can travel left (northwest) 2 miles along the ridgetop to 3,126-foot Mount Verdugo, highest peak in the range. Looking north and northwest you can see the San Gabriel Mountains and the mountains of Los Padres National Forest rising above Ojai.

You could also return to Glendale via an old road gone to ruin—Sunset Canyon Trail. At the end of the trail is 1 1/2 miles of street hiking on pleasant roads and sidewalks. The trail descends to to Villa Montana which you follow, making a left on Camino de Villas which becomes Tujunga Avenue and leads to Sunset Canyon Drive. Turn left on the Drive, which continues as Mountain Street and leads along the base of the hills to Brand Park.

East End of the Verdugos
Beaudry Road, Verdugo Road, Whiting Woods Road

Highlights: *Explore the eastern section of the Verdugos: valley views and views east and west over the city.*

Distance: Loop around Beaudry Canyon is 6-miles round trip with 1,300-foot gain; Beaudry Canyon to Henderson Canyon is 7 1/2 miles one way.

Directions: From the Foothill Freeway, take the Verdugo Road exit and head south. Just beyond the Oakmont Country Club, the road forks and you stay right, continuing on La Canada Boulevard. Turn right onto Santa Maria Avenue, then another right onto Country Club Drive. Turn left on Beaudry Boulevard and park near the trailhead, which is at the intersection of the boulevard and Beaudry Terrace.

Henderson Canyon trailhead: From the Foothill Freeway in La Crescenta, exit on Pennsylvania Avenue and head south. Just as Pennsylvania bends southeast, continuing as Honolulu Way, look right for Whiting Woods Drive and follow it to road's end.

THIS WALK ON THE EASTERN SIDE OF THE VERDUGO Mountains offers a number of options, including a 6-mile loop, a ridgeline ramble, and the chance to climb the range's 3,126-foot signature summit, Verdugo Peak. Also, a clear day walk to the top of the eastern crest offers a great geography lesson.

Begin along a paved length of fire road, pass a vehicle barrier, and continue on dirt road 1/4 mile to a fork in the road. Bear right on unsigned Beaudry North Fire Road. The road ascends a steep mile and passes a narrow ravine on the left. A rough path enters the ravine which is watered by a little creek. It's a tranquil, but often mosquito-plagued place to take a break.

Another mile's ascent brings you to the mountains main road—Verdugo Fire Road. Loop hikers will turn left and ascend 1/2 mile toward a forest of radio towers. From the antennae covered peak, the road descends another half-mile to a fork; the right branch drops down to Glendale's Sunshine Drive, but you descend left to the junction 1/4 mile short of the trailhead, then retrace your steps to your starting point.

Those hikers bound for Henderson Canyon will turn right on Verdugo Fire Road. The road levels for a bit and in a half-mile brings you to a major intersection, perhaps the "hub" of the Verdugo's trail network. Here two trails drop south off the mountain crest—to Brand Park and to Sunset Canyon. You can sit on a strategically placed bench and enjoy your geography lesson to the south, or you can stand and take in the view to the north.

Continue on Verdugo Fire Road a long mile to Whiting Woods Road on your right. (If you want to visit Verdugo Peak, it's another mile up the road.) Whiting Woods Road switchbacks down the ridge separating Sheep Corral Canyon to your left and Henderson Canyon to your right. Two winding miles of descent brings you to the bottom of Henderson Canyon and trail's end at paved Whiting Woods Road.

"Miradero," Leslie Brand's Estate, is now a park.

Descanso Gardens
Descanso Trail

Highlights: *Descanso is the Spanish word for "rest." The aptly named garden is a most restful place from its oak-shaded camellia garden (featuring 600 varieties, said to the be the world's largest) to its bird observation station overlooking Descanso Pond. Paths and hiking trails explore flora, native and exotic.*

Distance: A mile or so through the gardens

Directions: From the Glendale Freeway (2), just south of its junction with the Foothill Freeway (210) exit on Verdugo Boulevard. Head west a short distance to Descanso Drive, then turn right and follow the oak-lined street to Descanso Gardens.

Open daily 9 a.m. to 5 p.m.; closed Christmas.

The garden is a popular photography spot for celebrations of all kinds.

NATIVE OAKS OF THE OLD WEST MEET A Camellia forest of the Far East in Descanso Gardens, an eclectic collection of flora tucked away in a natural bowl in the San Rafael Hills.

The camellia gardens began as landscaping around the mansion built in 1938 by F. Manchester Boddy, owner of the Los Angeles Daily News. He named his property, known as Rancho San Rafael since Spanish days as Rancho del Descanso.

More than 100,000 camellias, whose native habitat is the mountainous valleys of eastern Asia, thrive in the gardens. Many of the shade loving (native oaks provide the shade) plants stand more than 20 feet tall—a veritable forest. Complementing the camellias are pools and landscaping created by L.A.'s Japanese-American community.

Six miles of garden paths as well as hiking trails in an adjacent watershed area beckon the walker. Two rose gardens—a historical one with varieties dating back to 1200 B.C. and a modern garden devoted to All-American Rose selections—are popular walking destinations, as is a lush fern collection.

Walkers who want to go native can wander among California cactus, shrubs and succulents. Nature trails meander creekside through oak woodland and past stands of pine.

On the west side of Descanso is a bird observation station, which overlooks a small lake. More than 150 kinds of land and water birds have been sighted from the station.

Flint Peak
Senator Flint Trail

Highlights: *The path to Flint Peak, like politics, is not always pretty, but it does have its rewards. Hike it on a brisk fall or winter day. The 1,889-foot peak, one of the more noteworthy peaks of the San Rafael Hills, offers fine clear day city views.*

Distance: 1-mile round trip with a 200-foot gain

Directions: From the Ventura Freeway (134) in Glendale, exit on Glendale Avenue. Head south and turn left at the first light—onto Lexington Avenue. Proceed a half-mile to Verdugo Road. Turn right, then make an immediate left onto Chevy Chase Drive, which you'll follow on a winding ascent to Linda Vista Road. Turn right and drive a mile to Figueroa Road. Turn right again and follow Figueroa to its end. The unsigned trail, a fire road, begins at a locked gate.

HISTORICALLY, POLITICIANS HAVE MORE OFTEN BEEN known for campaign trails rather than hiking trails, but one turn-of-the-century California politician, Senator Frank Flint, left us a namesake town, peak and path.

Frank Putnam Flint was born in Massachusetts in 1862. His family moved to San Francisco, where Flint received most of his schooling. After moving to Los Angeles and becoming a successful attorney, he served as a superior court judge and U.S. District Attorney. Flint, a Republican, was elected to the United States Senate in 1904 and served one term. As a Senator, he was involved in some of the behind-the-scenes maneuvering to bring Owens Valley Water to Los Angeles.

Flint's small place in history comes not from his Realpolitik career but from his real estate career. Flint is remembered as one of the major builders of urban and suburban Los Angeles.

Flint was well aware that turn-of-the-century Los Angeles had a housing shortage, and that immigrants from all over the U.S., indeed from all over the world, were flocking west to take advantage of the city's booming economy and Mediterranean climate. The well-connected Flint knew that good roads would soon be extended from downtown to the La Canada-Glendale area, so he began buying up hundreds of acres of foothill land, including a large piece of the old Rancho San Rafael.

Astride his horse, Flint rode over his property and designed the street plan for his new suburb. He envisioned a quiet community of luxury houses built on large lots, scattered seemingly at random on the wooded hills. The houses, which offered great arroyo and mountain views, had a country feel, yet were located within commuting distance of the growing city.

(Sounds like the modern suburbanite's dream, doesn't it?)

Flint's development—dubbed Flintridge—was a huge success. Frank Flint was an outdoors enthusiast, and he designed his suburb with more than twenty miles of riding/hiking trails.

Flint became a wealthy man, though he suffered a serious financial setback—and a nervous breakdown—after the stock market crash of 1929. In an attempt to recover his health, he signed on for a world cruise, but died aboard ship in the Philippines.

Follow the fire road, which ascends steeply for the first fifty yards, then proceeds at a more moderate incline toward the peak. Ignore the sight of—and, if the wind is just right, the smell of—Scholl Canyon Sanitary Landfill. Also ignore a few side roads that lead leftward.

A more pleasant perfume comes from the sage that lines Senator Flint Trail. And a more pleasant sight is the showy toyon, or Christmas berry, blooms during the holiday season on the shoulder of Flint Peak.

The top of the antennae-covered peak is fenced. If the gate at the end of the dirt road is locked, you'll have to peer through the brush to get the best view of the metropolis.

Chapter V

San Fernando Valley

Quote to remember: *At the end of World War II,
the San Fernando Valley was little more than some land north of
Los Angeles. The development of the real estate is the story of
the economic, social, and cultural development of post-war America.*

–KURT SECHOOLER, *The San Fernando Valley Past and Present*

San Fernando Valley

EXCEPT FOR A COUPLE OF INCORPORATED CITIES—
Burbank, Glendale and San Fernando—most of the
Valley is part of the city of Los Angeles. But the Valley
has never wholly been politically, socially or ecologically integrated into Los Angeles.

Geography: Far back in geologic time the Valley—and most
of the land around it—was flat and underwater. Over millions
of years mountains rose up and enclosed it. After numerous
uplifts and down-warpings, the Valley became an inland sea.
Geologists speculate that two of the Valley's current openings—San Fernando Pass and Santa Susana Pass—served as
inlets to this sea. Eventually the waters receded, pouring out
of the Verdugo Pass at the Valley's southeast corner. The path
taken by these waters is today the riverbed of the Los Angeles
River. One could, in fact, define the Valley as the watershed
for the Los Angeles River, though this once-impressive river is
now reduced to a concrete-lined flood control channel and
such a definition would most certainly lack geographical
grandeur. The historic power of the river became evident to
Valley residents during the winter of 1992 when it overflowed
its banks and inundated the Sepulveda Basin.

The alluvial-filled depression we now call the San Fernando
Valley is rectangular in shape, roughly twice as long as it is
wide. It extends 24 miles east to west and about 12 miles north
to south.

For most practical purposes, the Valley floor can be regarded as flat, though the astute walker or bicyclist may have
noticed otherwise. The Valley slopes in a general north to
south and west to east direction. Its high point is in the northwest corner, its low point in the southeast corner. If the Valley
was still in its natural state, water would drain across the tilted plain to the southeast into the Los Angeles River, which in
turn would flow across the neighboring Los Angeles Basin into
the Pacific.

On a clear day, enjoy cross-Valley views.

Natural attractions: At the walker's feet is an almost endless suburbia, 275 square miles of green lawns, swimming pools, imported trees and shrubs, parking lots and shopping malls, a strange combination of tidiness and unseemliness.

The Valley holds one of the most natural stretches of the Los Angeles River in Sepulveda Basin and a couple of botanic gems—Orcutt Ranch and Theodore Payne Foundation. To really get a glimpse of Valley ecology, you need to take a look at the surrounding mountains that wall the Valley off from the rest of Southern California. It's in the mountains surrounding the Valley, not the Valley itself, where traces of the natural and human history of the region can still be found.

Walling off the San Fernando Valley on the north and northeast and protecting it from the heat of the Mojave Desert are the San Gabriel Mountains. The Santa Monica Mountains, which extend from Calabasas in the northwest to Glendale in the southeast mark the Valley's southern boundary. The Agoura Hills, Simi Hills and Santa Susana Mountains bound the Valley on the west. On the eastern edge of the Valley are the Verdugo Hills, which almost connect with the Santa Monica Mountains to the south at Verdugo Pass.

Because the Valley floor has been almost completely urbanized/suburbanized, the walker must venture into the mountains to get to know the Valley. For example, the native needle grass that once covered the floor of the San Fernando Valley is now extinct in that area, and the intrepid botanist must venture to the far corners of the Verdugo Mountains to spot clumps of this once-dominant bunchgrass.

History: In 1769, Father Juan Crespi of the Portola expedition named the Valley De Valle Santa Catalina de Bononia de los Encinos. Mercifully, this mouthful was by the end of the century reduced to Valle de los Encinos, the Valley of the Oaks. The padres named the mission they built in 1797 after the canonized Spanish King Ferdinand III. A town and the Valley were two more places that were named after Saint Fernando.

Before the Europeans arrived, oak-dotted grassland covered much of the Valley floor. A relatively high population of Southern Shoshone and Chumash lived in the Valley and in the surrounding mountains. Game was abundant, as were acorns and seed-bearing plants. Only the lack of a dependable water supply limited the population in this land of plenty.

During the first third of the 19th Century, the Spanish and their Indian neophytes planted wheat, corn and beans, and tended horses and sheep. After the secularization of the missions, during the second third of the century, came that romantic era of the great ranchos and their huge cattle operations. In 1869, much of the southern part of the San Fernando Valley was acquired by two Isaacs—Lankershim and Van Nuys. During the last third of the century the Valley became a giant wheat field.

When the Los Angeles Aqueduct was completed in 1913, bringing High Sierra water to the Southland, the Valley was soon transformed into an agricultural region of citrus orchards and poultry farms. By the 1930s, the irrigated fields began to give way to residential housing, a process that accelerated rapidly after World War II. Some farm communities—Winnetka, Zelzah and Owensmouth—were swallowed up, while whole new cities of stucco seemed to instantly appear.

Administration: Various private botanical and historical foundations are attempting to preserve the natural and human history of the valley. Friends of the Los Angeles River have suggested the creation of the Sepulveda Wildlife Refuge.

Theodore Payne Foundation
Theodore Payne Trail

Highlights: *The Theodore Payne Foundation, dedicated to educating us about the culture and uses of native plants, is a great place to learn about local flora. A walk around the foundation's gardens is most informative; the short hike up Wildflower Hill, inspiring.*

Distance: 3/4-mile loop around the grounds

Directions: From Interstate 5 in Sun Valley, exit on Sunland Boulevard and head north a half-mile to Tuxford Street. Turn right and proceed two blocks to the entrance of the Theodore Payne Foundation. Follow the dirt driveway to the parking lot. Hours: Open 8:30-4:30 Tuesday-Saturday, Oct. 1 through June 30; open Wednesday-Saturday during the summer.

L OCATED IN SUN VALLEY—AN APT LOCATION IF ONLY for the name—is the Theodore Payne Foundation for Wildflowers and Native Plants. The nonprofit organization was incorporated in 1960 to carry on the work of its founder, botanist Theodore Payne.

Payne, who studied the nursery and seed business in his native England, moved to Southern California in 1893, where he continued to practice his trade. The botanist soon became interested in preserving the natural flora of his new home, particularly the wildflowers that were being lost to development even then.

Begin at the gift store, which offers gardening books and seeds for sale. Next, enter the nursery, where you'll find 600(!) varieties of native plants.

Several rare and endangered native species are preserved here, including a variety of manzanita that is now extinct in nature.

Join the footpath ascending Wildflower Hill. During spring, the aptly named hill displays a colorful array of at least 25 native wildflowers. The easy zigzag hike up the hill offers a delightful assortment of blooms, including poppies, lupine, owl's clover, cream cups and many more.

Sepulveda Dam Recreation Area

Los Angeles River Trail

Highlights: *Some greenery in the San Fernando Valley. Los Angeles River looks like a real river.*

Distance: 3 miles round trip

Directions: From the Ventura Freeway (101) in Encino, exit on Balboa Boulevard. Head north a half mile, crossing a bridge on the Los Angeles River and looking right for a drive leading to parking area for Sepulveda Dam Recreation Area.

THE LOS ANGELES RIVER, WHICH DRAINS THE SAN FERnando Valley at its southeast corner, is very much a part of the Valley's history and geography. Prior to the valley's subdivision and suburbanization, sand-filled arroyos extended across the valley. Winter storms filled the arroyos which in turn, swelled the river. Flooding has been a problem since recorded history.

Today, the Golden State Freeway parallels the cement-lined river channel as it crosses the Valley. But before extensive flood control measures were taken, winter and spring rains would wash out the trans-valley roads. Most travelers preferred journeying from the valley to downtown via Cahuenga Pass (now the site of the Hollywood Freeway), a higher, drier route.

In 1941 the U.S. Army Corps of Engineers rimmed the Sepulveda Basin with a 3-mile long earth-filled dam. Today the city leases some 2,000 acres of the the basin from the Army Corps of Engineers and established the Sepulveda Dam Recreation Area, complete with golf courses, sports fields and bike paths. Sepulveda Basin flooded—just as flood control engineers had designed—when the Los Angeles River overflowed in the winter of 1992.

One of the few semi-natural stretches of the Los Angeles River (and the only one along which the authorities encourage walking) flows through the basin.

The river attracts lots of birdlife. Finding the reeds, willows and cattails of the river to its liking is the red-winged blackbird. Look for its distinctive red and yellow banded wings and listen for its call—often described as "a rusty hinge."

Friends of the Los Angeles River and other conservation groups have called for the "Sepulveda Wildlife Reserve."

Begin walking on the dirt road by the river. Not long from the start you'll notice a river crossing. You can boulder-hop across the river on the return trip, if you want.

The ol' river looks pretty good along this stretch. Plenty of riparian growth and yeah, a few shopping carts.
You can make you way down to the river for a closer look and even bushwhack your way up-river through the jungle that thrives on the riverbanks.

You'll cross the river on the Burbank Boulevard bridge and resume walking on the other side. (Across Burbank Boulevard you can take a path to the foot of the Sepulveda Dam, but it isn't exactly a thrill a minute.) Your route passes two golf courses and leads you back to the aforementioned river crossing or, alternately if the river is up, to Balboa Boulevard, which you can follow back to the entrance of the recreation area and the beginning of your walk.

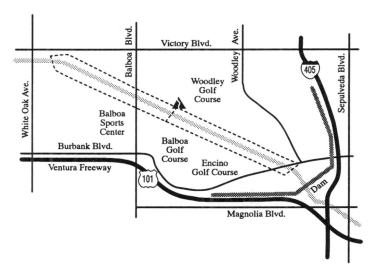

Valley Views from
Serrania Ridge
Serrania Ridge Trail

Highlights: *San Fernando Valley Views*
Distance: 2 1/2 miles round trip with 500-foot gain
Directions: From the Ventura Freeway (101) in Woodland Hills, exit on De Soto Ave. and head south. After crossing Ventura Boulevard, the avenue continues as Serrania and you proceed a mile to Serrania Park.

NOT MUCH OPEN SPACE REMAINS ON THE SOUTH RIM of the San Fernando Valley. The Santa Monica Mountains are located here, but they sometimes seem a world apart, more connected to the ocean side than the valley side of Los Angeles.

So it's with some relief that the eye travels over the Valley's south rim and finds a little green space that's not a golf course. That little green space in Woodland Hills is Serrania Ridge, a pocket of parkland on the suburban edge.

Join the path along the far eastern edge of the park and begin ascending south. The steep trail roller coasters up and down, but mostly up, offering one rise and then another from which to partake of the view.

West of the path is Woodland Hills Country Club and the hillside suburbs of Calabasas and Hidden Hills. Just east are— or once were—the Chalk Hills; so graded, contoured, terraced, plumbed and engineered for haciendas have the hills become, it's difficult to discern what was once there.

Your path climbs some more and eventually finds Mulholland Highway, your turnaround point.

Orcutt Ranch
Horticulture Center
Orcutt Ranch Trail

Highlights: *Rancho Sombre del Roble (Ranch in the Shadow of the Oak) was once a 200-acre estate owned by William Orcutt. Orcutt, a geologist with Union Oil Company, is credited with the discovery of the La Brea Tar Pits. His shady retreat in the Valley remains a haven for ancient oaks and groves of oranges.*

Distance: A half-mile or so around the ranch.

Directions: From the Ventura Freeway, exit on Topanga Canyon Boulevard and head north to Roscoe Boulevard. Turn west and drive to the park entrance, at 23600 Roscoe, a few blocks past Fallbrook.

Open daily 8 a.m. to 5 p.m.; closed major holidays

T UCKED AWAY AT THE WESTERN END OF THE SAN Fernando Valley, is a delectable slice of valley history, served up in the prettiest of surroundings—amidst a rose garden and ancient oaks.

Orcutt Ranch began as the vacation retreat of Los Angeles residents William and Mary Orcutt in 1914. Orcutt, a well respected geologist, is remembered not only for his considerable contributions to modern geology, but for his discovery of a fossil ground sloth in the La Brea Tar Pits; his discovery prompted great public and scientific interest, to say the least.

The Orcutts built a beautiful Spanish-style home and planted hundreds of acres of citrus and walnut groves. Many of the valley oaks and coast live oaks on the property were preserved.

In 1966, the Los Angeles City Parks Department purchased the estate and gardens and opened them to the public. Much of the "1920s look" has been preserved.

The large adobe house, the former Orcutt residence, is surrounded by several gardens decorated not only by interesting collections of varied plant species, but attractive fountains, statues and sundials as well.

109

The public is invited to cultivate the community garden plots and to participate in several events including the annual rose pruning demonstration in January and citrus pick in July.

Walkers can follow ranch paths for a look at an enormous valley oak—33-feet in circumference and estimated to be 700 years old. Gravel nature trails wind through the lushly vegetated estate, leading to a small creek with a bridge and a romantic rose garden.

Placerita Canyon Park
Placerita Canyon Trail

Highlights: *Placerita Canyon has a gentleness that is rare in the steep, severely faulted San Gabriel Mountains. A superb nature center, plus a walk through the oak- and sycamore-shaded canyon adds up to a nice outing for the whole family.*

Distance: Nature Center to Walker Ranch Picnic Area is 4 miles round trip with 300-foot elevation gain.

Directions: From Highway 14 (Antelope Valley Freeway) in Newhall, exit on Placerita Canyon Road and turn right (east) two miles to Placerita Canyon County Park. Park in the large lot near the Nature Center.

IN 1842, SEVEN YEARS BEFORE THE '49ERS RUSHED TO Sutter's Mill, California's first gold rush occurred in Placerita Canyon. Legend has it that herdsman Francisco Lopez awoke from his nap beneath a large shady oak tree, during which he had dreamed of gold and wealth. During the more mundane routine of fixing his evening meal, he dug up some onions to season his supper and there, clinging to the roots, were small gold nuggets. Miners from all over California, the San Fernando Placers, as they became known, poured into Placerita Canyon. The prospecting was good, though not exceptional, for several years. The spot where Lopez made his discovery is now called the Oak of the Golden Dream. A plaque marks his find.

Placerita Canyon has been the outdoor set for many a Western movie and 1950s television series, including *The Cisco Kid* and *Hopalong Cassidy*. Movie companies often used the cabin built in 1920 by Frank Walker. Walker, his wife, Hortense, and their 12 children had a rough time earning a living in what was then a wilderness. The family raised cows and pigs, gathered and sold leaf mold (fertilizer), panned for gold, and hosted movie companies. The family cabin, modified by moviemakers, stands by the park's nature center.

Placerita Canyon's nature center has some very well done natural history exhibits and live animal displays. Pamphlets, available at the center, help visitors enjoy park nature trails including: Ecology Trail, which interprets the canyon bottom and chaparral communities; Hillside Trail which offers a view of Placerita Canyon; Heritage Trail, which leads to the Oak of the Golden Dream.

From the parking lot, walk up-canyon, following the stream and enjoying the shade of oaks and sycamores. A 1979 fire scorched brush within a hundred feet of the nature center, but remarkably spared the oak woodland on the canyon bottom. Nature regenerates quickly in a chaparral community; Some of the chamise on the slopes may be a hundred years old and veterans of dozens of fires.

The canyon narrows, and after a mile the trail splits. Take your pick: the right branch stays on the south side of the canyon while the left branch joins the north side trail. The two intersect in a half-mile, a little short of the Walker Ranch Group Campground. Here you'll find a picnic area with tables, water and restrooms.

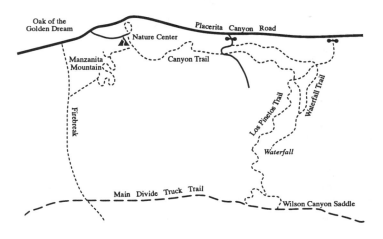

Los Pinetos Waterfall, Ridge
Los Pinetos Trail

Highlights: *A climb through chaparral and oak woodland to Los Pinetos Ridge for a view of the metropolis; during the wet seasons, Los Pinetos Waterfall is a pleasant excursion.*

Distance: Walker Ranch Campground to Los Pinetos Waterfall is 1 1/2 miles round trip with 300-foot gain; loop around Los Pinetos Ridge is 7 miles with 1,600 foot gain.

Directions: From Highway 14 (Antelope Valley Freeway) in Newhall, exit on Placerita Canyon Road and turn right (east) two miles to Placerita Canyon County Park. Continue past the turnoff to the park's nature center to Walker Ranch Group Campground.

WATERFALL TRAIL ASCENDS ALONG LOS PINETOS Canyon's west wall, then drops into the canyon for an up-close look at a fall.

Los Pinetos Trail explores the county park's high country, entering Angeles National Forest and taking you to Los

Big Leaf Maple

113

Pinetos Ridge. From the ridgetop, you can look northward over historic Placerita Canyon and Sand Canyon and southward over the San Fernando Valley sparkling below. Here on Los Pinetos Ridge, the 19th Century meets the 21st Century, and neither gives an inch.

(Waterfall Trail) The trail to the falls (not to be confused with Los Pinetos Trail) climbs into narrow Los Pinetos Canyon. Big cone spruce and live oak, plus a few stray big leaf maple shade the canyon walls. The waterfall, sometimes an impressive flow after a good rain, splashes into a grotto at trail's end.

(Los Pinetos Trail) Signed Los Pinetos Trail climbs the the south slopes above Placerita Canyon. It ascends first through chaparral-covered slopes, then through a sprinkling of walnut trees and an oak woodland. A few switchbacks from the summit, where fire fighters have stored an emergency water supply is Los Pinetos Spring (non drinkable water).

The trail reaches Wilson Canyon Saddle and a junction with Wilson Canyon Road and Santa Clara Divide Road. You might meet some fellow hikers or mountain bicyclists who have huffed and puffed their way up to the saddle via Wilson Canyon Road from Sylmar.

Enjoy views of the valleys—Santa Clarita and San Fernando—then head west on Sant Clara Divide Road. You ascend just a little bit more, then join a fire break, or fuel break, that drops off the ridge to the south. For almost two miles the break descends steeply and finally re-entering Placerita Canyon Park just above Manzanita Mountain.

A side trails leads to 2,063-foot Manzanita Mountain, which has lost much of its namesake shrub over the years to wildfire.

As you near a water tank, you can either join Hillside Trail and travel to the west end of the park's picnic area. or split to your right and follow a path to its junction with Placerita Canyon Trail; this latter trails leads two miles east through the canyon back to the trailhead.

Last of the Old West in Hart Park

William S. Hart Trail

Highlights: *A visit to the home and a hike around the ranch owned by cowboy and silent movie actor William S. Hart.*

Distance: 2-mile loop through William S. Hart County Park with 200-foot elevation gain.

Directions: From the Antelope Valley Freeway in Newhall, exit on San Fernando Road and head west 1 1/2 miles to Newhall Avenue. Turn left on Newhall and drive into William S. Hart County Park.

ON THE NIGHT STAGE, WILD BILL HICKOK,– *Hell's Hinges, the Narrow Trail.* These were some of the classic silent westerns starring movie cowboy great William S. Hart. Hart was the personification of

the strong, silent Western hero and his films were noted for their realism and authenticity.

There is a scene near the beginning of *Tumbleweeds*, Hart's last film, in which the cowboy/hero halts his horse atop a ridgetop. Removing his hat, he observes the last cattle drive over land settlers will soon claim. "Boys," says Hart, "It's the last of the West."

"Two-Gun Bill" in his Silent Movie days.

115

Tumbleweeds was also the last of the West for Hart, who retired in 1925 to his Newhall ranch. William S. Hart County Park preserves Hart's 22-room hacienda and his ranch. Hart's home, full of western memorabilia and mementoes from his film days, can be viewed on a guided tour. His ranch can be explored via a short hiking trail.

Hart Park displays the last of the West in other ways. A small zoo with barnyard animals recalls the Newhall area's ranching and farming heritage. The Saugus Train Station has been relocated to the park and offers Sunday tours of the old depot. Just outside the park is Pioneer Oil Refinery, the first refinery built in Southern California.

The hiker, too, can get a feel for the last of the West, Southern California-style, by wandering into the hills above Hart's home. From atop the hills, hikers can survey the Santa Clarita Valley and see the sometimes jarring meeting of past and present.

After Hart's retirement from acting, his company, William S. Hart Productions, filmed many westerns on his ranch. You can get a feeling for the Old West by hiking into the hills so beloved by Hart. Fire roads and a nature trail explore the ranch and offer easy hiking for the whole family.

Exit the park, walk along Newhall Avenue a short ways, then turn left on Market Street. Walk 150 yards to a senior citizens center on the left. At the edge of the center's parking lot is a Riding and Hiking Trail sign and a closed fire road.

Head up the dirt fire road, which climbs above a seasonal creek and winds into the brushy hills. The road crests at an overlook where you'll find a hitching post and some handsome cement and river rock benches.

You get good clear-day views of the Santa Clarita Valley and a glimpse of Hart's home, *La Loma de Los Vientos*, The Hill of the Winds. Inspired by this view, Hart wrote his autobiography, as well as some western fiction and poetry.

From the overlook, you can descend toward a campground and the old Saugus Train Station or head down toward Hart's home. After reaching the house, hikers may join a nature trail and descend to the main part of the park.

116

Chapter VI

Santa Susana Mountains

Quote to remember: *"Movie directors of countless old cowboy films used these sandstone hills to create the image of a rugged western setting to the point where millions of people grew up thinking the entire Old West looked like these hills."*

—L.J. HERRERA, *Santa Susana: Over the Pass into the Past*, 1973

Santa Susana Mountains

I N TERMS OF DEVELOPMENT, CONSERVATIONISTS SUG-
gest that the range resembles the Santa Monica Mountains
of 30 years ago. The middle and upper reaches of the
range are undeveloped except for a few oil wells and ranches.

The rocky peaks of the Santa Susanas.

Geography: The Santa Susana Mountains are bordered on
the south by the San Fernando Valley and the north by
Newhall, Valencia and fast-growing Santa Clarita Valley. To the
west the mountains adjoin the gentler Simi Hills and extend
into Ventura County. Granada Hills lies on the eastern end of
the range.

Geologists call the Santa Susana Mountains a transverse
range, that is to say, one of the east-west trending mountain
ranges of Southern California. Other Southland transverse
ranges are the Santa Ynez Mountains behind Santa Barbara
and the Santa Monica Mountains, to which the Santa Susanas
are often compared.

This comparison with the much better known Santa
Monicas reveals some interesting differences. One difference
is elevation: the highest peak (Oat Mountain) in the Santa

Susanas reaches 3,740 feet; the Santa Monicas can claim only one peak over 3,000 feet and most of the range is more than 1,000 feet lower than the Santa Susanas. A second difference: while the Santa Monicas are chaparral-cloaked, chaparral is absent from most of the Santa Susanas; it's grassland and oak woodland that predominates.

Natural Attractions: What you see when you look up at the Santa Susanas depends on where you stand. North-facing slopes are covered with coast live oak woodland and grassland, while the south-facing slopes present panoramas of coastal sage scrub and grassland. The upper ramparts of the range have a rich population of the valley oak, considered by many oak-lovers to be the most beautiful variety of *quercus*.

Many of the more colorful plant species of the mountains are survivors of the Pleistocene Era, or Ice Age, which ended about 11,000 years ago. Big cone spruce, big leaf maple and myrtlewood are vestiges of that cooler and moister period.

The mountains are a sanctuary for hawks—red-tailed and red-shouldered, and to owls—great-horned, barn, and long-eared. Golden eagles and prairie falcons have been spotted over the remote cliffs above Chatsworth. Roadrunners are common; stellar jays are found in the big cone spruce groves and you can see—and hear—acorn woodpeckers hammering away in the valley oaks.

History: The Santa Susanas were seen as a barrier to stagecoach (and later train) travel. About 1860 a steep stagecoach road was carved through the hills. Bandits preyed upon the stages, then headed for the hills to escape the law.

A railroad spur was built to haul sandstone from the mountains. The rock was used in the building of the Los Angeles Harbor breakwater around 1890. But it was not until the completion of the Santa Susana railroad tunnel, quite an engineering feat, in 1904 that the mountains were truly connected to points north and south.

Administration: O'Melveny Park, at 714 acres, is the city's second largest. Look for the state to take a more active role with Santa Susana Mountain State Park and proposed 6,000 acre Santa Clarita Woodland State Park. Hats off to the Santa Susana Mountain Park Association for its conservation efforts.

O'Melveny Park: Bee Canyon
Bee Canyon Trail

Highlights: *Exloring the wild side of the city's second largest park. Great walk for kids.*

Distance: 2 miles round trip

Directions: From the San Fernando Valley Freeway in Granada Hills, exit on Balboa Blvd. and head north to Orozco Street. Turn left and drive along the park's panhandle to parking for the picnic area.

ONE OF SOUTHERN CALIFORNIA'S MANY FAULTS, THE Santa Susana, tweaked the mountains of O'Melveny Park, with the happy result of helping to form Bee Canyon. The canyon is an ideal tyke hike; kids love poking around the lushly vegetated creek bottom.

The canyon—a narrow gorge, actually—has a creek that runs most of the year and a surprisingly wild ambiance. Oak and walnut trees line the base of the canyon's high sedimentary rock walls.

At the mouth of the canyon is the ranch house and barn that once belonged to the O'Melveny family. The canyon is a reminder of how much the family must have enjoyed their retreat during the 1940s at the edge of the then remote San Fernando Valley. The canyon also suggests some of the delights farther back in the Santa Susana Mountains that still need to be preserved.

Begin at the north end of the extensive picnic grounds and follow the trail into the canyon. To your right are dramatic, sky-scraping sedimentary cliffs; to your left some shady oaks.

A half-mile along the willow-crowded creek, you'll see a fire road on your left, ascending out of the canyon. You can loop back to the main part of the park on this road.

A rougher trail continues up-creek another half-mile to the park boundary.

120

O'Melveny Park: Mission Point
Mission Point Trail

Highlights: *Billowing grass and seasonal wildflowers paint a pastoral landscape on the slopes of L.A.'s second-largest city park. O'Melveny Park, located at the north end of the San Fernando Valley, is the principal recreation area in the Santa Susana Mountains.*

Distance: Bee Canyon to Mission Point is 4 1/2 miles round trip with 1,400-foot gain

Directions: From the San Fernando Valley Freeway in Granada Hills, exit on Balboa Boulevard and head north to Orozco Street. Turn left and drive along the park's panhandle to parking for the picnic area.

A second trailhead: From Balboa Boulevard, turn west on Jolette. Follow Jolette a mile to Sesnon Boulevard. (A right turn on Sesnon will take you to the main part of O'Melveny Park.) Turn left on Sesnon, then right on Neon Way. Park at the end of Neon Way. The fire road leading to Mission Point starts here.

O'MELVENY PARK TAKES ITS NAME FROM THE WELL-known famly of Los Angeles lawyers who once owned a "gentleman's ranch" here. Attorney John O'Melveny bought the land in 1941 and called it CJ Ranch. Cattle roamed the hills, a citrus orchard was planted, and family members enjoyed spending weekends roaming the Santa Susana Mountains. The family ranch house, barn and orchard still stand near the park entrance.

Although areas near the ranch were oil-rich, exploration on the ranch was unsuccessful. The O'Melvenys deeded half their ranch to Los Angeles, and the city purchased the rest. The 720-acre park, which opened to the public in 1981, includes a large developed picnic area and rugged wildland laced with 10 miles of trail.

In spring, a host of wildflowers—poppies, morning glory, Indian paintbrush and Mariposa lily—splash the hillsides. Fall wildflowers include the white trumpet-shaped jimson weed, scarlet California fuschia, and yellow goldenbrush. Wildlife in

O'Melveny Park includes deer, golden eagle, bobcat, rabbit, raccoon, and coyote. All this flora and fauna next to super-suburban San Fernando Valley!

A fire road ascends to Mission Point and explores the wild parts of the park. Bring a city map. As you climb high into the Santa Susana Mountains, you can pick out numerous natural and manmade points of interest. Views of the Southland from 2,771-foot Mission Point are often quite good.

Head west up the fire road past the park office (the former O'Melveny ranch house), rising above a walnut tree-lined canyon. You'll pass a junction with the fire road coming up from Neon Way, then join a wider road bound for Mission Point.

(From the Neon Way entrance, the fire road leads you past a seasonal brook and begins to climb high above the nearby residential area. This road soon joins the road coming up from the main part of the park.)

Evidence of the 1971 earthquake that damaged the nearby Golden State Freeway and Van Norman Dam is present in the form of fissures and slides. Seismically, the Santa Susana Mountain range is one of California's most active areas. Below, you can see the new Los Angeles Reservoir, replacement for the quake-damaged Van Norman Reservoir.

As you make your ascent, you'll notice quite a difference in vegetation between north and south slopes. The canyon's dry north slopes are blanketed with sage and other coastal scrub. To the south, the hills are covered with grasses punctuated with occasional live oak or California walnut.

As you near the top, you'll pass a small stand of Aleppo pine, which is a tree native to Mediterranean countries. This pine is successful in Southern California's Mediterranean climate, too.

Close to the top, a couple washed-out dirt roads and bulldozer lines converge. (All roads lead toward Mission Point, but the "main road" is easier walking.) Navigate toward four sturdy oaks, which offer a nice picnic or rest stop.

Just past the oaks, a dirt road branches left and leads to wind-blown Mission Point. A 1932 U.S. Geological Survey

Marker is atop the point. Two seasonal cow ponds are located on the southwest slope. Below Mission Point to the northwest are oil fields and natural gas underground storage areas.

Enjoy the view of the Santa Susana Mountains—including nearby Oat Mountain, highest peak in the range. The San Gabriel Mountains, Santa Monica Mountains, Santa Clarita Valley, and downtown Los Angeles are also part of the 360-degree panorama. Return the way you came.

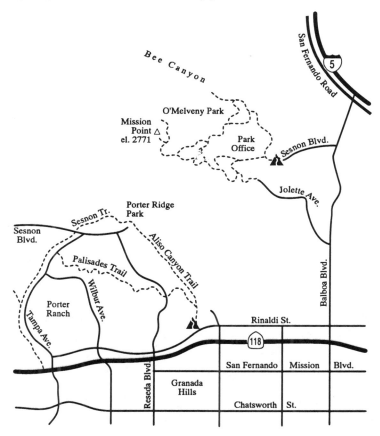

Porter Ranch Greenways
Aliso Canyon, Palisades, Sesnon and Limekiln Trails

Highlights: *A couple of quiet oak- and sycamore-shaded canyons and trails that lead through them; every community should have "greenways" like those in Porter Ranch.*

Distance: An Aliso Canyon ramble is a 5-mile round trip; a loop with Sesnon, Limekiln Canyon and Palisades Trails totals 8 miles with a 500-foot elevation gain.

Directions: From the San Fernando Valley Freeway (118) in Granada Hills, exit on Reseda Boulevard. Turn north to Rinaldi Street, and head east. Turn left on Chimineas Avenue or another nearby sidestreet and park. (There's no parking on Rinaldi.) Walk east on Rinaldi to the bridge over Aliso Canyon. Just before the bridge, on the north side of the street, is a dirt pathway leading down the embankment into Aliso Canyon.

If you wish to visit Limekiln Canyon first, or arrange some sort of car shuttle: Leave your car on Rinaldi just west of Tampa Avenue.

TWO OAK- AND SYCAMORE-SHADED CANYONS—ALISO and Limekiln—and eroded sedimentary outcroppings known as "The Palisades" are some of the highlights of a walk through the Porter Ranch portion of the Santa Susana

What will happen to these quiet canyons if development continues unchecked?

Mountains.

The good news for walkers is this part of the Southland is that the trail system is pretty good. Expect well-graded paths and good signs.

Less happy news is that Porter Ranch is, or at least scheduled to be, one of the largest subdivisions in Los Angles history. Political battles have taken place over the size and scope of this gigantic undertaking.

What happens in the next couple years to Limekiln and Aliso Canyons might very well indicate how—or if—the valley manages to preserve some precious open space. Take Limekiln for example: The lower reaches of the canyon are tree-lined and quiet. In the middle section of the canyon, a subdivision is blanketing the west wall. The upper reaches of the canyon are an oil field belonging to the Texaco Oil Co. and are off limits. What will the future be for places like Limekiln Canyon?

Descending the embankment from Rinaldi, you soon find yourself in quiet Aliso Canyon. The path passes a stables and meanders along the canyon bottom among oak, sycamore and eucalyptus.

On the canyon walls, which burned in a 1988 fire, watch for spring wildflowers—purple lupine, golden California poppies. You'll pass junctions with a couple of side trails, but the only one to note is Palisades Trail which climbs out of the canyon to your left.

Aliso Canyon Trail stays near the bottom of the narrow canyon for another mile, before it climbs out of the canyon to meet the end of Sesnon Boulevard. You'll then head west through Porter Ridge Park on Sesnon Trail, which heads behind some houses and ends at Limekiln Canyon, near the intersection of Sesnon Blvd. and Tampa Ave.

Head south on bridle-path-like Limekiln Trail which soon brings you to the signed intersection for Palisades Trail, which climbs eastward over some sedimentary outcroppings and offers you southern views of the San Fernando Valley. Palisades Trail crosses Reseda Boulevard, then drops you back down into Aliso Canyon. You then retrace your steps down-canyon back to Rinaldi St. and your starting point.

Devil Canyon
Devil Canyon Trail

Highlights: *A heavenly creekside retreat in Devil Canyon; handsome sandstone formations.*

Distance: 4 1/2 miles round trip; 400-foot gain

Directions: From the San Fernando Valley Freeway (118), exit on Topanga Canyon Boulevard. Park in the little dirt lot just north of the freeway.

S O PEACEFUL A RETREAT IS THIS CANYON THAT YOU wonder how it got its name. The canyon is cool, wet, and green, in contrast to the hot, dry northeast rim of the San Fernando Valley.

Decades before condominiums blossomed on the canyon walls, fire and flood ravaged the canyon, removing a road (and any possibility of vehicle travel). Nature healed itself just fine,

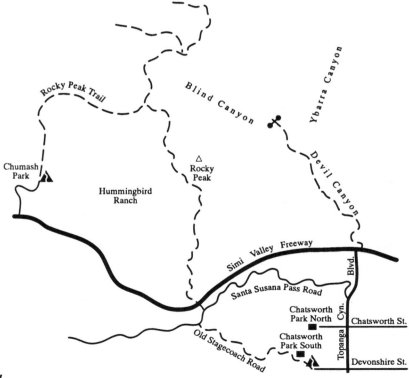

without human intrusion. Today, this oak-shaded canyon, through which a seasonal creek flows, is a welcoming oasis, particularly after winter rains swell Devil Canyon Creek.

Hunt for the beginning of the dirt road, in an area of new construction, that descends into the canyon. After a quarter-mile or so of less-than-inspiring walking under the shadow of the condominiums that line the west wall of the canyon, the road bends left and Los Angeles County Flood Control Dept. signs warn you about the dangers of Devil Canyon, in which you're now traveling.

The canyon bottom is a lovely place, shaded by oaks, alder and sycamore. The trail narrows as it heads up-creek.

A bit more than a mile along, just short of where Ybarra Canyon joins Devil Canyon, there a shady flat—an ideal picnic spot. Another mile along is trail's end; a gate with private property beyond.

Santa Susana Pass
Stagecoach Trail

Highlights: *A hike along a part of the old stagecoach route from San Francisco to Los Angeles, an infamous stretch through Santa Susana Pass known as the Devil's Slide.*

Distance: From Chatsworth Park South to Devil's Slide is 2 1/2 miles round trip with 500-foot elevation gain

Directions: From the Ventura Freeway (101) in Woodland Hills, exit on Topanga Canyon Boulevard and drive 6 1/4 miles north to Devonshire St. Turn left and proceed 3/4 mile to Chatsworth Park South, a city-owned park with wide lawns and picnic areas, located next to the new state park. If you're coming from the Simi Valley-San Fernando Valley Freeway (118), take the Topanga Canyon Boulevard exit in Chatsworth, drive 1 1/2 miles to Devonshire and turn right to the park.

ONE OF THE MAJOR OBSTACLES TO STAGECOACH travel between Los Angeles and San Francisco was a route out of the west end of the San Fernando Valley over the Simi Hills. About 1860, a steep road was carved out of the rock face of the hills. The steepest stretch, a peril to man and beast, was known as Devil's Slide.

The slide, the old stage road and a portion of the Simi Hills are preserved in a park in-the-making located just west of Chatsworth. In 1989, the state purchased 400 acres in the Santa Susana Pass area and added it to another 400 acres of state-owned parkland. Eventually Santa Susana State Park will be staffed with rangers, and have recreation facilities. The park represents two decades of organizing and lobbying efforts by San Fernando Valley and Simi Valley environmentalists, spearheaded by the Santa Susana Mountain Park Association.

Santa Susana as a park name is confusing because the Simi Hills, not the nearby Santa Susana Mountains, are protected by the park. Visually, the Simi Hills with their sky-scraping sedimentary rock formations are quite different from the rounder, taller Santa Susana Mountains to the north of Chatsworth.

The reddish-orange sandstone outcroppings of the Simi Hills, dating from the Tertiary and Mesozoic periods 60 to 80 million years ago, form a dramatic backdrop for the park. It's easy to see why these rugged hills were a popular setting for Western movies.

The hills overlook Chatsworth, named after Chatsworth England. Founded in the 1880s, it became a community of vegetable patches, orchards, cattle and horse ranches. Although one of the west San Fernando Valley's oldest towns, it's managed to hang on to its rural character somewhat better than most Valley communities.

A network of trails loop through the park, but the trails are unsigned and more than a little confusing. During your first

Historic Stage Road over the Devil's Slide.

visit to the park, expect to improvise a bit. Once you get the lay of the land, subsequent visits will be easier.

As you drive up Devonshire you'll notice signed Stagecoach Trail, an equestrian trail. Leave your car and pick up this trail if you wish, but it's more convenient continuing to the ample parking area in the main part of Chatsworth Park South.

From the parking lot, walk across the wide lawn (or take one of the dirt paths that border the lawn). With the park recreation center directly behind you, navigate toward a couple of oaks and join a gravel path that begins just below a water tower on your right.

Begin a moderate ascent. When presented with confusing choices and unsigned junctions, try to keep ascending straight up the hill. Don't drift too far to the south where there's a line of electrical transmission towers, or too far to the north where the Southern Pacific railroad tracks penetrate the mountains.

A half-mile from the trailhead you'll intersect a paved road, which winds up to a small hydroelectric pumping plant. You, however, will almost immediately abandon this road at a break in a chain link fence by two telephone poles. Here you'll find the old stage road and begin to climb more earnestly toward Devil's Slide.

A century ago, the road was in much better shape. Erosion has carved wagon-wheel-sized potholes into the soft rock. The Devil's Slide is more like the Devil's Stairs these days.

Near the top of the slide is a historical marker placed by the Native Daughters of the American West commemorating "Old Santa Susana Stagecoach Road, 1859-90." This is a great place to pull up a rock, sit a spell and survey the San Fernando Valley, which spreads south and east. Just below is Chatsworth, a mixture of old ranchland and new townhouses. If you're lucky, you'll sight a train snaking through the Simi Hills and disappearing into the Santa Susana tunnel.

After enjoying the view, you can continue another 1/4 mile up the Stagecoach Trail and inspect the rest of Devil's Slide. Or retrace your steps and take one the side trails leading southeast over to the park's intriguing rock formations.

Rocky Peak
Rocky Peak, Chumash Trails

Highlights: *Well-named rocky peak, oak-lined canyons, and a new trail that offers valley and coastal views.*

Distance: 6 miles round trip with 1,200 foot elevation gain to Rocky Peak via Rocky Peak Trail; 7 miles round trip with 1,400-foot elevation gain to Rocky Peak via Chumash Trail.

Directions: To reach the Rocky Peak trailhead, take Highway 118 through the Simi Valley and exit on Rocky Peak Road (that's one exit west of Topanga Canyon Boulevard). The trailhead is immediately opposite the end of the freeway offramp. Caution: You can exit on Rocky Peak Road only by traveling west on Highway 118.

To Chumash trailhead: From Highway 118 (Simi Valley-San Fernando Valley Freeway) in Simi Valley, exit on Yosemite Avenue. Head north 1/2 mile to Flanagan Drive, turn right, and drive 3/4 of a mile to road's end and Chumash Park.

ONE CONSERVATION SUCCESS STORY IS THE PRESERVATION of Runkle Ranch, now Rocky Peak Park. The park, which straddles the Los Angeles/Ventura County line, sets aside some much needed parkland for fast-growing Simi Valley. Until purchased by the Santa Monica Mountains Conservancy in 1991, the Rocky Peak area was owned by entertainer Bob Hope.

The rocks of Rocky Peak are sandstone outcroppings that geologists say were formed some 65 million years ago during the Cretaceous Period of the Mesozoic Era. Besides its namesake promontory, 4,369-acre Rocky Peak Park includes Las Llajas and Blind Canyons. These canyons have two of the most pleasant seasonal streams in the mountains. After a good rain, waterfalls cascade down the canyons.

Chumash Trail begins in Chumash Park on the outskirts of Simi Valley and leads 2 1/2 miles to a junction with Rocky Peak Trail, which leads to the peak. Park trails provide access to Blind Canyon and the rolling meadowlands of the Santa Susana Mountains to the north. The trail is a good introduction to the charms of the Santa Susanas.

Aptly named Rocky Peak area.

(Via Rocky Peak Trail) Begin at the locked gate of the fire road (closed to vehicles) and begin the ascent. Soon you'll get grand view (if you turn around, that is) across the freeway to the historic Santa Susana Pass, once crossed by stagecoaches.

The fire road continues up and up, with only a lone oak along the trail for shade. Rocky Peak is off to the right (east) of the trail. From the peak and related smaller peaks, you'll get vistas of the San Fernando Valley, Simi Valley, high peaks of Los Padres National Forest, Anacapa Island and the Santa Barbara Channel. Way off to the right (west) is the new Ronald Reagan Presidential Library.

From Chumash Park, Chumash Trail heads north from the end of Flanagan Drive. The path soon parallels a creek, makes a half-circle around a minor hill, then begins climbing in earnest high above Blind Canyon.

Two-and-a-half miles of steady ascent brings you to an intersection with Rocky Peak Trail. If you turn right (south) on this trail, it's about a mile's walk to Rocky Peak. A left turn leads 2 1/2 miles to the park boundary and a large oak savanna.

Bell Canyon, Castle Peak
Bell Canyon, Castle Peak Trails

Highlights: *Stand in the 19th Century and gaze into the 21st; grand views from atop Castle Peak.*

Distance: 2 miles round trip with 700-foot gain

Directions: From the Ventura Freeway (101) in Woodland Hills, exit on Valley Circle Blvd. and head north all the way to Vanowen Street. Turn left and drive a short ways, parking near where the street curves to meet Sunset Ridge Drive and Castle Peak Estates. At the west end of Vanowen is Bell Canyon Park.

O N THE BORDER BETWEEN THE SANTA SUSANA Mountains and the Simi Hills, between Los Angeles County and Ventura County, between Rockwell International's Santa Susana Field Laboratory and the pricey West Hills suburbs, is rarely visited Bell Canyon Park.

The walker may opt for a peaceful stroll among the park's valley oaks or an assault on Castle Peak, which offers a commanding view of the west valley.

You head west along a dirt road and soon come to a junction; two parallel tracks penetrate Bell Canyon Park. If you intend to meander among the oaks, take either fork; however, if you're bound for Castle Peak, go right, then turn right again when you see an extremely steep path angling toward the summit.

After pausing several times to catch your breath, you reach the castellated summit. You can see Simi Valley; it was covered with farms as late as World War II but now seems to be merging with the San Fernando Valley into the great urban metropolis. From Castle Peak, the Valley looks like a valley— surrounded by mountains. The valley is developing a skyline, you notice, as you observe the high-rises around Warner Center and elsewhere.

After your valley views, carefully descend the precipitous path back to the park flatlands. Follow one of the two flatland trails westward among the valley oaks until you run out of parkland; alas, a chain-link fence blocks further exploration of the delightful Simi Hills.

133

Cheeseboro Canyon
Cheeseboro Canyon Trail

Highlights: *A lovely place, where the Southern California of old faces the Southern California of the future. Cheeseboro Canyon is a pleasant walk, gentle enough for the whole family.*

Distance: From NPS Parking Lot to Sulfur Springs is 6 miles round trip with 100-foot elevation gain; to Sheep Corral is 9 1/2 miles round trip with 200-foot elevation gain

Directions: From the Ventura Freeway (U.S. 101) in Agoura, exit on Chesebro Road. Loop inland very briefly on Palo Comado Canyon Road, then turn right on Chesebro Road, which leads to the National Park Service's gravel entrance road and parking lot.

I T'S THE OLD CALIFORNIA OF THE RANCHOS: OAK-STUD-ded Potreros, rolling foothills that glow amber in the dry months, emerald green in springtime. It's easy to imagine vaqueros rounding up tough Mexican range cattle.

Vultures roost in the ancient oaks of Cheeseboro Canyon.

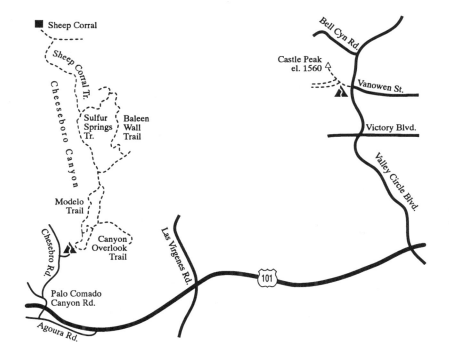

For years this last vestige of old California faced an uncertain future, but thanks to the efforts of conservationists it was saved from golf course and suburban development in 1991.

In times past, the Chumash occupied this land. The Indians came to gather acorns, a staple of their diet. A family required about 500 pounds of acorns a year, anthropologists estimate. It was quite an operation to gather, dry, and grind the acorns into meal, then leach the meal to remove the tannic acid.

From the days of the ranchos to 1985, Cheeseboro Canyon was heavily grazed by cattle. Grazing altered canyon ecology by displacing native flora and allowing opportunistic plants such as mustard and thistle to invade. As you walk through the canyon, you'll see signs indicating research areas. The National Park Service is attempting to re-colonize native flora and eradicate nonnatives.

Note your return route, Modello Trail, snaking north up the wall of the canyon, but follow the fire road east into Cheeseboro Canyon. The fire road soon swings north and dips into the canyon. You'll pass a signed intersection with Canyon Overlook Trail, a less-than-thrilling side trail that leads to a knoll overlooking the Lost Hills landfill.

After this junction, the main canyon trail, now known as Sulfur Springs Trail, winds through valley oak-dotted grassland and coast live oak-lined canyon. Watch for mule deer browsing in the meadows and a multitude of squirrels scurrying amongst the oaks.

The old road crisscrosses an (usually) all-but-dry streambed. About 3 miles from the trailhead, your nose will tell you that you've arrived at Sulfur Springs. You can turn around here or continue another 1 3/4 miles up a narrowing trail and narrowing canyon to an old sheep corral.

Return the way you came on Sulfur Springs Trail to a junction 3/4 mile from the trailhead. Join signed Modello Trail which ascends the west wall of the canyon. From the ridgetop you can get a good view of Cheeseboro Canyon and one of the finest remaining oak woodlands in Southern California.

At a signed junction, stay with Modello Trail, which loops around the head of a ravine, then descends to the trailhead.

Chapter VII

The New Arroyo Seco Bridge Pasadena, Cal.

San Gabriel Valley

Quote to remember: *"It would be difficult to suit a
pleasure-seeker who could not be satisfied in this land—this veritable
land of milk and honey, where Nature pours out her bounties
and her beauties in lavish abundance, and the air of heaven conspires
with the cunning of man to confirm health and to sanctify happiness."*

—JEANNE C. CARR, describing the San Gabriel Valley in
West of the Rocky Mountains, 1888

San Gabriel Valley

EXTENDING EASTWARD ALONG THE BASE OF THE SAN Gabriel Mountains, from Pasadena to Glendora, this former orange-growing empire is now throughly suburbanized. The valley's natural history is preserved in some terrific botanic gardens and in some hilltop retreats.

Geography: The San Gabriel Valley may not seem very valley-like to the commuter speeding along the Foothill Freeway; however, the valley, as a geographic entity, is apparent to the hiker standing on high and to the geologist reading the valley's long history in the rocks.

The valley is that area drained (or rather, once drained) by tributaries of the San Gabriel River. Nowadays the river and its offshoots are tamed by concrete flood control channels, but in geologic ages past they spread the alluvium that now makes up the valley floor.

More evidence that the valley is a valley: it's surrounded by mountains. The San Gabriel Mountains border the valley on its northern edge, South Hills on the northeast, Puente Hills on the south and southeast, the hills of Montebello and the San Rafael Hills on the west.

Natural Attractions: Much of today's valley is typical late 20th Century Southern Californian in appearance, but bits and pieces of its ecological past have been preserved.

What natural history remains is found along its waterways and atop its hills. Walnut Creek and Marshall Canyon preserve important riparian communities. At Whittier Narrows some last natural vestiges of the San Gabriel River can be seen.

Like the San Fernando Valley, the San Gabriel Valley's flora and fauna is best preserved not on the valley floor but in the surrounding hills. The brush-covered Puente Hills and San Jose Hills deliver up-close views of native chaparral as well as far-reaching panoramas of the valley.

History: The valley was once Gabrielino Indian territory. Spanish missionaries established Mission San Gabriel on the banks of the San Gabriel River in 1771. Because of flooding, the nission was moved inland a few years later. At its height, it was the wealthiest of California missions with thousands of acres of vineyards and grain fields under cultivation and many thousands of head of cattle.

At the base of the San Gabriel Mountains are the cities of Siera Madre, Monrovia, Duarte, Azusa and Glendora. After American settlers displaced the Spanish in the middle of the 19th Century, these valley communities emerged as one of the Southland's famed citrus belts.

Today, when you look down at the San Gabriel Valley, it's obvious that the Foothill Freeway is the main transportation corridor. But much earlier in this century, it was the Pacific Electric redcars that linked these rural suburbs to Los Angeles and to to the rest of Southern California.

The "capital" of the San Gabriel Valley has long been Pasadena, known worldwide for its beautiful setting and civic promotions: the Rose Parade and Rose Bowl game. Beginning in the latter part of the last century, the city became a health resort, eventually a desirable suburb. Tree-lined boulevards and its celebrated architecture put Pasadena on the map and continue to attract visitors today.

Administration: Los Angeles County Department of Parks and Recreation holds much of the valley's greenery, including Schabarum, Bonelli, Walnut Creek, Whittier Narrows and Marshall Canyon parks. The Los Angeles County Arboretum and the private Rancho Santa Ana Botanic Garden are two valley highlights.

San Gabriel Valley home, circa 1870.

139

Pasadena's Arroyo Seco
Arroyo Seco Trail

Highlights: *Since before the turn of the century, the arroyo has been a pleasuring ground for nature-loving Pasadenans. Old photos show a verdant canyon, with trails meandering along wooded banks. Engineers, not ecologists, have controlled nature in the arroyo; still, some tranquil places remain.*

Distance: From Arroyo Seco Park to the Rose Bowl is 3 miles round trip.

Directions: From the Pasadena Freeway in South Pasadena, exit on Marmion Way/Avenue 64. Bear left and follow the signs to York Avenue. Turn right on York and then almost immediately turn left on San Rafael Avenue. Drive three-quarters of a mile to Arroyo Seco Park, where there's plenty of parking. Best bet for hikers is the small lot near the softball field. Arroyo Seco Trail departs from San Pasqual Stables, just up the avenue on the left side of the road. Don't park in the stables' lot.

ARROYO SECO IS UNDOUBTEDLY THE BEST-KNOWN canyon in Southern California. It's the site of the Rose Bowl and has the dubious distinction of hosting California's first freeway. The arroyo includes ten miles of urban canyon and ten miles of wild and rugged watershed spilling from the shoulder of Mount Wilson.

In Pasadena, between the end of the freeway and the beginning of the Angeles National Forest, the arroyo takes on a third dimension, what land use planners, in the peculiar jargon of their trade refer to as "the urban/rural interface." Here the arroyo has been domesticated, but not destroyed. And here the walker will find a little leg-stretcher of a hike that recalls the Pasadena of a century ago. Rose Bowl-goers will find a fun way to reach the stadium.

During the last decade of the last century and the first decade of this one, the banks of the Arroyo Seco hosted a way of life historians now call Arroyo Culture. Artists, writers, wealthy eccentrics and assorted nonconformists settled in this suburb, so uniquely positioned between the wilderness and fast-growing Los Angeles. Many decades before today's "Southwest Look" became so trendy, Arroyo residents gloried in Indian and Mexican cultures. They filled their homes with Indian blankets and pottery, stained glass and colored tile.

Historian Kevin Starr, in *Inventing the Dream: California through the Progressive Era*: sums up Arroyo Culture: "To build homes on the Arroyo, as did these bohemians, was to embrace the symbol of the desert wilderness and to glory in Southern California's resistant, elemental culture. On Orange Grove Avenue the Pasadenan looked out on a lawn and a trimmed hedge. On the Arroyo Seco, he looked out on jackrabbits and chaparral."

One tireless promoter of Arroyo Culture was Charles Fletcher Lummis, city editor of the *Los Angeles Times*, editor of *Out West* magazine and founder of the Southwest Museum.

Graceful bridge spans Pasadena's Arroyo Seco.

(You can see the Lummis Home at 300 East Avenue 43.)

Another booster was George Wharton James, author of *Wonders of the Colorado Desert* and innumerable articles about the natural and cultural history of the Southwest. Two of the many writers whose careers were influenced by their contact with Arroyo Culture included Mary Austin and a young Occidental College student/blossoming poet, Robinson Jeffers.

Pasadena purchased the arroyo from the Pasadena Land & Water Company in 1912. Over the years, the arroyo hasn't always been so "seco"; in fact during some winters, quite a torrent rushed down the arroyo. Devil's Gate Dam and Reservoir were built to capture the arroyo's runoff and a cement channel built to direct its flow. Today, as a result of all these flood control measures, the trail along the Arroyo Seco is no wilderness adventure, but it does afford a a pleasant walk into Pasadena's past.

The trail, signed "Horseback Riding Trail," begins at the north end of the stable grounds. A 50-yard walk brings you to a small bridge over the arroyo flood control channel. Here you may choose which side of the arroyo you'd like to walk upon; equestrian trails parallel both sides of the channel for about a mile.

Arroyo Seco Trail passes native oak, alder and sycamore, as well as arboreal imports from faraway lands—eucalyptus, palm and pepper trees. Pasadenans have been cultivating gardens at the arroyo's edge for about a century, and some mighty strange flora has escaped from these gardens and sprouted on the canyon walls and bottom: bougainvillea, bird of paradise, and dozens of other exotic plants.

High above you, atop the arroyo walls, are some fine old homes—Bavarian, Victorian, Tudor and Anyone's Guess in style—and all but hidden by the profligate vegetation.

As you approach an archery range, note the huge castle-like structure high on the arroyo's east bank. This is the Vista del Arroyo Hotel, finished in 1936 and now a federal government office building.

The trail takes you beneath a trio of bridges arching over the Arroyo Seco. Unlike the arroyo flood control channel, the bridges are an aesthetic triumph. Particularly pleasing to the eye is the Colorado Boulevard Bridge, known in the 1930s as "Suicide Bridge." Many wealthy Pasadenans were hard hit by the 1929 stock market crash and decided to leave this world by leaping off the bridge. Seventy-nine people were reported to have taken a dive. Arroyo homeowners, upset by the effect this leaping was having on their property values and the unseemliness of it all, pressed the city to correct the situation. The city responded in 1937 by building a high fence and stationing a guard on the bridge.

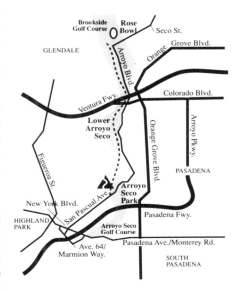

Somewhat ironically, the most natural part of the arroyo that you'll encounter along this trail is found beneath the Colorado Boulevard and Ventura Freeway bridges. Eastside and westside arroyo trails join together near a spillway and finally depart from the straight line course of the cement flood control channel. The path follows a little creek, which hints at what the arroyo might have looked like before its ecology was forever altered by engineers.

Arroyo Seco Trail emerges from the greenery near the corner of Arroyo Boulevard and Seco Street. The Rose Bowl is dead ahead. Walk along Arroyo Boulevard a short distance to Brookside Park, where you can picnic in the shadow of the Rose Bowl.

A signed "Horseback Riding Trail" continues north another mile, first passing through the Rose Bowl parking lot, then continuing alongside West Drive past Brookside Golf Course. Skip this boring path, eat your lunch at Brookside Park and return the same way.

Los Angeles State and County Arboretum

Arboretum Trail

Highlights: *Tropical Greenhouse, the Garden for All Seasons, Sunset Demonstration Home Gardens and specialty gardens featuring plants from around the world. Colorful peacocks strut the gardens; a collection of ducks populate the 4-acre lake. A 50-foot waterfall forms a beautiful backdrop for a collection of ferns and water-loving species.*

Distance: A mile or so.

Directions: From the San Bernardino Freeway (10) in El Monte, exit on Baldwin Avenue and drive north to the entrance of the Los Angeles County Arboretum on the west side of the street. From the Foothill Freeway (210) in Arcadia, exit on Baldwin Avenue and go south a short distance to the arboretum entrance.

Open 9 a.m. to 4:30 p.m.; closed Christmas

THE FORMER ESTATE OF E.J. "LUCKY" BALDWIN IS NOW home to 30,000 plants. Businessman and developer Baldwin purchased the old Rancho Santa Anita in 1875 and constructed a striking Queen Anne-style home on his property overlooking a natural lagoon. While the arboretum gets plenty of visitors (a half-million a year), many more head for that other Baldwin-inspired creation across the street—the Santa Anita racetrack.

If the arboretum scene looks familiar, it's because you've seen it on the screen: old Tarzan flicks, the *Fantasy Island* television series, and much more. With Katharine Hepburn along, Humphrey Bogart pulled the African Queen through the arboretum jungle.

In terms of exercise, the road circling the arboretum offers the walker the best workout. But to really see the flora, get off the road onto the garden paths.

Paths wind past some of America's tallest palm trees,streams and a waterfall to greenhouses–for bromeliads,

144

orchids, begonias and tropical plants. Particularly fun is a stroll through the Jungle Garden. The stands of eucalyptus in the Australian section look right at home here in Southern California.

For a good clear-day view of Mt. Wilson, follow the path up Tallac Knoll, and in the process you will encounter a stand of the rare Pasadena oak.

Amidst the colorful flora, the walker will likely encounter the arboretum's dominant fauna—peacocks, descendants of a couple of peafowl brought from India by Lucky Baldwin at the turn of the century.

Fern-lined waterfall: a cool and tranquil corner of the arboretum.

145

Whittier Narrows
Nature Center
Aquatecos Lake Trail

Highlights: *A glimpse at the natural world that once flour-ished along the banks of the San Gabriel River.*

Distance: 1 mile round trip. Energetic walkers can join nearby San Gabriel River Trail and travel many miles along a paved pathway that follows the river from Azusa to Long Beach.

Directions: From the Pomona Freeway in South El Monte, exit on Peck Road. Pick up Durfee Avenue, south of the freeway overpass, and follow it into Whittier Narrows Recreation Area. Turn left into the parking lot for Whittier Narrows Nature Center.

BIRDS, LOTS OF THEM, HAVE LONG ATTRACTED birders to Whittier Narrows. At last count, more than 250 species had been recorded in the area between the San Gabriel and Rio Hondo Rivers. Diverse habitats—lakes and rivers, sandbars and mudflats, riparian vegetation and open fields—account for the high number of species.

Abundant birdlife was one of the reasons the National Audubon Society established its Southern California head-quarters in Whittier Narrows during the 1930s. San Gabriel River Wildlife Refuge was how the area was known then.

A wild river, vines that climbed high into the trees, and jun-gle-like vegetation attracted moviemakers to Whittier Narrows. The Narrows doubled for deepest darkest Africa in the Tarzan movies starring Johnny Weismuller.

Over the years Whittier Narrows survived fire and floods, but nearly perished, as a wildlife sanctuary anyway, when the Audubon Society was displaced by the Army Corps of Engineers, who built berms, dams and concrete channels.

Today's 127-acre Whittier Narrows Nature Center is but a fraction of the much larger Whittier Narrows Recreation Area, which is a developed area that includes Legg Lake and all manner of sports fields and facilities.

A cliff above the Whittier Narrows section of the San Gabriel

146

River was the original site of Mission San Gabriel, established here in 1771. Spanish missionaries regarded the San Gabriel as a dependable source of water and could well imagine the possibilities for a settlement in the river valley.

However, the padres did not foresee how the river could rage when swollen by winter rains. After losing their first structures in a flood, they moved their settlement away from the river (to its present site in San Gabriel) in 1775.

While thousands of motorists on the 605 (San Gabriel River) Freeway whiz through Whittier Narrows, undoubtedly very few of them think about how the narrows came to be. Normally, narrows come into existence by young rivers carving old mountains; however, this is not the case with the Whittier Narrows. Geologic evidence suggests that the San Gabriel River was here first and that the Whittier Hills were slowly uplifted across its path. So slow was this uplift that the river was able to maintain its course. The San Gabriel is known as an antecedent river (very rare) because it anteceded (came before) the hills.

You can explore the ecology—what's left of it, anyway—of the San Gabriel River via a path that loops around the Whittier Narrows Nature Center. To get more out of the walk, pick up a leaflet at the nature center. Stop by the small nature museum which exhibits native flora and fauna.

The path, paved at first, explores riparian vegetation—willows, sycamores and elderberry. Eventually, the trail reaches bullrush-and cattail-lined Lake Aquatecos, a pond that attracts many birds.

Walkers more in the mood for exercise than education will join nearby San Gabriel River Trail or Rio Hondo River Trail and power walk to their hearts' content.

Puente Hills
Puente Hills Skyline Trail

Highlights: *This tramp through the Puente Hills offers both short and lengthy samples of the Skyline Trail. All the options offer fine clear-day views of the metropolis from scenic overlooks.*

Distance: From Seventh Avenue to Overlook is 5 miles round trip with a 800-foot elevation gain; to Rio Hondo College is 5 miles round trip with 800-foot gain; to Schabarum Park is 12 miles one-way with 1,000-foot gain

Directions: Exit the Pomona Freeway (60) on Seventh Avenue and drive four blocks south to its end at Orange Avenue. Park near the traffic barrier. (To reach Schabarum County Park, end point for one of this day hike's options, exit the Pomona Freeway on Azusa Avenue. Proceed south and turn left on Colima, then right into the park.)

THE PUENTE HILLS DIVIDE THE LOS ANGELES BASIN into a Northern one-third and a southern two-thirds. North is the San Gabriel Valley, an alluvium-filled basin. South of the hills is a coastal plain, a flatland tilted gently toward the Pacific. The Whittier Fault, which pushes the hills around a bit, extends along the south base of the range and ends west of Whittier Narrows.

Puente Hills Skyline Trail, under the jurisdiction of the Los Angeles County Parks Department, is a riding and hiking trail that rambles through the canyons and over the mustard-covered crests of the hills.

Ramble up Seventh Avenue Trail, which is a bulldozed dirt road beyond the traffic barrier. Pass some private horse corrals and ascend briefly on a paved road to a San Gabriel Water Company facility. Here a dirt trail picks up and you begin ascending a mile though a small forest of thistle and mustard. You reach a long plateau and are treated to views of the San Gabriel Valley. Atop the plateau, you intersect the Puente Hills Skyline Trail.

Bear right on the Puente Hills Skyline Trail, following a fence

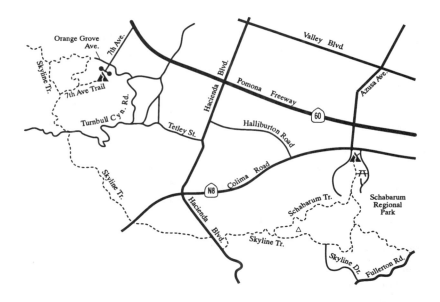

along the plateau's perimeter. The land belongs to Rose Hills Memorial Park, but the county has easements for its trail system. The cemetery is located just on the other side of the hill.

After hiking the length of the mustard-smothered plateau, you'll reach an unmarked junction. Bear left here and ascend the hill. From the overlook, where a missile facility once stood, you can see Whittier to the south, San Gabriel Valley to the north. It's an urban view—sometimes you can even see dump trucks chugging up to Puente Hills Landfill. On clear winter days, you'll spot the Pacific and Catalina on one side, and snow-capped Mount Baldy and the San Gabriel Mountains on the other.

You can return the same way, loop back by another trail back to Seventh Avenue Trail, or continue on to Rio Hondo College.

To reach Rio Hondo College: From the overlook, the trail stays briefly with a crumbling road, passes another picnic area, then veers off from the road at an unsigned junction. You look down at the gardens of Rose Hills Memorial Park.

Noisome civilization grows more evident as you descend toward Workman Mill Road. The trail leads to North Drive at Rio Hondo College.

For the full Puente Hills experience, Schabarum Park-bound hikers will bear left on the Skyline Trail. A thicket of prickly pear cactus lines the trail. A right turn at an unmarked junction keeps you on the trail, which descends through sage and monkeyflowers into Turnbull Canyon. After a short ascent, the trail reaches and crosses Turnbull Canyon Road. More climbing brings you to an overlook for fine views of downtown Los Angeles, the westside and the Pacific.

The trail angles toward the suburb of Hacienda Heights, and actually passes right behind some homes (with swimming pools that look inviting on a hot day), before dropping down to Colima Road. Follow the pedestrian/equestrian underpass underneath Colima. The trail then ascends to Hacienda Boulevard, where the hiker makes use of another pedestrian/equestrian underpass.

The Skyline Trail is anything-but for the next half-mile as it turns southeast and follows a culvert alongside Hacienda Boulevard. This trail ends at Leucadia Road, where the hiker joins a fire road and begins ascending above La Habra Heights. Stay right on the fire road at a junction and pass a locked gate. The trail ascends through a eucalyptus grove and passes another of the many microwave towers in the Puente Hills. Civilization—in the form of Puente Hills Mall and the Pomona Freeway—appears close-in to the north. The trail descends a last mile to the wide lawns and picnic areas of Schabarum Park.

Puente Hills: Schabarum Park
Schabarum Trail

Highlights: *San Gabriel Valley views from Schabarum Park at west end of Puente Hills.*

Distance: 5 mile round trip loop of park with 700-foot elevation gain.

Directions: From the Pomona Freeway in Hacienda Heights, exit on Azusa Avenue. Head south a short ways to Colima and turn left to the entrance to the park on your right. The signed trail begins behind some restrooms near the park entrance.

COUNTY SUPERVISOR (FROM 1972-1990) PETER Schabarum is remembered by Schabarum Avenue in Irwindale, Schabarum Senior Center in South El Monte. More surprisingly, to conservationists, are Schabarum Regional Park and Schabarum Trail. Park-lovers were not at the top of his list.

For a decade-and-a-half, Otterbein was the name of this Regional Park; in 1989 it was renamed for Schabarum. At the park office is a Presidential library-like display of Schabarum's political career, complete with trophies, newspaper clippings and photos and plaques.

Schabarum Park is a mile-long band of green full of happy picnickers. Schabarum Trail explores the brush-covered slopes—the wilder part of the park.

The trail tacks this way and that as it ascends a steep hillside. Almost a mile out, you reach a junction and Schabarum Trail splits. (The left branch goes to a corral and horse rental facility). Take the right branch, which climbs steeply for a long mile toward the brushy hilltops.

When you meet Skyline Trail, turn left (east) climbing a little bit more of a hillock, then beginning your descent back to the park. When you reach the park equestrian center, you can return to the trailhead either via a bridle path that parallels the park road, or by way of an asphalt path that bisects the park's long picnic grounds.

Galster Nature Park
Covina Hills Trail

Highlights: *The wild West Covina Hills, plus views of the southeastern San Gabriel Valley.*

Distance: 1/2-1 mile round trip

Directions: From the San Bernardino Freeway (10) in West Covina, exit on Azusa Avenue and head south. Turn left on Aroma Drive and follow it to the lower entrance of Galster Nature Park.

GEOLOGISTS SAY THE SAN JOSE HILLS (SOMETIMES called the Covina Hills), which extend from Covina to Pomona, bound the southeastern portion of the San Gabriel Valley. Azusa Avenue crosses the range, which is part natural landforms and part elaborately disguised landfills.

Galster Nature Park, situated on a north slope, was a gift to the city of West Covina from the Galster family. Native and imported trees and shrubs attract many birds and their watchers.

You begin walking up a dirt road through a narrow, tree shaded ravine, soon passing Spring Eternal, a little bubbling spring, as well as a plaque honoring West Covina's first park director.

Past a small picnic area, the trail system is catch as catch can. You can circle a hilltop, and hide behind a bird blind, taking a bird's-eye-view of the valley. Select another trail and descend back to the trailhead.

152

Walnut Creek Regional County Park
Walnut Creek Trail

Highlights: *On the map, Walnut Creek County Park appears as a green worm wriggling through a suburbanized corner of the San Jose Hills. On the ground, the long, narrow park seems even more removed from its civic surroundings than indicated on the map.*

Distance: 2 miles one way with a 500-foot elevation gain.

Directions: You can reach the lower trailhead in Walnut Creek County Park by exiting the Foothill Freeway (210) on Covina Boulevard. Head west to Valley Center Avenue, turn left and proceed to Cypress Street, where you turn right. At Lyman Avenue, make a left. When you reach Scarborough Lane, turn left and park in the dirt lot.

The upper trailhead is easier to reach. Exit the Foothill Freeway (210) on San Dimas Avenue. Head south a short ways, passing under the freeway overpass and park on the Avenue's shoulder on your right. Signed Walnut Creek Trail begins here.

W ALNUT CREEK IS REALLY A CREEK. NO CEMENT channel to contain it. It runs even during drought years. You might even get your feet wet crossing it.

Sure, it eventually meets the fate of all county waterways and becomes incarcerated by various flood control works, but for more than two miles, through Walnut Creek County Park, the creek runs free.

The two-mile creekside trail can be enjoyed in a couple of different ways. You can walk it one way with a car shuttle, or as a 4-mile out and back. If you want a longer, 10-mile day hike, cross San Dimas Avenue and add a 6-mile loop of Frank G. Bonelli Regional County Park.

(From the lower trailhead) The wide trail begins a gentle creekside ascent under the shade of live oak and the California black walnut that gave this creek, canyon and park their names.

153

You'll soon make the first of your half-dozen creek crossing en route. A mile along, you pass through an equestrian parking area in a grove of eucalyptus and cross the paved road leading to Pacific Coast Baptist College.

As you ascend, the canyon seems to narrow, isolating you from the busy world beyond. After crossing a bridge and the creek a couple more times, the trail rises out of the tranquil canyon toward the noisome freeway and San Dimas Avenue. You can either return the same way or cross San Dimas Avenue and enter Frank G. Bonelli Regional Park. (See Bonelli walk description in this guide.)

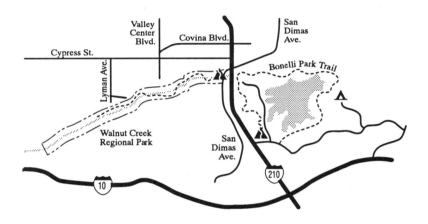

Bonelli Regional Park
Bonelli Park Trail

Highlights: *Considering that two of the park's borders are the Foothill and San Bernardino Freeways, and that it's the site of "Raging Waters," Bonelli offers more peace and solitude than one might expect. Fourteen miles of trail cross the park's chaparral-covered hills and lead through quiet canyons shaded by oak and walnut groves.*

Distance: 6-mile loop of Frank G. Bonelli Park

Directions: Frank G. Bonelli Regional Park has two main entrances. (1) Exit the San Bernardino Freeway (10) on Ganesha Boulevard, then turn left (west) on Via Verde Park Road. Continue a couple of miles to park headquarters, where you can pick up an equestrian trails map. Park in Picnic Valley off Via Verde Park Road or continue following this road out of Bonelli to the Caltrans parking lot located just west of the Foothill Freeway. (2) Exit the Foothill Freeway (210) on Via Verde Road. Park in the CalTrans lot just west of the freeway. There is a vehicle parking fee; no charge to walk in.

T HE LOS ANGELES COUNTY FLOOD CONTROL DIStrict built Puddingstone Dam in the San Jose Hills near San Dimas in 1928. The dam created a 250-acre lake, which soon attracted swimmers and fishermen, and has remained a popular destination ever since.

As the population of the San Gabriel Valley mushroomed during the 1950s and 1960s, the State Department of Parks and Recreation began purchasing land around the reservoir. Puddingstone Reservoir State Park as it was known, remained a little-developed, low-key place until 1970, when the property was transferred to Los Angeles County.

Today, the park features the aquatic amusement park Raging Waters, a golf course, giant RV campground and a hot tub rental establishment. Plans are in the works for a hotel, cocktail lounge and a second golf course.

The 2,000-acre park, the county's second-largest, has long been the center of controversy between those who want to further develop the park and those who would prefer that the park's hills and canyons remain wild. These conflicting senti-ments are even etched onto the lakeside plaque dedicated to former County Supervisor and park namesake Frank G. Bonelli. The plaque proclaims that the park is dedicated for "use as a county regional recreation and wilderness area for the enjoyment of all."

As most outdoor enthusiasts know, the words "recreation" and "wilderness" mean different things to different people. For the last decade and a half, the County Parks Department has leaned heavily toward intensive recreation at the park, which is visited by more than two million people each year.

Plantations of pepper, eucalyptus, cedar and pine have been planted in the park. Wildlife includes squirrels, cottontail rab-bits, blacktail rabbits, raccoons and deer. About 130 bird species have been sighted in the park.

Bonelli's trail system is poorly marked and oriented toward equestrians, not pedestrians. It's the hiker with a sense of direction—and a sense of humor—who will most enjoy a walk in this park. Trails and trail junctions are rarely signed, but the paths don't stray too far from park roads and landmarks, so you won't get lost.

From the CalTrans parking lot, cross (with caution) to the south side of Via Verde Road and follow the sidewalk over the freeway overpass into the park. Look right (south) for the path signed "Equestrian Trail." (If you want to pick up a park map, you'll continue a short distance farther up Via Verde Road to the headquarters/administration office.) The trail enters the bougainvillea-draped mouth of the underpass beneath Via Verde. Ever-adapative mud swallows have affixed their nests to the ceiling of the underpass.

Emerging from the underpass, you'll follow the horse trail into a quieter world. The din of the freeway fades away, and you can hear the call of the birds. Crossing slopes covered with ceanothus, thistle and prickly pear cactus, the trail soon offers its first view of Puddingstone Reservoir. Depending on the day's ozone level, the San Gabriel Mountains rise majesti-cally or murkily before you. In spring, the hills are green and brightened with mustard and California poppies, but most of the year, they're bare and brown.

The trail descends into a shallow, walnut-shaded canyon, and crosses a (usually dry) creek. Nearing the park's equestrian center, the path emerges from the greenery and reaches a fork located by a thicket of blackberry bushes. The left fork ascends a hillock and dead-ends at an overlook high above Raging Waters. On clear days, this overlook offers a panorama from Mount Baldy to San Bernardino. You'll take the right fork, proceed along a fence line, then switchback up a jimson weed- and monkeyflower-dotted slope to Boater Picnic Area. The trail descends an oak- and pine-shaded draw, passes a fig tree, then joins a fire road that leads near the Raging Waters amusement park.

Crossing Puddingstone Road, near the entrance to Raging Waters, you'll pick up the signed Equestrian Trail, which soon deposits you at a boat-launching area on the north side of the reservoir. Now your improvisation begins in earnest.

Join the paved walkway and head east along the north shore of the reservoir. When the walkway gives out, pick up the unmarked dirt trail that continues east then south along the moist, willow-choked lakeshore. Perched on the hill above you is the park's campground. You'll join a paved bike path and pass several picnic areas.

After passing through well-named Picnic Valley walk up Eucalyptus Park Road to its junction with Via Verde Park Road. At this point you're just about opposite park headquarters. A right turn and a short walk along Via Verde will return you to the starting point.

Marshall Canyon Park
Marshall Canyon Trail

Highlights: *Marshall Canyon and its neighbor, Live Oak Canyon, are shaded with oak, alder and sycamore. From atop the canyon walls, walkers gain great clear-day views of the mountains to the north and San Gabriel Valley to the south.*

Distance: 7-mile loop through Marshall Canyon with 800-foot elevation gain. Shorter walks possible.

Directions: Follow the Foothill Freeway (210) to its end, continuing east on Highway 30 and still farther east on Foothill Boulevard. Turn left, north on Wheeler Avenue, ascend to Golden Hill Road and turn right. You'll see signs for Marshall Canyon Golf Course. Just before the road turns right toward Live Oak Reservoir, turn left into a dirt parking lot.

FOR SEVERAL YEARS THIS SEMI-WILD AREA ABOVE SAN Dimas and Claremont has been something of a secret—frequented only by a few horseback riders and a very few hikers. Los Angeles County park planners say their intention is to leave Marshall Canyon more or less alone—that is to say undeveloped, with minimum facilities. Marshall Canyon will remain as "open space"—something to be thankful for in the fast-growing eastern edge of the metropolis.

A good network of equestrian/hiking trails explores the brushy ridges and lush canyon bottoms of the park. Much of the network is fire roads, which may sometimes be closed during the dry summer months.

Depending on time and inclination, the walker can fashion a number of loop trips ranging from 2 to 8 miles. Park trails and roads are unsigned, so expect to improvise a little.

The trail begins at the east end of the lot and begins descending into Marshall Canyon. During winter, the snow-covered peaks of the San Gabriel Mountains framed by oaks are a picturesque sight. Just before a creek crossing, the trail splits. Marshall Canyon is to the left, Live Oak Canyon to the right. (The trails intersect again, so you may choose either.)

158

Marshall Canyon Trail crosses the creek a couple times, then rises out of the canyon as a dirt road. You'll pass a side road leading to the park's nursery, and a couple side trails offering access to the canyon bottom.

Rather than traveling a northeast course through the canyon, it's enjoyable to wind along in a half-circle toward a prominent water tower and partake of the fine ridgetop views.

Atop the ridgeline, the trail rollercoasters along. You turn left on signed Miller Road, then descend into Live Oak Canyon. You'll reach a three-way junction and continue a hundred yards along the main fire road to a picnic area. Enjoy this oak-shaded retreat, then double back and look sharply right for an unsigned footpath descending into Live Oak Canyon.

The canyon's oaks are accompanied by sycamores, walnuts, cottonwoods, mosses and ferns. It's a most delightful half-mile descent to the canyon bottom. You'll continue your descent to an unsigned junction. The right fork follows Marshall Canyon back to the trailhead. Bear left and meander along with Live Oak Canyon 1 1/2 miles back to the trailhead.

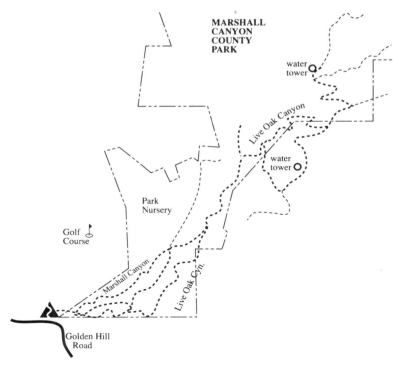

Rancho Santa Ana
Botanic Garden
Woodland Trail, Riparian Trail

Highlights: *Located in the foothills of the San Gabriel Valley, this botanical research and educational institution features a 40-acre collection of native California plants. Trails lead to desert, coastal, woodland and riparian plant communities.*

Distance: A mile or so round trip

Directions: Rancho Santa Ana Botanic Garden is located on College Avenue, north of Foothill Boulevard and east of Indian Hill Boulevard in Claremont. From the San Bernardino Freeway (10) exit on Indian Hill Boulevard, travel 2 miles north to Foothill Boulevard, turn right, and proceed 3 blocks east to College Avenue.

Open 8 a.m. to 5 p.m. daily; closed major holidays.

O N THE RIGHT DAY, IN THE RIGHT LIGHT, THIS Botanic Garden offers a scene from a 1920s postcard: wildflower- bedecked fields in the foreground, snow-capped Mt. Baldy in the background.

Native California flora (more than 1,500 species) is the emphasis at Ranch Santa Ana Botanic Garden. Particularly prominent are a multitude of manzanita and a ceanothus collection that's attracted nationwide attention.

Although the garden welcomes walkers, it's main orientation is toward science. Affiliated with the Claremont Colleges, it has a modern botany lab and a huge herbarium. The garden has developed, nurtured and introduced to nurseries many varieties of plants that have in turn greatly influenced Southern California landscaping.

The walker will enjoy stepping down the garden paths, which explore several representative plant communities. Highlights include a collection of more than two dozen California conifers, the Coastal Garden, and the Desert Garden which displays California cactus species plus related succulents and desert shrubs.

Chapter VIII

San Gabriel Mountains

Southern California

San Gabriel Mountains

Quote to remember: "Hither come the San Gabriels
lads and lassies, to gather ferns and dabble away their hot
holidays in the cool waters. glad to escape
their common-place palm gardens and orange groves."

—JOHN MUIR, *The Mountains of California,* 1877

San Gabriel Mountains

MOST OF THE SAN GABRIEL MOUNTAINS ARE included within the 700,000 acres of the Angeles National Forest, one of the most heavily used national forests in America. For more than a century the front range of the San Gabriels has delighted Southland residents seeking quiet reteats and tranquil trails.

Geography: Sixty miles long, twenty miles wide, the San Gabriels extend from Soledad Canyon on the west to Cajon Pass on the east. The mountains bless Los Angeles by keeping out hot desert winds, and curse it by keeping in the smog.

The San Gabriels are the only major mountain range in California that is considered a Transverse Range; that is, extending east-west across the state. Once the mountains formed a nearly impassable barrier to travel and blocked the northward expansion of Los Angeles into the Mojave Desert. A glance at a modern map attests to the fact that the San Gabriels are no longer a barrier to transportation and settlement.

The range is young (less than a million years in its present location), dynamic (it moves and grooves with the San Andreas Earthquake Fault), and complex; geologists claim the fractured and shattered mountains are composed of many different kinds of rocks of diverse ages.

The San Gabriels are divided lengthwise into a steeper southern front range and a taller northern range by a series of east-west trending canyons. It is the rugged front range, the mountains on the urban edge, that are explored by this guide.

Natural Attractions: "The slopes are exceptionally steep and insecure to the foot and they are covered with thorny bushes from five to ten feet high," was how the great naturalist John Muir described the front range of the San Gabriels. The "thorny bushes" of Muir's description belong to the dominant plant community of the mountains—the chaparral. Higher elevations have a wealth of taller trees: oaks, pines, incense cedar and big cone spruce.

Other front range attractions are arroyos. These boulder-strewn washes may seem lifeless on the bottomland; however, a walker following an arroyo's course upward may soon find lush creekside flora, including ferns and wildflowers, shaded by sycamore, alder and antiquarian oaks.

Wildlife-watchers are sure to spot lots of California ground squirrels and lizards, and hear the rat-tat-tat of woodpeckers. Red-tailed hawks circle above. Lucky adventurers might glimpse more elusive creatures: bighorn sheep, fox or black bear.

History: First to use the mountains were the Shoshone (or Gabrielino) Indians as the Spanish called them. For the most part they lived in the valleys and lowlands, and used the mountains for gathering food and hunting animals.

The Spaniards made little use of the mountains except as a water source, but gave the range its name; two names, in fact: the Sierra Madre (Mother Range) and Sierra de San Gabriel. Both were used until 1927 when the United States Board of Geographic Names decided upon the latter.

As early as the 1880s, it became obvious to Southern Californians the mountains should be protected from the destruction caused by logging and other ventures. In 1892, the San Gabriel Timberland Reserve was proclaimed by President Harrison. It was the first forest reserve in California, and the second in the United States. (The first was Yellowstone.) The name was changed to the San Gabriel National Forest in 1907, and to the Angeles National Forest a year later.

From 1895 to 1938 the San Gabriels hosted "The Great Hiking Era" as thousands of hikers headed into the backcountry every weekend and a multitude of trail resorts opened to serve them. The great flood of 1938, which wiped out trails, camps and resorts, as well as the paved roads that were extended across the mountains, put an end to this colorful era.

Administration: With the exception of some small city and county parks located at the base of the mountains, the bulk of the San Gabriels, including 800 miles of trail, is under the jurisdiction of the Angeles National Forest.

Where the L.A. River Springs Forth

Oak Spring Trail, Doc Larsen Trail

Highlights: *Tucked away in the foothills of the San Gabriel Mountains is inviting Oak Spring, one of the sources of the Los Angeles River, and a delightful destination.*

Distance: To Oak Spring is 3 1/2 miles round trip with 1,000 foot gain; to Yerba Buena Ridge Road is 7 miles round trip with 1,800-foot gain

Directions: From the Foothill Freeway (210) in Pacoima, exit on Osborne Street. Head north on Osborne, which soon becomes Little Tujunga Canyon Road and travel 4 miles to Gold Creek Road. Turn right and wind a short mile to signed Oak Spring trailhead on your right. Park carefully in one of the dirt turnouts off the road.

WE WALKERS—NOT TO MENTION FREEWAY COMmuters—know the Los Angeles River as a cement-lined flood control channel. It's surely not a thing of beauty. Ah, but the river's source is another story; it hasn't been tamed or touched by engineers, nor engulfed by the metropolis. Oak Spring is a rver source and a great place to relax.

Oak Spring Trail follows Gold Creek, a tributary of Little Tujunga Creek. True to its name, Gold Creek yielded some fair-sized nuggets.   The gold is long-gone and these days the land belongs to Angeles National Forest and a few private ranchers.

Another lure of this trail is the views of city and forest from Yerba Buena Ridge. Vistas to the south take in the San Fernando Valley while those to the north include the one time Paradise Movie Ranch where many a western was filmed.

This walk offers a couple options. You could begin or conclude the hike at the Tujunga District Office by utilizing the Doc Larsen Trail, which leads east from the forest service office to an intersection with Oak Spring Trail. Just up Oak Spring Trail from this intersection is Fascination Spring, another oak-shaded retreat.

The path immediately begins its ascent, soon leaving shady Gold Creek Canyon and heading into the high chaparral. You top one minor ridge, then another, and enjoy good clear-day views of the San Fernando Valley as well as the handsome foothill country to the north.

The trail then descends to Oak Spring. The spring is a modest enough source for the Los Angeles River, but the shady surroundings are a delight. You'll want to linger at this tranquil spot before deciding whether to head back the way you came or climb Yerba Buena Ridge for the fine view.

The Los Angeles River of a century ago flowed wild and free.

Trail Canyon Trail

Highlights: *A creekside saunter, a visit to a waterfall and a restful trail camp.*

Distance: 3 miles round trip with a 700-foot elevation gain to Trail Canyon Falls; 8 miles round trip with a 2,000-foot gain to Tom Lucas Camp.

Directions: From the Foothill Freeway (210) in Sunland, exit on Sunland Boulevard. Head east on Sunland, which soon merges with Foothill Boulevard. Continue to Mt. Gleason Avenue, turn north(left) and drive to its end at a "T" at Big Tujunga Canyon Road. Turn right and proceed 5 miles to a dirt road on the left, where a sign indicates parking for Trail Canyon. The road ascends a quarter-mile then forks; descend a quarter-mile to the right to an oak-shaded parking area.

T RAIL CANYON TRAIL ISN'T QUITE AS REDUNDANT AS it sounds. the "Trail" in Trail Canyon refers not to a footpath but to the "trail" left by tiny flakes of gold found in the gravel of the canyon's creekbed. Turn-of-the-century placer miners worked the creek, but the "trail" didn't lead to any riches.

The real wealth of Trail Canyon is its scenery: steep canyon walls conceal a bubbling creek and a surprising waterfall. During dry months and drought years, the creek is a pokey watercourse, but swollen by rain and runoff it becomes lively, even raging. The path to the falls and to the trail camp crosses the creek numerous times; be careful at times of high water.

Beyond the falls, the trail leads to shady Tom Lucas Camp, named for grizzly bear hunter and one of the first forest rangers in that forerunner of the Angeles National Forest, the San Gabriel Timberland Reserve.

The trail, a closed fire road, passes some private cabins that date from the 1920s and 1930s and arrives at the creek. The road ends and the footpath begins 3/4 mile from the trailhead at a creek crossing.

Trail Canyon Trail heads up-creek in the shade of

sycamores, oak and alder. After a half-mile, the path switch-backs up the canyon's chaparral-covered west wall. After a couple of bends in the trail, look for Trail Canyon Falls below.

The side trail to the falls is a precipitous path, made by use, not design; proceed at your own risk. An alternative route to the falls is to simply bushwhack up Trail Canyon from the point back where the trail leaves the canyon. The latter route is safer, except at times of high water.

Past the side trail to the falls, Trail Canyon Trail drops back into the canyon, crossing and recrossing the creek for 2 1/2 miles to Tom Lucas Trail Camp. This oak-and alder-shaded camp is perched on the edge of a meadow watered by the headwaters of Trail Canyon Creek. The meadowland is known as Big Cienega.

The energetic will savor a late afternoon or early morning assault on 5,440-foot Condor Peak. Ascend Trail Canyon Trail a long steep mile to a firebreak, then climb another long steep mile to a point just below the peak. Clamber a hundred yards over fractured granite to the summit. Rewarding the peak-bag-ger are views of the San Fernando Valley, Santa Monica Bay and Catalina Island.

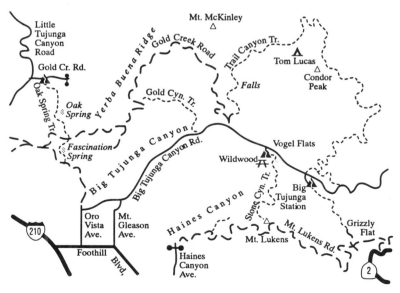

City's Highest Peak: Mt. Lukens
Stone Canyon Trail

Highlights: *Mount Lukens, a gray whale of a mountain beached on the eastern boundary of Los Angeles, is the highest peak within the city limits. A hike up this mile-high mountain offers a great aerobic workout and terrific clear-day views of the metropolis.*

Distance: Vogel Flats to Mount Lukens is 8 miles round trip with 3,200-foot gain.

Directions: From Foothill Boulevard in Sunland, turn north on Mount Gleason Avenue and drive 1 1/2 miles to Big Tujunga Canyon Road. Turn right and proceed 6 miles to signed Vogel Flats Road. Turn right and drive into the Forest Service's Vogel Flats Campground and Picnic Area. Turn right on the Forest Service road. Leave your car in one of the many day use parking spaces, near water, restrooms and picnic tables; or proceed another quarter-mile through a private residential area to the end of the road where parking is limited to a few cars and there are no facilities.

THEODORE P. LUKENS, FOR WHOM THE MOUNTAIN IS named, was a Pasadena civic and business leader, and an early supporter of the first scientific reforestation effort in California. A self-taught botanist, Lukens believed that burnt-over mountainsides could be successfully replanted. During 1899 alone, Lukens and fellow mountaineers planted some 65,000 seeds in the mountains above Pasadena.

After the death of Lukens in 1918, a 5,074-foot peak was named to honor the one-time Angeles National Forest Supervisor and Southern California's "Father of Forestry."

Stone Canyon Trail is by far the nicest way to ascend Mount Lukens. (Other routes are via long wearisome fire roads.) The trail climbs very steeply from Big Tujunga Canyon over the north slope of Lukens to the peak.

Carry plenty of water on this trail; none is available en route. It's fun to unfold a city map on the summit to help you identify natural and manmade points of interest.

One warning: In order to reach the beginning of the Stone

Canyon Trail, you must cross the creek flowing through Big Tujunga Canyon. During times of high water, this creek crossing can be difficult and dangerous—even impossible. Use care and your very best judgement when approaching this creek.

From the Forest Service parking area, saunter a quarter-mile northwest along the paved road past some cabins. The road ends at a barrier and you continue on a trail which travels 150 yards or so along and above the Big Tujunga Canyon creekbed. Look leftward for 1) A good place to cross the creek 2) a metal trail registry on the other side of the creek that marks the beginning of the Stone Canyon Trail 3) well-named Stone Canyon itself, which resembles a waterfall of white boulders. Stone Canyon Trail runs just to the left of Stone Canyon.

After you've signed the trail registry, begin the vigorous ascent, which first parallels Stone Canyon, then switchbacks to the east above it. Pausing to catch your breath, enjoy the view of Big Tujunga Canyon.

Rugged Mount Lukens, highest peak in Los Angeles.

The trail leads through chamise, ceanothus and high chaparral. The 1975 Big Tujunga Fire scorched the slopes of Mount Lukens. Stone Canyon Trail could use a few more shady big cone spruce and a little less brush. Theodore Lukens and his band of tree planters would today be most welcome on the mountain's north slopes!

Three-and-a-half miles from the trailhead, you'll intersect an old fire road and bear left toward the summit. Atop the peak is a forest of radio antennae.

Enjoy the sweeping panorama of the Santa Monica and Verdugo Mountains, Santa Monica Bay and the Palos Verdes Peninsula, and the huge city spreading from the San Gabriel Mountains to the sea.

"Big T" Creek and Canyon
Grizzly Flat Trail

Highlights: *These days you won't find any grizzlies atop Grizzly Flat, just a few hikers enjoying a pine-shaded retreat above one of L.A.'s more renown canyons—Big Tujunga.*

Distance: Big Tujunga Creek to Grizzly Flat is 5 miles round trip with 900-foot elevation gain

Directions: From the Foothill Freeway (210) in Sunland, exit on Sunland Boulevard and head west to Foothill, continuing west to Mount Gleason Avenue. Turn left and drive 1 1/2 miles to a stop sign. Turn right, proceed 6 miles to Vogel Flat Road, and turn right again. The road drops to a stop sign. To the right is a Forest Service fire station. Turn left and park by Stonyvale Picnic Area.

DURING THE LAST CENTURY, A LARGE POPULATION of grizzlies roamed the San Gabriel Mountains. The bears frightened early miners and settlers, and in later years, had many a run-in with sportsmen and forest rangers. Big Tujunga Canyon was particularly attractive habitat to the big bears; in fact, the last wild grizzly in Southern California was killed in the lower reaches of the canyon in 1916.

Grizzly Flat Trail explores Tujunga Canyon, then rises into the storied hills where notorious highwayman Tiburcio Vasquez eluded a posse in 1874. Vasquez, after robbing a San Gabriel Valley rancher, rode over the top of the San Gabriels, descended north along a then-unnamed creek to Big Tujunga Canyon, and made good his escape. The unnamed creek, which cuts through the eastern edge of Grizzly Flat, has since been known as Vasquez Creek.

Big Tujunga Canyon—or "Big T" as it's sometimes nick-named—has certainly felt the hand of man. Its creek has been dammed and diverted by the Los Angeles County Flood Control District. The purpose of these flood control efforts is to control the runoff of Big Tujunga Creek and prevent it from rushing into the eastern lowlands of the San Fernando Valley.

Damming a wild, but seasonal, mountain stream such as Big

Tujunga solves one problem but creates another: when rains swell the creek, millions of cubic yards of sand and gravel are carried downstream and clog up flood control structures. Obviously, to be effective, a flood control reservoir should not be filled with rock debris. So the debris must be hauled away. But where?

The urban mountaineer may ponder a not altogether facetious question: If Los Angeles and its flood control projects keep growing and we keep carting away rock debris, will we one day haul our mountains entirely away?

Grizzly Flat Trail departs from Stonyvale Picnic Area, one of the less-visited locales in the front range of the San Gabriel Mountains. The trail, while not difficult, does require four crossings of Big Tujunga Creek, and should be avoided after heavy rains and during times of high water.

The trail, signed with the international hiking symbol, begins at a vehicle barrier at the east end of Stonyvale Picnic Area. Almost immediately you cross Big Tujunga Creek. Small trail markers keep you on the path, which crosses a boulder field and fords the creek three more times.

A bit more than a mile from the trailhead, Big Tujunga creek and canyon bend northeast, but the trail heads right, south. Soon you'll pass an abandoned trail register and begin ascending up oak- and chaparral-covered slopes. After a mile, you'll dip to a seasonal fern-lined creek, then ascend briefly to grassy Grizzly Flat. The Forest Service planted pines here in 1959, shortly after a fire scorched the slopes above Big Tujunga.

From Grizzly Flat you can make your way northeast a few hundred yards to Vasquez Creek. Picnic here or at Grizzly Flat and return the same way.

George Deukmejian Wilderness Park
Dunsmore Canyon Trail

Highlights: *George Deukmejian Wilderness Park preserves 702 acres in the foothills of the San Gabriel Mountains just above Glendale/La Crescenta. Two steep canyons— Dunsmore and Cook—make up the bulk of the park, which adjoins Angeles National Forest.*

Distance: 2-3 miles round trip with 500-foot gain

Directions: From the Foothill Freeway (210) in Glendale, exit on Pennsylvania Avenue, and head a half-mile north to Foothill Boulevard. Turn left and travel 1 1/4 miles to Dunsmore Avenue, turn right and drive a short mile to the avenue's end at George Deukmejian Wilderness Park. Proceed up a long asphalt driveway and park in the dirt lot.

THE GEORGE DEUKMEJIAN WILDERNESS. COULD IT BE A mapmakers mistake? An oxymoron of the great outdoors? Sarcasm from some curmudgeonly conservationist?

Even the former governor's most ardent supporters concede that naming a wilderness after George Deukmejian was, to say the least, surprising. Ecology was most certainly not the centerpiece of Deukmejian's two terms as governor of California. Naming a prison or a highway after the governor would be more in-synch with the ex-governor's political philosophy, some citizens opine.

The city of Glendale purchased the property in 1989 with

monies from park bond funds and from the Santa Monica Mountains Conservancy. The conservation group SWAP (Small Wilderness Area Preservation) was particularly effective in saving the canyons from subdivision and helping to secure the necessary park funds. Off the record, conservationists involved in the creation of the park note that then-Governor Deukmejian opposed preserving the area as parkland until it was suggested that the park be named for him.

Long before anyone talked about a park, Gabrielino Indians roamed the foothill canyons. In later years, Dunsmore Canyon was part of a Spanish land grant and known as a favorite hideout of bandit Tiburcio Vasquez. Legend has it that from a lookout at a prominent oak (still standing on the property), Vasquez watched for the pursuing posse.

Early in this century, a French immigrant planted a vineyard and built a little winery in Dunsmore Canyon. The grapes grown in the canyon were used in the making of fortified brandies. In Los Angeles, the brandies were bottled and marketed under the "Old Heritage" label.

The stone walls of the winery still stand today, though the roof has more than a few holes. A private equestrian center, which provides board and training for horses, uses part of the building as a tack room.

George Deukmejian Wilderness is very much a park-in-the-making. No facilities or interpretive displays have been constructed.

Most of the park consists of chaparral-cloaked hillsides and a seasonal stream lined with oak and alder. On the higher slopes grow scattered big cone spruce.

Bird-watchers will find many native and migrant species: the California towhee, rufous-sided towhee, Berwick's wren, yellow-rumped warbler and that most ubiquitous of chaparral dwellers, the wrentit.

The park's trail system consists of a couple miles of dirt roads (closed to vehicles). One rocky road leads a long mile up Dunsmore Canyon and dead-ends. Another road circles a hill and offers good San Fernando Valley views. In the future, hikers hope the trail system can be extended to connect with trails and fire roads in the adjacent Angeles National Forest.

From the stables, walk up-canyon on unsigned Dunsmore Canyon Trail, which is the main park road. About a hundred yards past a check-dam in the canyon bottom, look left for a dirt road; this is an alternate route back to the trailhead.

173

The dam and flood control works you see below are mentioned in John McPhee's book, *The Control of Nature*. Anyone who wants to know more about Los Angeles ecology and how engineers have battled the forces of nature in the front range of the San Gabriel Mountains will find the book fascinating.

The route up Dunsmore Canyon stays above the creekbed and finally dead-ends at a woodsy perch above the seasonal creek. If you want to proceed from here, the route is trail-less. You can bushwhack and boulder-hop up either of two ravines.

As you return down-canyon, look right for the alternate return trail and ascend a short distance up to a good viewpoint of the San Fernando Valley. The trail then skirts Cook Canyon, reaches another overlook by some eucalyptus, and descends back to the trailhead.

Dunsmore Canyon: Nature tamed but not controlled.

Afoot in the Arroyo Seco

Arroyo Seco Trail
(Gabrielino National
Recreation Trail)

Highlights: *Hikers walk an abandoned 1920s auto road and newer Forest Service trails through the Southland's most storied canyon. Several quiet picnic areas beckon the walker.*

Distance: To Teddy's Outpost is 3 miles round trip; to Gould Mesa Campground is 4 miles round trip; to Paul Little Picnic Area is 6 1/2 miles round trip with a 400-foot elevation gain; to Oakwilde Trail Camp is 10 miles round trip with a 900-foot elevation gain.

Directions: From the Foothill Freeway (210) in Pasadena, take the Arroyo Boulevard/ Windsor Avenue exit. Head north on Arroyo, which almost immediately becomes Windsor, and travel 3/4 mile. Just before Windsor's intersection with Ventura Street, turn into the parking lot on your left. From the small lot you can look down into the bottom of the Arroyo Seco and see the Jet Propulsion Laboratory.

EARLY IN THIS CENTURY, ARROYO SECO WAS AN extremely popular place for a weekend outing. About halfway up the wild section of the canyon stood Camp Oak Wilde, a rustic resort constructed in 1911. Hikers and horsemen stayed a night or two or used the hostelry as a rest stop on the way up to Mt. Wilson. During the 1920s, a road was constructed and automobilists traveled the Arroyo to Camp Oak Wilde.

Southern California's "flood of the century" wiped out Oak Wilde in 1938. The awesome torrent also washed away the road and many vacation cabins. A few stone steps and foundations, ivy-covered walls and bridges give today's hiker hints of a time gone by.

Besides the Southern California history lesson, oak-, sycamore- and bay-filled Arroyo Seco has much to offer. The modern-day traveler can walk the old 1920s auto road and newer Forest Service trails to quiet picnic areas. Because the path up the Arroyo Seco is officially part of the Gabrielino National Recreation Trail, it's usually in very good condition.

This is a great morning walk. On hot afternoons, however, you might want to exercise elsewhere; smog fills the Arroyo Seco.

As you walk up Windsor you'll spot two roads. The leftward road descends to JPL. You head right on a narrow asphalt road, closed to vehicle traffic. You'll pass some fenced-off areas and facilities belonging to the Pasadena Water Department and a junction with Lower Brown Mountain Road. A short mile from the trailhead are some Forest Service residences.

The road, dirt now, penetrates the arroyo and enters a more sylvan scene, shaded by oaks and sycamores. Often you can't

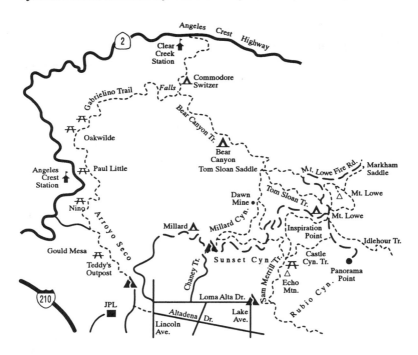

help but chuckle at the "No Fishing" signs posted next to the creekbed; most of the time the arroyo is quite "seco" and if there are any fish around, they must have walked here.

Teddy's Outpost Picnic Area is your first destination. In 1915 Theodore Syvertson had a tiny roadside hostelry at this site. A half-mile beyond Teddy's is large Gould Mesa Campground, with plenty of picnic tables. Next stop, a short distance past the campground is a small picnic area called Nino. A mile beyond Gould Mesa Campground is Paul Little Picnic Area.

Now you leave the bottom of the arroyo and climb moderately to steeply up the east wall of the canyon. After curving along high on the wall, the trail then drops back to the canyon floor, where oak-shaded Oakwilde Trail Camp offers a tranquil rest stop. A few stone foundations remind the walker that Arroyo Seco was once Pasadena's most popular place for a weekend outing.

**The Arroyo isn't always dry: rain and snowmelt
sometimes swell the creek.**

Millard Canyon, Dawn Mine
Millard Canyon Trail

Highlights: *Hidden from the metropolis by Sunset Ridge, lush Millard Canyon is one of the more secluded spots in the front range of the San Gabriels. A cold stream tumbling over handsome boulders, a trail meandering beneath a canopy of alder, oak and sycamore, a waterfall and a historic mine, are a few of Millard's attractions.*

Distance: To Millard Canyon Falls is 1 mile round trip; to Dawn Mine is 5 miles round trip with 800-foot elevation gain

Directions: From the Foothill Freeway (210) in Pasadena, exit on Lake Avenue. Drive north four miles, at which point Lake veers left and becomes Loma Alta Drive. Continue a mile to Chaney Trail and turn right. Proceed another mile to a junction atop Sunset Ridge. If you're hiking to Dawn Mine, you'll bear right at this junction and park just outside the gate blocking Sunset Ridge Fire Road. If you're bound for Millard Canyon Falls, you'll stay left at the junction and descend to a parking lot at the bottom of the canyon.

MILLARD CANYON IS BEST-KNOWN AS THE SITE OF the dawn Mine which, unfortunately for its investors, produced more stories than gold. The mine was worked off and on from 1895, when gold was first discovered, until the 1950s. Enough gold was mined to keep ever-optimistic prospectors certain that they would soon strike a rich ore-bearing vein, but the big bonzana was never found.

You can explore Millard Canyon by two different routes, which lack an official name, but are often referred to as Millard Canyon Trail. An easy half-mile path meanders along the canyon floor to 50-foot Millard Falls. This is a pleasant walk, suitable for the whole family.

More experienced hikers will enjoy the challenge of following an abandoned trail through Millard Canyon to the site of the Dawn Mine. Enough of the old trail remains to keep you on track, but it's slow going with many stream crossings en route.

(To Millard Canyon Falls) From the parking area at the bottom of Millard Canyon, you'll walk a hundred yards up a fire road to Millard Canyon Campground. Walk through the campground and pick up the signed trail leading to the falls. The trail heads east along the woodsy canyon bottom, crosses the stream a couple times, and arrives at the base of the waterfall. Don't try to climb up, over, or around the falls; people have been injured attempting this foolhardy ascent.

(To Dawn Mine). From the Sunset Ridge parking area, head up the fire road. Enjoy the clear-day ridgetop views of the metropolis. You'll soon pass a junction on your left with a trail leading down to Millard Canyon Campground.

A short quarter-mile from the trailhead, you'll spot signed Sunset Ridge Trail, which you'll join and begin descending into Millard Canyon. A few minutes of walking down the well-graded path will reward you with an eagle's-eye-view of Millard Canyon Falls.

Near the canyon bottom, you'll meet a trail junction. Sunset Ridge Trail continues along the canyon wall, but you bear left and descend past a cabin to the canyon floor. As you begin hiking up–canyon, turn around and take a mental photograph of the trail that brought you down to the canyon; it's easy to miss on your return trip.

As you pick your way stream-side amongst the boulders and fallen trees on the canyon floor, you'll follow vestiges of the old trail. Typically, you'll follow a fifty- or hundred-yard stretch of trail, boulder-hop for a bit, cross the stream, then pick up another length of trail.

The canyon floor is strewn with lengths of rusting pipe and assorted mining machinery. Several pools, cascades, and flat rocks suggest a stream-side picnic.

After hiking a bit more than a mile up-canyon, you'll find that Millard Canyon turns north. From this turn, it's a bit less than a mile to the Dawn Mine site. Don't go into the mine shaft. Darkness and deep holes filled with water make it very dangerous.

Return the same way, and remember to keep a sharp lookout for the trail that leads out of the canyon back to the trailhead.

Scaling the Ghostly Ruins of Echo Mountain Resort
Sam Merrill Trail

Highlights: *Professor Thaddeus Sobreski Coulincourt Lowe's Echo Mountain Resort area can be visited not only by retracing the tracks of his "Railway to the Clouds" (See Mt. Lowe Railway walk) but by a fine urban edge trail that ascends from the outskirts of Altadena.*

Distance: Cobb Estate to Echo Mountain is 5 miles round trip with 1,400-foot elevation gain.

Directions: From the Foothill Freeway (210) in Pasadena, exit on Lake Avenue and travel north 3 1/2 miles to its end at Loma Alta Drive. Park along Lake Avenue.

THIS HISTORIC HIKE VISITS THE RUINS OF THE ONE-time "White City" atop Echo Mountain. From the steps of the old Echo Mountain House are great clear-day views of the megalopolis. Energetic hikers can join trails leading to Inspiration Point and Idlehour campground.

Pasadena and Altadena citizens have been proud to share their fascination with the front range of the San Gabriel

ON MT. LOWE INCLINE, ELEVATION 3,000 FEET, MT. LOWE, CALIFORNIA.

Mountains. This pride has extended to the trails ascending from these muncipalities into the mountains.

It was local citizens, under the auspices of the Forest Conservation Club, who built a trail from the outskirts of Altadena to Echo Mountain during the 1930s. During the next decade, retired Los Angeles Superior Court clerk Samuel Merrill overhauled and maintained the path. When Merrill died in 1948, the trail was named for him.

Sam Merrill Trail begins at the former Cobb Estate, now a part of Angeles National Forest. A plaque placed by the Altadena Historical Society dedicates the estate ground as "a quiet place for people and wildlife forever."

From the great iron gate of the old Cobb Estate, follow the trail along the chain-link fence. Sign in at the trail register.

The path dips into Las Flores Canyon, crosses a seasonal creek in the canyon bottom, then begins to climb. As you begin your earnest, but well-graded ascent, enjoy good, over-the-shoulder views of the San Gabriel Valley and downtown Los Angeles. Two long, steep and mostly shadeless miles of travel brings you to a signed junction. Bear right and walk 100 yards along the bed of the old Mount Lowe Railway to the Echo Mountain ruins. Just before the ruins is a drinking fountain, very welcome if it's a hot day.

Up top, you'll spot the railway's huge bull wheel, now embedded in cement, and just below is a pile of concrete rubble, all that remains of the railway depot after it was dynamited by the Forest Service in 1959.

Energetic hikers can join signed trails that lead to Mt. Lowe Camp and to Inspiration Point and Idlehour Campground.

The steps and foundation of the Echo Mountain House are great places to take a break and enjoy the view straight down precipitous Rubio Canyon, the route of Lowe's railway. A bit down the mountain to the east stood another hotel—the Chalet—but nothing remains of it.

Echo Mountain takes its name from the echo that bounces around the semicircle of mountain walls. I've never managed to get very good feedback; perhaps even echoes fade with time.

A Railway to the Clouds
Mount Lowe Railway Trail

Highlights: *Historic walk along the old railway bed of Professor Thaddeus Lowe's "Railway to the Clouds" with stops at such places as Cape of Good Hope, Granite Gate and Horseshoe Curve. Atop Inspiration Point are really inspiring metropolitan views—on clear days of course.*

Distance: To Mt. Lowe Trail Camp; 10 miles round trip with 2,700-foot gain; to Inspiration Point is 11 miles round trip.

Directions: Exit the Foothill Freeway (210) at Lake Avenue and follow it north to its end. Turn left on Loma Alta Drive. Go one mile to Chaney Trail Road and turn right. At a "Y" in the road, take the right fork to the Sunset Ridge parking area. The trailhead is located at the locked gate, which bars vehicles from Sunset Ridge Fire Road.

PROFESSOR THADDEUS LOWE, CIVIL WAR BALLOONIST, man of fame and fortune, was the quintessential California dreamer. His dream was to build a railway into—and a resort complex atop—the San Gabriel Mountains high above Pasadena. In the 1890s, his dream became a reality.

During the height of its popularity, millions took Professor Lowe's "Railway to the Clouds" to fine hotels and spectacular views of Southern California. Until it was abandoned in the 1930s, it was the Southland's most popular tourist attraction.

From Pasadena, visitors rode a trolley up Rubio Canyon, where a pavilion and hotel were located. After taking refreshments, they boarded the "airships" of the great cable incline, where carried them 3,000 feet (gaining 1,300 feet) straight up to the Echo Mountain Resort Area. "Breathtaking" and "hair-raising" were the most frequent descriptions of this thrilling ride. Atop Echo Mountain was the White City, with a hotel, observatory, and a magnificent searchlight purchased from the Chicago World's Fair. When the searchlight swept the mountaintop, the white buildings of the resort were visible from all over Los Angeles. From Echo Mountain, tourists could board a trolley and ride another few miles to Mount Lowe Tavern at the end of the line.

This historic walk follows the old railway bed, visits the ruins of the White City and Mount Lowe Tavern, and concludes with some fine views of Los Angeles from Inspiration Point. The old railway bed with its gentle seven percent grade makes for easy walking.

An interpretive brochure is (sometimes) available from Angeles National Forest headquarters in Arcadia.

The trail begins just past the locked gate. Follow the paved Sunset Ridge Fire Road. You may follow the fire road two miles to the junction with Echo Mountain Trail, but a more attractive alternative is described below.

Follow the road one-quarter mile to the signed Sunset Ridge Trail on your left. Join this trail, which for the most part parallels the fire road, and leads into peaceful Millard Canyon. Near the canyon bottom, the trail forks at a signed junction. Bear right and ascend back up to Sunset Ridge Fire Road. Follow the fire road about 75 yards, and on your right you'll spot the signed junction with Echo Mountain Trail.

To Echo Mountain: Bear right on Echo Mountain Trail, which leads one-half mile over the old railway bed to Echo Mountain. Echo Mountain takes its name from an echo that bounces around the semicircle of mountain walls.

On Echo Mountain are the foundations of Echo Mountain House and the chalet. The most prominent ruin is the large iron bull wheel that pulled the cars up the steep incline fromm Rubio Canyon. A fire swept Echo Mountain in 1900, leveling all of the White City except the observatory. Picnic tables suggest a lunch stop among the ruins. Leave behind the ruins of the White City, return to Sunset Ridge Fire Road and bear right.

The paved road soon becomes dirt and an interpretive sign at "Cape of Good Hope" lets you know you've joined the Mount Lowe Railway tour. Continue along the railway bed, passing the tourist attractions that impressed an earlier generation of travelers: Granite Gate, Horseshoe Curve, and the site of the Great Circular Bridge.

Near the top, you'll come to the site of Mount Lowe Tavern, which burned in 1936. Almost all signs of the tavern are gone, but this peaceful spot under oaks and big cone spruce still extends its hospitality. On the old tavern site is Mount Lowe Trail Camp, which welcomes day hikers with its shade, water, restrooms and picnic tables.

Before heading down, follow the fire road east and then south for one-half mile to Inspiration Point. Where the fire road makes a hairpin left to Mount Wilson, go right. At Inspiration Point, you can gaze through several telescope-like sighting tubes aimed at Santa Monica, Hollywood and the Rose Bowl. After you've found a sight that inspires you, return the same way.

Professor Lowe's "Railway to the Clouds."

Eaton Canyon
Eaton Canyon Trail

Highlights: *Eaton Canyon Nature Center, situated at the base of Mt. Wilson, offers flora and fauna displays and a nature trail. A path leads to Eaton Canyon Falls.*

Distance: From the Nature Center to Eaton Falls is 3 miles round trip with 200-foot gain.

Directions: From the Foothill Freeway (210) in Pasadena, exit on Altadena Drive. Proceed north 1 3/4 miles to the signed entrance of Eaton Canyon County Park. Turn right into the park and leave your car in the large lot near the Nature Center.

"It is a charming little thing, with a low, sweet voice, singing like a bird, as it pours from a notch in a short ledge, some thirty-five or forty feet into a round mirror-pool."

Eaton Falls, as admired by John Muir in 1877
—*The Mountains of California*

LATE ONE AUGUST AFTERNOON IN 1877, JOHN MUIR set out from Pasadena to begin his exploration of the San Gabriel Mountains. He spent the night camped with a blindly optimistic, half-Irish, half-Spanish water prospector, who was convinced that his digging would soon result in a wealth of water. Muir was dubious of this cash flow, and the next morning bade his acquaintance farewell and began tramping up the canyon. After enjoying Eaton Falls, Muir followed bear trails, sometimes on all fours, up the chaparral-smothered ridges of the San Gabriel Mountains.

It was not the water-seeker Muir met, but Judge Benjamin Eaton, who channeled and piped the canyon's waters to nearby ranches. The judge's neighbors laughed when he planted grapevines, but the vines were quite successful and commanded a high price. San Gabriel Valley farmers knew a good thing when they saw it, and soon grapes joined oranges as the crop of choice.

Much of the canyon named for Judge Eaton is now part of

Eaton Canyon County Park. The park's nature center has exhibits which emphasize Southern California flora and fauna. Kids will love the park's Naturalist's Room, which features live animals. Park nature trails explore a variety of native plant communities—chaparral, coastal sage, and oak-sycamore woodland.

Eaton Canyon County Park is a busy place on weekends. Family nature walks are conducted by docent naturalists; the park also has bird walks, natural history classes and "nature-cize" hikes

The walk up Eaton Canyon to the falls is an easy one, suitable for the whole family. Eaton Canyon Trail leads through a wide wash along the east side of the canyon to a junction with Mount Wilson Toll Road. In fact, Eaton Canyon Trail was once a toll road itself; fees were collected from 1890 to 1911.

The hiker seeking strenuous exercise can swing right on Mount Wilson Road for a steep, 8-mile ascent of Mount Wilson.

From the parking lot, head north on the wide dirt road. You meander beneath the boughs of large oak trees and pass a junction with a connector trail that leads to the Mount Wilson Toll Road.

To the east, you'll spy the plateau overlooking Eaton Canyon. A hundred years ago this land belonged to wealthy capitalist and pioneer forester, public libary founder and builder of Venice, Abbott Kinney and his Kinneloa Ranch. Kinney loved this area and was a bit miffed when a nearby peak was named Mount Harvard for the university that built an observatory atop the mountain, rather than for him.

The trail leads along the wide arroyo. Eaton Canyon was widened considerably by a 1969 flood that washed away canyon walls. This flood, and the many floods before and since, have spread alluvium, or water-transported sand and rock, across the canyon floor. It takes a hearty group of drought-resistant plants to survive in this soil and Southern California's sometimes not-so-benign Mediterranean climate.

Notice the steepness of the canyon's walls. Early Spanish settlers called the canyon "El Precipio."

A mile's travel from the Nature Center brings you to the

186

Mount Wilson Toll Road bridge. A right turn on the toll road will take you on a long, steep ascent to the top of Mount Wilson. A left turn on Mount Wilson Toll Road will bring you a very short distance to the unsigned junction with Altadena Crest Trail. This rather dull trail travels two miles above the reservoirs and backyards of residential Altadena. Walking a half-mile on Altadena Crest Trail to a vista point

For more than a century, pleasure-seekers have enjoyed Eaton Canyon Falls.

will reward you with great clear-day views of the Los Angeles Basin.

To reach Eaton Falls, continue straight up Eaton Canyon wash. You'll rock-hop across the creek several times as you walk to trail's end at the falls.

When John Muir visited the canyon a century ago, the great naturalist reported: "Hither come the San Gabriel lads and lassies, to gather ferns and dabble away their hot holidays in the cool waters, glad to escape their common-place palm gardens and orange groves."

Alas, the local youth of today isn't quite as well-mannered. Cretins have desecrated some of the canyon's boulders with graffiti. After you've enjoyed the falls Muir called "the finest yet discovered in the San Gabriel Mountains," return the same way.

Bailey Canyon
Bailey Canyon Trail

Highlights: *The attraction is the view: clear-day vistas of the San Gabriel Valley are your reward for scaling many a steep switchback. If you want to get a feel for the area's geography, take a map along a San Gabriel Valley map.*

Distance: 5 miles round trip with a 1,300-foot elevation gain.

Directions: From the Foothill Freeway (210) in Arcadia, take the Rosemead Blvd./Michillinda exit and head north on Michillinda. Continue a bit more than a mile to Grand View Avenue, turn right and proceed a few blocks to Grove Street. Follow Grove to its end at Bailey Canyon Park. There's ample parking here.

WHEN THE LIGHT IS HARSH AND THE AIR IS DIRTY, the foothills above the San Gabriel Valley seem a sight for sore eyes: fire-scarred, eroded, brush smothered, laced with roads and power lines. But when the light is right and the air is clean, these flaws disappear and the purple mountains beckon with the sweet smell of sage and many a winding trail.

One of these inviting trails leads up Bailey Canyon from the town of Sierra Madre. Bailey Canyon Trail doesn't really go anywhere; it simply ascends halfway up the canyon to a viewpoint and dead-ends.

Most of what you see of the San Gabriel Valley from Bailey Canyon Trail is commercial and residential. However, there are two significant splotches of green almost due south of the canyon: the Los Angeles County Arboretum and the Santa Anita Golf Course. Between the green is Santa Anita racetrack.

In 1875, this canyon on the outskirts of Sierra Madre was homesteaded by R.J. Bailey, who left little behind but his name. The canyon, in its early, wild days, was worked by local trappers, who snared fox and coyote and shipped the pelts to furriers in Chicago. Bailey sold his property in 1881 to Palmer Reed, a clerk at the Sierra Madre Villa Hotel.

Over the years the property was divided. The Sierra Madre Municipal Water Company acquired part of the canyon, as did the Passionist Fathers, who built a monastery. The Carter family owned the lower part of the canyon and in 1965 donated land to the city of Sierra Madre for Bailey Canyon Park. For quite some time, the path leading up Bailey Canyon was known as the Carter Trail.

The trail has for several decades been something of an orphan. Angeles National Forest officials have paid scant attention to what is depicted as Trail 11W11 on their map. Conservation groups and Boy Scouts have pitched in with periodic maintenance, but the trail is neglected and it shows. No trail signs are in evidence and some of the switchbacks are badly eroded.

Bailey Canyon Trail begins just one mile west of one of the Southland's most famous footpaths—the Mt. Wilson Trail. Hikers have long dreamed of extending Bailey Canyon Trail and connecting it with the trail to Wilson. (Easier said than done, as a hike up Bailey Canyon will make abundantly clear.)

Time out on steep Bailey Canyon Trail.

Angle northwest through the park's picnic area and proceed through an ancient turnstile to a road leading past a check-dam. The road peters out and you join a trail alongside the Bailey Canyon creekbed. Some maps call this part of the canyon bottom Bailey Canyon Wilderness Park; it's far from a wilderness, but trees grow here, offering just about the last shade you'll find en route.

The trail begins its no-nonsense climb and, after a couple of switchbacks, it's good-bye shade, hello steep ascent. Below you, adding a touch of European style, is the Passionist Fathers Retreat, a monastery.

Many a switchback takes you up the steep, brushy, east wall of the canyon and then north, higher and higher into the San Gabriel Mountains. Near trail's end, Bailey Canyon narrows.

At the head of the canyon is a grove of oak and bay. From the stone foundation of an old cabin, you can contemplate the mountains above, the San Gabriel Valley below. In the late afternoon or early morning, you might spot deer traveling through the canyon.

Henninger Flats:
Where Trees Come From
Mt. Wilson Toll Road

Highlights: *Perched halfway between Altadena and Mt. Wilson, Henninger Flats is the site of Southern California's finest tree plantation. On the flats you'll be able to view trees in all shapes and sizes, from seedlings to mature stands. A museum with reforestation exhibits, a nature trail, and the Los Angles County foresters on duty will help you understand where trees come from.*

Distance: From Altadena to Henninger Flats is 6 miles round trip with 1,400-foot elevation gain.

Directions: From the Foothill Freeway (210) in Pasadena, exit on Lake Avenue. Turn north and continue to Altadena Drive. Make a right, continue about ten blocks, and look closely to your left. Turn left on Pinecrest Drive and wind a few blocks throughn a residential area to the trailhead. The trailhead is found in the 2200 block of Pinecrest. You'll spot a locked gate across the fire road that leads down into Eaton Canyon.

CONSIDER THE CONIFERS. A WIND-BOWED LIMBER pine clinging to a rocky summit. A sweet-smelling grove of incense cedar. The deep shade and primeval gloom of a spruce forest. Where do trees come from?

I know, I know. "Only God can make a tree."

Keep your Joyce Kilmer. Hold the metaphysical questions. Our inquiry here is limited to what happens in the aftermath of a fire or flood, when great numbers of trees lie dead or dying.

Fortunately for California's cone-bearing tree population— and tree lovers—there is a place where trees, more than 120,000 a year, are grown to replace those lost to the capriciousness of nature and the carelessness of man. The place is Henninger Flats, home of the Los Angeles County Experimental Nursery.

The Flats have a colorful history. After careers as a gold miner, Indian fighter and first Sheriff of Santa Clara County,

Captain William Henninger came to Los Angeles to retire in the early 1880s. While doing a little prospecting, Henninger discovered the little mesa that one day would bear his name. He constructed a trail over which he could lead his burros.

Atop the flats he built a cabin, planted fruit trees, raised hay and corn. His solitude ended in 1890 when the Mt. Wilson Toll Road was constructed for the purpose of carrying the great telescope up to the new observatory. Captain Henninger's Flats soon became a water and rest stop for hikers, riders and fishermen who trooped into the mountains.

After Henninger's death in 1895, the flats were used by the U.S. Forest Service as a tree nursery. Foresters emphasized the nurturing of fire- and drought-resistant varieties of conifers. Many thousands of seedlings were transplanted to fire- and flood-ravaged slopes all over the Southland. Since 1928, Los Angeles County foresters have continued the good work at Henninger Flats.

The Pasadena and Mt. Wilson Toll Road Company in 1891 fashioned a trail to the summit of Mt. Wilson. Fees were fifty cents per rider, twenty-five cents per hiker. A twelve-foot wide road followed two decades later. Senior Southland residents might recall a somewhat hair-raising Sunday drive up the steep grade. During the 1920s, the road was the scene of an annual auto race, similar to the Pikes Peak hillclimb. In 1936 the Angeles Crest Highway opened and rendered the toll road obsolete. Since then the toll road has been closed to public traffic and maintained as a fire road.

A moderate outing of just under six miles, on good fire road, the trail up to Henninger Flats is suitable for the whole family. The Flats offer a large picnic area and fine clear day city views.

Proceed down the fire road to the bottom of Eaton Canyon. After crossing a bridge, the road begins a series of switchbacks up chaparral-covered slopes. Occasional painted pipes mark your progress.

Henninger Flats welcomes the hiker with water, shade, and two campgrounds where you may enjoy a lunch stop. Growing on the flats are some of the more common cone-bearing trees of the California mountains including knobcone, Coulter, sugar, digger and Jeffrey pine, as well as such exotics as Japanese black pine and Himalayan white pine. Visit the interesting exhibits at the new Henninger Flats Museum.

Ultra-energetic hikers will continue up the old toll road to Mt. Wilson; the journey from Altadena to the summit is 9 miles one-way with an elevation gain of 4,500 feet.

Young trees grown on Henninger Flats are transplanted throughout L.A. County's mountains.

Mt. Wilson Trail

Highlights: *This hike takes you up Little Santa Anita Canyon, visits Orchard Camp, and climbs to the top of Mt. Wilson. It's a classic climb, one of the nicest all-day hikes in the Southland.*

Distance: From Sierra Madre to Orchard Camp is 9 miles round trip with a 2,000-foot gain; to Mt. Wilson is 15 miles round trip with a 4,500-foot gain.

Directions: From the Foothill Freeway (210) in Arcadia, exit on Baldwin Avenue and head north. Turn right on Miramonte Avenue near the junction of Mt. Wilson Trail Road, which is on your left. The trail begins 150 yards up this road and is marked by a large wooden sign. After passing some homes, the trail shortly intersects the main trail.

MT. WILSON TRAIL UP LITTLE SANTA ANITA CANYON is the oldest pioneer's trail into the San Gabriels. It was built in 1864 by Benjamin Wilson, who overhauled a Gabrielino Indian path in order to log the stands of incense cedar and sugar pine on the mountain that now bears his name.

The first telescope was carried up this trail to Mt. Wilson in 1904. During the Great Hiking Era, thousands of hikers rode the Red Cars to Sierra Madre, disembarked, and hiked up this path to the popular trail resort to Orchard Camp. Forty thousand hikers and horseback riders passed over the trail in 1911, its peak year.

After the passing of the Great Hiking Era in the 1930s, the trail was all but abandoned until the late 1950s when rebuilding efforts began. Sierra Madre citizens, aided by Boy Scout troops, rebuilt the trail all the way up canyon to its junction with the old Mt. Wilson Toll Road.

Sierra Madre citizens also prevented county flood control engineers from bulldozing and check-damming Little Santa Anita Canyon. The aroused citizenry established Sierra Madre Historical Wilderness Area to preserve the canyon. This area is patterned after federal Wilderness Areas; the land is to be

194

preserved forever without development or mechanized use.

After trudging 1 1/2 miles up Santa Anita Canyon you reach a junction with a side trail, which leads to the nearby canyon bottom. Here you can lean against an old oak, cool your heels in the rushing water, relax and watch the river flow.

Continue hiking on the ridge trail as it climbs higher and higher above the canyon floor onto sunny, exposed slopes. A hot 3 miles of walking bring you to Decker Spring and another 1/2 mile to Orchard Camp, a shady glen dotted with oak and spruce trees. When Wilson was building his trail, a construction camp called Halfway House was built here. Later homesteaders tried their hand planting apple and cherry trees—hence the name Orchard Camp.

During the Great Hiking Era, a succession of entrepreneurs utilized Orchard Camp as a trail resort and welcomed thousands of hikers. Hikers traveling through the canyon in the 1920s reported seeing "The Nature Man of Mt. Wilson," a tall bronzed hermit who looked like he stepped out of the pages of the Old Testament. The nature man carried a stone axe and worked on the trail for his keep. Some say he's still around, protecting the canyon—though he no longer springs out of the brush and greets every hiker who passes.

Benjamin D. Wilson

The trail continues through thick chaparral up Santa Anita Canyon to its head. It contours on the shelf-like trail, heads east on a firebreak and crosses over a steep manzanita-covered ridge. At the intersection with Winter Creek Trail, turn left (west) and ascend steeply to Mt. Wilson Toll Road, 2 miles from Orchard Camp.

Turn right on the Toll Road and follow it a mile as it ascends through well-spaced spruce to Mt. Wilson Road.

Big Santa Anita Canyon
Gabrielino National Recreation Trail

Highlights: *Cascades, a waterfall and giant woodwardia ferns are a few of the many delights of historic Big Santa Anita Canyon. The bucolic canyon has been popular with Southern California hikers for a hundred years.*

Distance: Chantry Flat to Sturtevant Falls is 3 1/2 miles round trip with 500-foot gain; to Spruce Grove Camp is 8 miles round trip with 1,400-foot gain; to Mt. Wilson is 8 miles one-way with 4,000-foot gain.

Directions: From the Foothill Freeway (210) in Arcadia, exit on Santa Anita Avenue and drive six miles north to its end at Chantry Flat. The trail begins across the road from the parking area. A tiny store at the edge of the parking lot sells maps and refreshments.

WILLIAM STURTEVANT, KNOWN TO HIS FRIENDS AS "Sturde," pioneered many miles of San Gabriel Mountains trails. He traveled from California to Colorado in the early 1880s with forty burros. A packer *par excellence,* he soon found his services to be in great demand in the San Gabriels.

Sturtevant hewed out a trail over the ridge from Winter Creek to the top of the canyon and in 1898 opened Sturtevant Camp. The rustic resort consisted of a dining hall, tents, and a store and was a popular trail resort well into the 1930s.

In Santa Anita Canyon today some eighty-odd cabins are serviced by a burro train from Chantry Flats, named for another early packer, Charlie Chantry. One of the more colorful sights in the local mountains—and a look backward into a bygone era—is a glimpse at the pack animals plodding up the trail to Sturtevant Camp, now a Methodist Church retreat.

Sturtevant's trail is now a section of the 28-mile long Gabrielino National Recreation Trail. The trail to Sturtevant Falls is very popular on weekends—but not as popular as it was on Fourth of July weekend 1919 when 5,000 people tramped into the canyon and signed the trail register! The ambitious hiker may continue past the falls to Spruce Grove

Camp and even as far as the top of Mount Wilson.

Descend on the paved fire road, part of the Gabrielino Trail, into Big Santa Anita Canyon. At the bottom of the canyon you'll cross a footbridge near the confluence of Big Santa Anita and Winter Creeks. Here a small sign commemorates Roberts Camp, a resort camp founded in 1912. Owner Otto Lyn Robers and other canyon boosters really "sold" the charms of the canyon to Southern Californians in need of a quiet weekend. As you follow the path up-canyon along the oak- and alder-shaded creek, you'll soon determine that the canyon "sells" itself.

The only blemish on the pristine scene is a series of check-dams constructed of giant cement "Lincoln logs," by the Los Angeles County Flood Control District and the Forest Service in the early 1960s. In their zeal to tame Big Santa Anita Creek, engineers apparently forgot that fast-moving water is supposed to erode canyon bottoms; floods are what originally sculpted this beautiful canyon. Today, thanks to the check-dams, the creek flows in well-organized fashion, lin-

The type of retreat we all long to find—a mile's walk from the parking lot.

gering in tranquil pools, then spilling over the dams in fifteen-foot cascades. Over the years, moss, ferns, alders and other creekside flora have softened the appearance of the dams and they now fit much better into the lovely surroundings.

The trail passes some private cabins and reaches a three-way trail junction. To visit Sturtevant Falls, continue straight ahead. You'll cross Big Santa Anita Creek, then re-cross where the creek veers leftward. Pick your way along the boulder-strewn creek bank a final hundred yards to the falls. The falls drops in a silver stream fifty feet to a natural rock bowl. (Caution: Climbing the wet rocks near the falls can be extremely hazardous to your health. Stay off.)

Return the same way, or hike onward and upward to Spruce Grove Trail Camp.

Two signed trails lead toward Spruce Grove. The leftward one zigzags high up on the canyon wall while the other passes above the falls. The left trail is easier hiking while the right trail heads through the heart of the canyon and is prettier. Either trail is good walking and they rejoin in a mile.

After the trails rejoin, you'll continue along the spruce-shaded path to Cascade Picnic Area. You can call it a day here or ascend another mile to Spruce Grove Trail Camp. Both locales have plenty of tables and shade.

Still feeling frisky? Hikers in top condition will charge up the trail to Mt. Wilson—an 8-mile (one way) journey from Chantry Flat. Continue on the trail up-canyon a short distance, cross the creek and you'll find a trail junction. A left brings you to historic Sturtevant Camp, now owned by the Methodist Church. The trail to Mt. Wilson soon departs Big Santa Anita Canyon and travels many a switchback through the thick forest to Mt. Wilson Skyline Park.

Monrovia Canyon Park
Waterfall Trail

Highlights: *Shaded by live oak and sycamore, Monrovia Canyon is delightful retreat, complete with a little waterfall and a nature museum. Ah, if only every canyon in the front range of the San Gabriels was this delightful.*

Distance: 1 1/2 miles round trip with 200-foot elevation gain.

Directions: From the Foothill Freeway (210) in Monrovia, exit on Myrtle Avenue and proceed two miles north. Turn right on Scenic Drive, jogging right, then left, and turning north on Scenic as it becomes Canyon Blvd. and continues another mile to the entrance of Monrovia Canyon Park. The park is open short hours: 12-5 weekdays, 9-5 weekends, and there's a small entrance fee. Signed Waterfall Trail begins opposite the Mal Parker Mesa Picnic Area near the park's small nature museum.

MONROVIA CANYON PARK PRESERVES ITS NAMESAKE canyon as well as one other: Sawpit Canyon. At the junction of these two canyons was once a sawpit. Two sawyers, one standing at ground level, the other in a pit, operated huge handsaws.

Sawing logs put the canyons on the map, but it was water that attracted civic attention in the 1880s. William P. Monroe's new city of Monrovia wanted the water and built a reservoir. L.H. Emerson wanted it too and a court battle ensued. City Hall won. Eventually, the name Monrovia was applied to a canyon, a peak and a park.

A pleasant goal of a 3/4 mile stroll is a two-tiered waterfall, which cascades into an oak- and spruce-shaded grotto in the midst of Monrovia Canyon. Walkers can extend their hike a bit by joining the park's nature trail.

Before you descend into the canyon, look behind you at the distinct V-shaped gorge, which frames a pie-shaped view of Monrovia and the San Gabriel Valley.

Waterfall Trail descends to the canyon bottom where you'll see the park's trail heading down-canyon. But head up-canyon, passing a series of check dams, to the little falls.

199

The Long Road to Mt. Bliss
Van Tassel Trail

Highlights: *The ascent of Mt. Bliss constitutes what hikers call a "conditioning hike," that is to say a real aerobic workout. The incline is quite steep, the cardiovascular system gets revved up, and clear-day views from the summit of this San Gabriel Mountains peak offer a good reward.*

Distance: Valley View Park to Overlook is 1 mile round trip with 200-foot gain; to Mt. Bliss is 8 miles round trip with 3,000-foot gain

Directions: From the Foothill Freeway (210) in Duarte, exit on Mt. Olive Drive and head north to Royal Oaks Drive. Turn right and continue to Greenbank where you'll turn left, then Deer Lane, where you'll turn right, then Mel Canyon Drive where you'll turn left and park near Valley View Park.

T HE ROUTE TO BLISS UTILIZES BOTH VAN TASSEL FIRE road and Van Tassel Trail. The fire road—and others in the front range of the San Gabriels—came into existence after the monstrous fire of September 1924, the worst fire in the history of the mountains. The fire began in San Gabriel Canyon and rapidly spread westward. Despite the best efforts of firefighters, the blaze burned for three weeks and for a time threatened the town of Monrovia.

As then Angeles National Forest Superintendent Rush Charleton put it: "The greatest difficulty in fighting the fires was the lack of roads over which to transport supplies to the men." Determined to prevent the occurence of another fire of this size, the Forest Service began an ambitious program to build roads and firebreaks throughout the San Gabriels. One of these roads was the Van Tassel Fire Road.

The new Van Tassel Trail, a footpath that leads from Valley View Park on the outskirts of Duarte a short ways to an intersection with Van Tassel Road, also came into existence thanks to the efforts of firefighters. Captain Ross Marshall of the Los Angeles County Fire Department supervised a hardworking CDC (California Division of Corrections) crew from Camp 19. The crew cut brush and dug trail—skills employed when fighting a fire. Their efforts earned the men time off their setences.

From the end of Mel Canyon Drive, follow the unsigned footpath up the brushy slope. The view down at first isn't too inspiring. You'll see the 605 and 210 freeways, as well as the huge gravel pits of Irwindale, including the "Raider Crater" the stadium site once proposed as a new home for the Los Angeles Raiders. The view east, where a quarry has chewed up mountainsides, isn't too inspiring either.

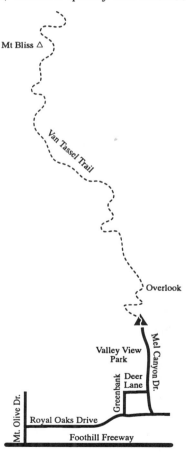

The trail briefly joins a road, and continues ascending to a fire department helipad, which does offer a pretty good view. On clear day, you'll have the San Gabriel Valley, downtown Los Angeles, and Santa Monica Bay at your feet.

Continue on the trail, a short ways past the helipad to an unsigned junction, where the trail joins Van Tassel Fire Road. You'll hike around a locked gate, and begin some steep switchbacks. The dirt road climbs to a ridgeline and takes you past some big cone spruce, which frame great views of the higher snow-covered San Gabriel peaks. Enjoy the panorama from 3,720-foot Mt. Bliss, catch your breath, and return the same way.

Angling Toward West Fork
West Fork National Scenic Trail

Highlights: *The West Fork of the San Gabriel River is known for its trout. The level trail that follows along the river is popular with hikers, joggers, cyclists and, of course, fishermen.*

Distance: From Highway 39 to Glenn Camp is 14 miles round trip, but (much) shorter trips are possible.

Directions: Weekend and holiday visitors to the popular San Gabriel Canyon area must obtain a parking permit ($3 a day) for parking along Highway 39 as far as the Crystal Lake turnoff. You can get a permit from the Forest Service San Gabriel Entrance Station, open 8-5 Saturday and Sunday; early risers will can buy permits from selected all-night businesses on Azusa Avenue, Azusa.

From the Foothill Freeway (210) in Azusa, exit on Azusa Ave (Highway 39) and head north. Fourteen miles later, and 1/2 mile past the Forest Service's San Gabriel Canyon Off Road Vehicle Area and Rincon Station, look for a parking lot and locked gate on your left. Signed West Fork National Scenic Trail is the asphalt road descending into the canyon.

DOWNRIVER, THE SAN GABRIEL (ALONG WITH ITS SISTER streams the Santa Ana and the Los Angeles) is best-known for depositing the alluvium that now covers the surface of the Los Angeles Basin. Upriver, the San Gabriel has two major forks—East Fork is known for its gold, West Fork for its trout.

For more than a century, Southern California anglers have been hooking trout in the San Gabriel River. The Pasadena Bait Club was the most prominent of several early West Fork fishing camps catering to men looking for camaraderie, rustic accomodation and good fishing.

Most of the West Fork has been set aside as a wild trout preserve. Fishing is of the "catch and release" variety. Barbless hooks must be used and the daily limit is zero. Fishing for keeps is permitted along a portion of the West Fork—the first 1 1/2 mile stretch of river reached by trail from Highway 39.

West Fork, as trout habitat, is still recovering from the

desilting of Cogswell Dam, which lies upriver. Some years ago, during less enlightened times, Cogswell Dam was cleaned out and tons of silt dumped into West Fork, thus wiping out most of the fish population.

West Fork Scenic Trail is actually an asphalt road that was built at the same time as Cogswell Dam. Closed to vehicle traffic, the road is popular with hikers, joggers and mountain bicyclists.

West Fork Trail meanders seven miles with the river to shady Glenn Camp. (The road continues another 1 1/2 miles past Glenn Camp to Cogswell Reservoir, which is closed to the public, and connects with forest service fire roads heading west.) You can walk the whole way to Glenn Camp or pick a picnic or fishing spot anywhere you choose.

Head past the locked gate and down the road into the canyon. On the weekends, you'll be joined by canyon visitors toting coolers, lawn chairs and fishing poles.

After a mile you'll pass a flat area, the site of the Pasadena Bait Club. The fishermen's headquarters burned in 1924, and the ruins washed away during the great flood of 1938. You'll also intersect the unsigned Bear Creek Trail that leads north into the San Gabriel Wilderness. Pioneers had many an encounter with a grizzly along this creek, which is how this tributary of the San Gabriel River got its name. After another half-mile's travel, you'll recross the river and enter the designated wild trout preserve.

The road, which climbs very slowly, but steadily, upriver leads past many, tranquil, oak- and sycamore-shaded pools.

Seven miles from the trailhead is Glenn Camp, set on a shady flat right by the river. It's a peaceful place with a half-dozen tables that invite a picnic.

The Nature of Crystal Lake

Pinyon Ridge, Cedar Canyon, Soldier Creek, Tototngna Nature, Lake Trails

Highlights: *Just below the crest of the Angeles Crest is a well-watered, cedar- and pine-forested basin. This basin has no outlet and thus gathers rainwater and snowmelt from the San Gabriel Mountains above. A happy result of this geographical happenstance is Crystal Lake, the only natural lake in the San Gabriel Mountains.*

Distance: Pinyon Ridge (1 mile loop), Cedar Canyon (1/2 mile), Soldier Creek (3/4 mile), Totogongna Nature Trail (3/4 mile loop), Lake Trail (2 miles round trip)

Directions: From the Foothill Freeway (210) in Azusa, take the Highway 39/Azusa Ave. exit. Drive north on Highway 39 for 24 miles to the turnoff for Crystal Lake Recreation Area. After a mile you'll reach the Forest Service entry station. Continue another mile to Crystal Lake Visitor Center, which is open weekends. Park in the lot next to the visitor center.

D URING THE 19TH CENTURY, THE LAKE WAS KNOWN as Sycamore Lake; that is, until Judge Benjamin Eaton visited in 1887 and proclaimed: "The water is clear as a crystal and the party found it good to drink." Crystal Lake it has remained.

Crystal Lake came under the protection of the U.S. Forest Service, first under the old San Gabriel Timberland Reserve, later under the Angeles National Forest. During the early years of this century, it was a popular beat-the-heat getaway for residents of the San Gabriel Valley. It was also a favorite summer vacation spot for Occidental College students, who built cabins near the lake.

During the 1930s, Los Angeles County took over Crystal Lake and operated it as a county park, complete with swimming, camping and recreation facilities. World War II, with its gas rationing and driving restrictions drastically reduced visitation, compelling the county to hand the lake back to the Forest Service.

Today, the Forest Service, along with dedicated volunteers,

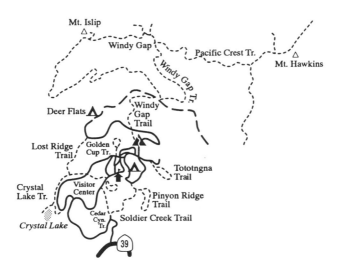

has made Crystal Lake Recreation Area an attractive destination, complete with nature trails, a pleasant campground and a visitors information center.

Crystal Lake itself, however, often disappoints first-time visitors. Drought has reduced the lake's size, overuse has dirtied the lakeshore. The lake suffers from heat pollution, human pollution and heavy algae growth.

The Forest Service is trying to help the little lake. The agency has installed an aeration system to provide the lake with more oxygen, and to mix surface and bottom waters in order to reduce water temperatures.

No swimming is allowed in the lake, but the lake is popular with fishermen, particularly after it's stocked during spring, early summer and late fall with rainbow trout.

While a visit to the lake might be underwhelming, a saunter along one of the recreation area's nature trails may provide the tranquility you're seeking. The nature trails provide a good introduction to the natural history of the San Gabriel Mountains.

Drop in at the Crystal Lake Visitor Center (open weekends) to pick up maps, pamphlets, and the latest trail information.

Pinyon Ridge Nature Trail (1 mile) Begin southeast of the visitors center. It introduces you to several mountain ecosystems including meadowland, a yucca grove and a pinyon pine woodland. Particularly evident are the big-coned trees—sugar pine, big cone spruce, and white fir. You'll also gain an appreciation for the natural forces—earthquakes, landslides, frost and flood—that have shaped the Crystal Lake Basin and the San Gabriel Mountains.

Cedar Canyon Trail follows an incense cedar-shaded canyon along a spring-fed creek. You can return via Soldier Creek Trail.

Soldier Creek Trail offers good views of San Gabriel Canyon as it winds through a mixed pine and oak forest. It connects to Cedar Canyon Trail.

Tototngna Nature Trail is an interpreted path (pick up a brochure at the visitor center) that leads through "the place of stones." You'll explore an earthquake fault and several ecologically unusual Crystal Lake communities.

Lake Trail goes where you would guess it goes—to Crystal Lake via an up-and-down route over rocky slopes. You'll appreciate the lake more if you arrive at its shores on foot.

Crystal Lake Basin: Tall trees, fresh air.

Mt. Islip
Islip Ridge Trail

Highlights: *Mt. Islip is by no means one of the tallest San Gabriel Mountains peaks, but its relatively isolated position on the spine of the range makes its stand out. Its summit offers the hiker fine views of the middle portion of the Angeles National Forest high country and of the metropolis.*

Distance: From Crystal Lake to Mt. Islip is 9 miles round trip with 2,200-foot elevation gain

Directions: From the Foothill Freeway (210) in Azusa, take the Highway 39/Azusa Ave exit. Drive north on Highway 39 for 24 miles to the turnoff for Crystal Lake Recreation Area. After a mile you'll reach the Forest Service entry station.

Continue another mile to Crystal Lake Visitor Center, which is open on the weekends, then another half-mile to a large dirt parking lot on your right and signed Windy Gap Trail on your left.

MT. ISLIP, (PRONOUNCED EYE-SLIP) IS NOT NAMED, as you might guess, for a clumsy mountaineer, but for Canadian George Islip, who homesteaded in San Gabriel Canyon a century ago.

Mt. Islip has long been a popular destination for hikers. The mountain was particularly popular with Occidental College students who in 1909 built a huge cairn (heap of boulders), dubbed the "Occidental Monument" atop the summit. The monument, which had the name Occidental on top, stood about two decades, until the Forest Service cleared the summit of Mt. Islip to make room for a fire lookout tower. Today, the monument and the fire lookout are long gone, but the stone foundation of the fire lookout's living quarters still remains.

Trail connoisseurs will appreciate the look—and feel—of handbuilt Islip Ridge Trail. The moderate grade, well-engineered switchbacks, the rock work and the way the path gently crosses the land are due to the skill and hard work of many dedicated volunteers, particularly the San Gabriel Mountains

Hand-hewn trail constructed by hard-working volunteers.

Trail Builders.

This trail to Mt. Islip climbs the forested shoulder of the mountain, and intersects a summit trail that leads to the peak.

Ascend moderately on Windy Gap Trail, which passes near a campground and heads into the cool of the forest. The trail crosses a forest service road leading to Deer Flat Campground, ascends some more and reaches the dirt South Mount Hawkins Truck Road. Cross the road and look left for the beginning of Islip Ridge Trail, sometimes called Big Cienega Cut-off because it passes near Big Cienega Spring.

Enjoy the pleasant trail as it ascends moderately more or less west through pine, spruce and cedar forest. A bit more than a mile from the top, Islip Ridge Trail turns sharply north into a more sparse alpine forest.

The trail intersects the path coming from Windy Gap. Turn left and walk a short, but steep distance to the summit of 8,250-foot Mt. Islip.

Take a Bite Out of Potato Mountain
Evey Canyon Trail

Highlights: *Hikers, for all you do, this spud's for you. Potato Mountain, which sits above Claremont, offers the hiker great clear-day vistas of the San Gabriel Valley, eastern Los Angeles County, and parts of San Bernardino County. The 3,360-foot, russet-brown mountain, is a refuge from the busy metropolis and its far-flung suburbs.*

Distance: Through Evey Canyon to the top of Potato Mountain is 5 miles round trip with 1,000-foot elevation gain

Directions: From the San Bernardino Freeway (10) in Claremont, exit on Indian Hill Boulevard. Head north to Foothill Boulevard and turn right. Turn left on Mills Avenue which, after reaching the outskirts of Claremont, veers right to become Mt. Baldy Road. Follow this road 2 1/2 miles. Soon after you see San Antonio Dam on your right, you'll see roadside turnouts on both your right and left. Park in a safe manner in either turnout. The trail begins on the left (west side) of Mt. Baldy Road. For further reference, there's a Stop sign and a road paddle reading "569" at the trailhead. (If you're driving

Evey Canyon: preserved for study and for contemplation.

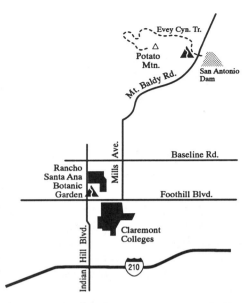

up Mt. Baldy Road and see signs welcoming you to the Angeles National Forest, you overshot the trailhead by a bit.)

To walk Evey Canyon you must secure an entry permit by calling Claremont Colleges, Biology Department, at (714) 621-8000, ext. 2950.

SPLITTING POTATO MOUNTAIN IS ATTRACTIVE EVEY Canyon. a little creek bubbles through an oak woodland and a tangle of vines and gooseberries.

Herman Garner saved the canyon from home development and gave it to Pomona College (one of the Claremont Colleges) Department of Biology with the condition that it remain pristine. Herman Garner Biological Preserve is used today for student field research, and for long walks away from it all.

The trail through Evey Canyon and up Potato Mountain consists of two fire roads (Evey Motorway and Palmer Motorway on some maps). Generally speaking, the first half of this hike is along a wide shady road through Evey Canyon and the second half is a hot ascent up a second fire road to the top of Potato Mountain.

Couch potatoes and the small fry will enjoy strolling through Evey Canyon. More ambitious walkers will head for the top of the tater.

Squeeze past the locked gate (the canyon is closed to vehicle traffic) and descend into Evey Canyon. After a brief descent, the fire road begins ascending moderately through the oak- and alder-shaded canyon. Beneath the tall trees is a lush understory of grasses and vines.

Two miles of walking takes you out of the canyon to an unsigned junction with another fire road. Evey Motorway descends to the west, but you turn sharply left. Peel off your jacket and continue a steep half-mile to the top of Potato Mountain.

From the summit are metropolitan views, as well as a panorama ranging from the appallingly ugly U.S. Army Corps of Engineers-built San Antonio Dam and flood control basin to the sparkling peaks of the Angeles National Forest.

Half-baked hiker atop Potato Mountain.

Baldy Views From Sunset Peak

Sunset Peak Trail

Highlights: *Sunset Peak gives you the best view of Old Baldy. When the higher peaks are snow-covered, consider this hike to the top of Sunset Peak. The view of the metropolis below is notoriously undependable; however, the panorama of peaks above is always an inspiring sight.*

Distance: From Glendora Ridge Road to Sunset Peak is 5 miles round trip with 1,200-foot gain

Directions: From the San Bernardino Freeway (10) in Claremont, exit on Indian Hill Boulevard and head north. Drive 2 miles to Foothill Boulevard (old Route 66 for the nostalgic). Turn right and proceed 3/4 mile Mills Avenue, then turn left and follow Mills 2 miles to a stop sign, where the avenue becomes Mount Baldy Road; continue another 8 miles to Glendora Ridge Road, which you'll spot on your left just short of the hamlet of Mount Baldy. Turn left and follow Glendora Ridge Road a mile to a gravel parking lot on the right. The trailhead is on the opposite (left) side of the road.

FOR MOST OF THE WINTER AND EARLY SPRING, 5,796-foot Sunset Peak seems strategically positioned just below the snow line and just above the smog line. You'll get great clear-day views of Claremont and the San Gabriel Valley below and of Baldy and its neighboring peaks above.

Sunset views, as the name of the peak suggests, are often glorious. If you plan an evening hike, remember to bring warm clothing and flashlights.

Sunset Peak Trail, a Forest Service fire road closed to vehicles, begins at a candy-cane striped barrier. The trail ascends moderately, but steadily up the pine- and big cone spruce-shaded north side of Sunset Peak.

About halfway to the peak, you'll ascend out of the shade into chaparral country. A 1975 fire scorched these upper slopes, and it will be a while before tall trees grow here again.

A very steep fire break offers a route to the summit, but it

Sunset Peak: best view of Old Baldy.

would be wise to ignore it and continue on the main trail. A half-mile from the top, at a wide bend in the road, the trail swings sharp left.

Just below the peak the fire road gives way to a steep foot-path and you'll ascend a final hundred yards to the summit. Up top are a couple of cement pillars and other debris, remains of a Forest Service fire lookout tower that was abandoned because of several reasons: Encroaching smog hindered visibility, Forest Service policy called for replacement of human lookouts with automated surveillance and ironically, a fire burned the peak.

San Antonio Falls, Canyon
Ski Hut Trail

Highlights: *Hikers of all ages and abilities will enjoy the half-mile walk to San Antonio Falls. After a little rain, the three-tiered, 60-foot waterfall is an impressive sight. Beyond the falls is the Sierra Club ski hut, where there's a cool spring, and a high ridge overlooking San Antonio Canyon.*

Distance: From Manker Flat to San Antonio Falls is 1 mile round trip with a 200-foot gain; to San Antonio Canyon Overlook is 6 1/2 miles round trip with a 2,600-foot gain.

Directions: Take the San Bernardino Freeway to Claremont, exit on Mountain Avenue and head north, joining Mount Baldy Road in San Antonio Canyon, and winding about 11 miles to Manker Campground. One-third mile past the campground entrance, look to the left for an unsigned paved road with a vehicle barrier across it. Park in the dirt lot just below the beginning of the road.

THIS WALK LEADS TO IMPRESSIVE SAN ANTONIO Falls, then utilizes a pretty but not-so-well-known trail that ascends San Antonio Canyon to the top of Baldy. Locals call it the Ski Hut Trail because the Sierra Club maintains a hut halfway up the path. The trail doesn't have an official name and it's not on the Angeles National Forest map.

Walkers in top form, with good trail sense (the last mile of trail to the peak is rough and tentative), will relish the challenge of a Mt. Baldy summit climb.

Head up the fire road, which is closed to all motor vehicles except those belonging to ski-lift maintenance workers. After a modest ascent, you will hear the sound of falling water and soon behold San Antonio Falls. If you decide to walk down to the base of the falls, watch for loose rock and use caution on the rough trail.

Resume walking along the road (unpaved beyond the falls). After about 10 minutes of walking at a moderate pace, look sharply left for an unsigned trail. Ducks (piles of rock) on both sides of the road mark the trail. (If you find yourself heading north up Manker Canyon and getting good views of the ski lift, you missed the turnoff.)

The no-nonsense trail ascends very steeply along the side of San Antonio Canyon. You'll get great over-the-shoulder views of the canyon bottom and of Mount Baldy Village. Trail connoisseurs will appreciate this path, which, despite its steepness, has a hand-hewn, unobtrusive look and follows the natural contours of the land. Jeffrey pine, ponderosa pine and fir shade the well-constructed path, which is seasonally decorated with red Indian paintbrush and creamy yucca blossoms.

From the ski lift road, it's 1 3/4 miles by trail to the Sierra Club ski hut. Near the hut, which was built in 1935, is a cool and refreshing spring.

Just past the ski hut the trail crosses a tiny creek, then snakes through a boulder field. Beyond the boulders, the trail ascends via a half-mile series of steep switchbacks to a ridgetop overlooking the headwaters of San Antonio Canyon. There's a great view from the tree-shaded ridgetop, and if you aren't quite up for an assault on the peak, this is a good picnic spot or turnaround point. Peak-baggers will continue up the extremely rugged trail for another mile to the summit.

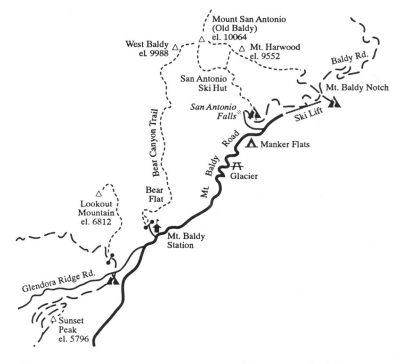

On Top of Old Baldy
Devil's Backbone Trail

Highlights: *Devil's Backbone Trail is a very popular trail and the one most hikers associate with Mount Baldy. A clear-day view from the top offers a panorama of desert and ocean, the sprawling Southland and the southern High Sierra.*

Distance: From Baldy Notch to Mount Baldy summit is 7 miles round trip to 2,200-foot gain

Directions: From the San Bernardino Freeway (10), exit on Mountain Avenue. Head north on Mountain, which joins Mount Baldy Road in San Antonio Canyon and winds 12 miles to road's end just beyond Manker Campground. Park in the ski lift parking area.

Purchase a ticket and ride the ski lift up to Baldy Notch. The lift is operated weekends and holidays all year.

An alternative is to walk up a fire road to Baldy Notch. This option adds three miles each way and a 1,300-foot gain to the walk. The fire road switchbacks up the west side of the steep San Antonio Canyon, offers a good view of San Antonio Falls, then climbs northward to the top.

THREE SAINTLY MOUNTAINS—SAN GORGONIO, SAN Jacinto and San Antonio—tower over the City of the Angels. Lowest of the three, but by far the best-known is Mount San Antonio, more commonly known as Mount Baldy. The 10,064-foot peak, highest in the San Gabriel Mountains, is visible from much of the Southland. Its summit gleams white in winter and early spring, gray in summer and fall. Old Baldy is so big and bare that it seems to be snow-covered even when it's not.

Legend has it, the padres of Mission San Gabriel, circa 1790, named the massive stone bulwark after Saint Anthony of Padua, Italy. The 13th-Century Franciscan friar was evidently a favorite of California missionaries; a number of geographical features, both in Monterey County and around Southern California, honor San Antonio. In the 1870s, San Antonio

216

Canyon and the nearby high country swarmed with gold-seek-ers, who dubbed the massive peak a more earthly "Old Baldy."

During the quarter-century from 1890 to 1915, often referred to as the "Great Hiking Era" in Southern California, many San Gabriel Mountain resorts opened to meet the demand of hik-ers. Surely one of the most unique resorts in the San Gabriels was the Baldy Summit Inn, perched just below the summit of the great mountain. Gale-force winds battered the above-tim-berline camp, which consisted of two stone buildings and a cluster of tents. William Dewey, the owner/guide, and Mrs. Dewey, the chef, welcomed guests to their summer resort of 1910 through 1912. Advertised rates were a dollar a meal, a dollar a bed. The camp burned in 1913 and never reopened.

Baldy is a bit austere from afar, but up-close, the white granite shoulders of the mountain are softened by a forest of pine and fir. Dress warmly for this trip and keep an eye out for rapidly changing weather conditions.

From Baldy Notch, a wide gravel path leads to a commanding view of the desert. You then join a chair lift access/fire road, and ascend a broad slope forested in Jeffrey pine and incense cedar. The road ends in about 1 1/4 miles at the top of a ski lift.

From the top of the ski lift, a trail leads out onto a sharp ridge known as the Devil's Backbone. To the north, you can look down into the deep gorge of Lytle Creek, and to the south into San Antonio Canyon. You'll then pass around the south side of Mount Harwood, "Little Baldy," and up through scattered stands of lodgepole pine.

The trail reaches a tempestuous saddle. (Hold onto your hat!) From the saddle, a steep rock-strewn pathway zigzags past a few wind-bowed limber pine to the summit.

Boulders are scattered atop Baldy's crown. A couple of rock windbreaks offer some shelter. Enjoy the view of San Gabriel and San Bernardino mountain peaks, the Mojave and the metropolis, and return the same way.

Chapter IX

Surf Scene at Long Beach, California.

The Coast

Quote to remember: *"Looking eastward from the cliff on which
I stood, I could see the long wharf at Santa Monica, and, beyond, a long
curve of shore that ran to Palos Verdes and the promontory of
Point Fermin. The roar of the sea close by met me with a sort of boister-
ous friendliness, like the welcome of some tremendous mastiff."*

—JOSEPH SMEATON CHASE
California Coast Trails, 1913

The Coast

WHEN THE SUMMER SUN BEATS DOWN ON THE metropolis and the smog thickens, half the the Southland flees to Los Angeles County's seventy-five miles of coastline. More than sixty million visits a year are made to county beaches, although, as walkers soon discover, most folks cluster blanket-to-blanket on the same beaches, leaving less-accessible areas to those willing to walk.

Geography: At the south end of the county is long, breakwater protected Long Beach and the Long Beach-San Pedro Harbor complex. Rocky Palos Verdes Peninsula's 15 miles of reefs, tidepools, coves and crescent beaches, will surprise those energetic enough to hike them.

The hills of the Palos Verdes peninsula anchor the south end of crescent-shape Santa Monica Bay, a series of wide sandy beaches extending 30 miles from Redondo Beach to Pt. Dume.

The northern part of the county's coastline, beginning about Malibu, is decidedly different from the south. The Santa Monica Mountains veer toward the coast, creating a series of bluffs, rocky points, coves, and sandy beaches. The coastline is the most rural in the county, although there are occasional clusters of expensive homes built, it seems, right over the surfline. The State Coastal Commission and Coastal Conservancy have worked to improve access to a number of secluded beaches.

Natural attractions: Palos Verdes Peninsula is famous for its rocky cliffs, which rise from 50 to 300 feet above the ocean and for its thirteen wave-cut terraces. These terraces, or platforms, resulted from a combination of uplift and sea-level fluctuations caused by the formation and melting of glaciers.

At Zuma Beach is one of Los Angeles County's largest

sand beaches and one of the finest white sand strands in California. Above the beach is Pt. Dume, a good place to watch for migrating California gray whales.

Bird-watchers will head for the Ballona Wetlands, undergoing restoration, or Malibu Lagoon at the mouth of Malibu Creek. Grunion-catchers make midnight runs to Cabrillo Beach. Anglers cast for surfperch, abundant in the surf zone along sandy beaches and Pacific mackerel, caught in near-shore waters.

History: Santa Monica was developed as a beachside resort in 1875, Long Beach in 1880, Redondo Beach in 1892. For many years, these towns competed to become the great port of Los Angeles. San Pedro Harbor next to Long Beach got the dredging and improvement monies and the other two remained/became laid-back suburban beach towns.

Then there's quintessential Southern California—Malibu Beach. Known more formally as Malibu Lagoon State Beach or Surfrider Beach, this is the site of beach-blanket movies and Beach Boys songs. Just down-coast is Zonker Harris Accessway, honoring a character from the Doonesbury comic strip who once had the goal of acquiring the perfect tan. Just up-coast is the exclusive Malibu Colony, which began attracting movie stars in the late 1920s.

Today, the typical mass-use L.A. beach includes acres of hot sand, waves ranging from the gentle to the inspired, a lifeguard every few hundred feet, and a boardwalk full of roller skaters, restaurants and beach toy rental establishments. Before dawn, huge mechanized sand rakes scoop up trash, doing a good job of picking up after sloppy beach-goers.

The walker will find that each city and beach has a unique history and personality: Venice with its canals and zany boardwalk, Hermosa with its surfer population, Marina del Rey with the largest man-made pleasure craft harbor in the world.

Administration: Most of the shoreline—including many of the sand strands called state beaches—are patrolled by Los Angeles County.

Santa Monica Bay
Santa Monica Bay Trails

Highlights: *Fringed by palm trees, with the Santa Monica Mountains as dramatic backdrop, the wide sand beaches along Santa Monica Bay draw visitors from around the world.*

Distance: About 40 miles around the bay from Torrance to Pt. Dume; join the beach path wherever you wish.

Directions: Pacific Coast Highway and various beach-feeder roads provide great access to Santa Monica Bay. Street parking is often restricted in beach areas so watch the signs carefully. Except for the warmest weekends and holidays, you can usually find space in the county's mega-beachfront parking lots.

SANTA MONICA BAY IS A MELLOW INTRUSION BY THE Pacific Ocean into the western edge of the Los Angeles lowlands. The bay's magnificent curving beaches are cooled by a prevailing ocean breeze, which protects the coast from the temperature extremes—and smog—chracteristic to the interior.

But, all is not postcard views along Santa Monica Bay; the bay has its share of environmental problems. Sewers and storm drains empty (sometimes purposely, sometimes accidentally) into the bay. Environmental organizations such as Heal the Bay have undertaken the herculean task of educating the public and public officials that the bay is not merely a series of sand strands, but a living, dynamic ecosystem.

For the walker, the bay offers short strolls and long strides along the sand, plus a chance to tour Santa Monica, Venice, as well as Malibu and the distinctive beach towns of the South Bay.

Bird-watchers and nature-lovers will want to explore the Ballona Wetlands, one of the last remaining wetlands in Los Angeles County. A plan to restore 175 acres of Ballona has been proposed; even in its current sorry state, the wetlands serves as a refuge for migratory birds and as breeding habitat for the endangered California least tern. Guided walks are regulary conducted by conservation organizations.

Favorite bay walks enjoyed by tourists include Venice Beach and the Venice Boardwalk, the Santa Monica Pier, and Santa Monica's Palisades Park.

Super-jocks will want to try what I call the Triathalon Trail: Run/walk the 19 miles from Torrance County Beach to the Santa Monica Pier, cycle the South Bay Bicycle Path, then take a long refreshing swim.

Walkers will find plenty of parking and coastal accessways around the bay. Use the walk description below to fashion an exploration of the bay; begin or end your walk according to your time, inclination and craving for exercise.

As the cliffs recede, the trail crosses RAT (Right at Torrance) Beach, popular with surfers and swimmers. Marching over the white sands, walkers soon arrive at wide Redondo State Beach. The town of Redondo Beach was founded in 1892; its name is derived from nearby Rancho Sausal Redondo (Round Willow Grove).

Ahead, toward the north end of the state beach, is King Harbor. In the 1890s, it appeared that this harbor might become the great port of Los Angeles. Great vessels anchored off shore, goods from Asia and the Pacific Islands were unloaded at the wharves, and railroad tracks ran from Redondo docks to downtown Los Angeles. Congress considered Santa Monica, San Pedro and Redondo for federal funding to build a seaport. San Pedro Harbor got the dredging and improvement monies and Redondo became a resort. An amusement park and salt water plunge hosted generations of Southern Californians. During Prohibition, "entertainment" boats anchored off Redondo shores, just outside the 3-mile limit.

King Harbor today bears little resemblance to Redondos busy little port of the 1890s. The harbor area is dominated by piers, full of restaurants and shops.

Walkers improvise a route through King Harbor, dawdle along the walkways around the boat basins, or follow the South Bay Bicycle Path to the east. Note Seaside Lagoon, a 2.5-acre warm saltwater swimming hole with a a sandy bottom, located between Basins 2 and 3.

Next is Hermosa Beach Municipal Pier, a 1320-foot fishing pier at the south end of Hermosa City Beach. Hermosa is Spanish for beautiful; the name was supplied by a real estate developer. Hermosa's two-mile long, wide sandy beach is paralleled by a scenic walkway established in 1908 known as the Strand. It hosts every beach culture activity imaginable. During the 1950s, crowds of beatniks hung out in Hermosa Beach coffee houses and bookstores, listening to jazz and poetry read to music.

Next is Manhattan State Beach, yet another wide sandy beach, which also features The Strand. Manhattan Pier, a fish-

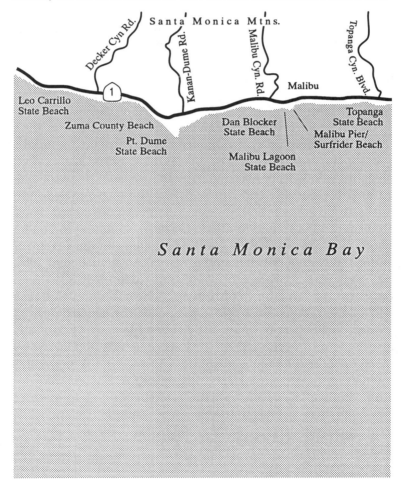

ing pier, is located at the south end of the beach. In the early 1900s, a wave-powered generator was located here, which produced electricity to light The Strand.

A mile past the pier, you'll pass low dunes which served as a "desert" location for many silent movies. Inland squats a massive power plant and "the plumber's nightmare"—the Hyperion Waste Treatment Plant. As the story goes, Aldous Huxley and Thomas Mann were hiking along this beach one day, discussing Shakespeare and Huxley's Brave New World, and other lofty subjects, when Huxley noticed what appeared to be thousands of wriggling, pale-colored worms. On closer

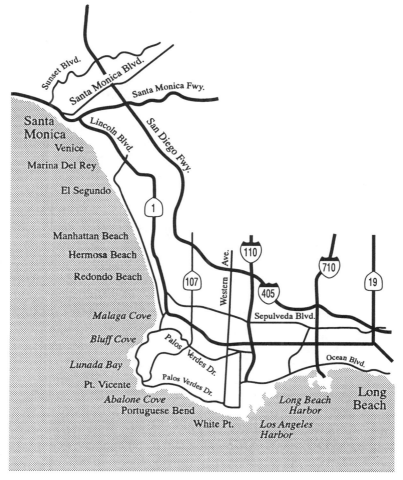

inspection, the worms turned out to be condoms. At first Huxley suspected typical Southern California orgiastic excess, but soon realized that the Hyperion Sewage Plant was discharging into the sea and the love aids had washed in with the tide. Huxley's beach walk and discovery led him to some profound speculation about man, civilization and sewage and he published a fine essay entitled "Hyperion to a Satyr."

After passing an ugly oil pier, you'll walk along Dockweiller Beach, which is wide, clean, sandy, and mostly pleasant—considering it's backed by Los Angeles International Airport. Dockweiller, usually referred to as Playa del Rey, extends to Marina Del Rey.

When you reach the Ballona Creek Channel, cross the bridge to the harbor jetty and follow the bikeway atop the jetty inland. On your left sailboats tack in and out of the harbor entrance. Occasionally a skipper goofs and sails his craft into the Ballona Creek Channel, inevitably getting marooned on the rocks.

On your right is a remnant of Ballona Wetland, a once extensive marshy area that extended from Playa del Rey bluffs to Venice. Housing developments, Army Corps of Engineers flood control projects, and Marina del Rey all but obliterated the marsh. Still, some pickleweed wetlands and mudflats remain, providing an important rest stop for birds along the Pacific Flyway. Ballona Creek is the winter home for many species of ducks, grebes and loons.

Past the UCLA rowing crew headquarters and some apartment buildings, the bikeway you've been following forks. You continue left, following a bike route and walkway past Fishermen's Village and various boat basins, and crossing Admiralty Way. Here you follow the landscaped bikeway along a bird refuge to Washington Street, then head west on Washington toward Venice Beach. On the west side of Washington Street, note one of the famed canals. Venice-by-the-Sea was the hallucination of Abott Kinney, the manufacturer of Sweet Caporeal Cigarettes. He was, as they say, a rich man with artistic impulses. He proceeded to drain the swampland here and build cottages connected by canals. He imported gondolas and gondoliers from that other Venice across the

Atlantic. Then, as now, however, the tawdry amusements of the boardwalk proved to be more popular than art and education. Today, the canals look a bit worse for wear. The system is choked with weeds and not much thrives there except ducks.

You return to the beach at the Venice Fishing Pier. Marina Peninsula (Venice Beach) extends down-coast one mile to the Marina Del Rey Channel entrance. Head up-coast along wide, sandy Venice City Beach. Venice is one of the county's oldest beaches; lifeguard service has been provided since the 1920s. The quiet of this beach is a marked contrast to the hubub of Ocean Front Walk paralleling the length of it. Almost every facet of zany California beach culture can be found on the boardwalk—jugglers, mimes, daring roller skaters, and more sidewalk cafes, offbeat outlets, junk-food and health-food eateries than one could sample in a year of Sundays.

Next, cross Santa Monica Beach, an extremely wide beach, bisected by the Santa Monica pier. The southern section has more sun-worshipers per square yard than does the north. This beach is perhaps no longer the glamour spot it was of old, but 5,000 parking spaces attest to the fact that a lot people find it quite attractive.

Rising 40-60 feet above Santa Monica Beach are the Palisades cliffs. The alluvial sands and gravels are in nearly horizontal layers and subject to severe erosion. The alluvium was deposited here by streams cascading down from the Santa Monica Mountains. Ages ago, Pacific waves found these deposits easy going and cut back extensively at the terraces, forming the Palisades. Palisades Park atop the cliffs at the north end of Santa Monica Beach is popular with joggers, tourists and sunset promenaders, although in recent years a sizeable homeless population has claimed this area.

Santa Monica Municipal Pier features the Playland Amusement Arcade, a relic from palmier days, and a wonderful carousel with elaborately carved prancing horses.

Walk past the pier on the wide sandy beach. The Palisades rise higher and higher, to more than one hundred feet above the beach and highway. Extraordinary (or comical, or tragic, depending on your point of view) attempts to stabilize the cliffs may be seen along this section of the cliffs. Three more miles of sandy beach follow as you cross Will Rogers State Beach, named for the famed cowboy and radio personality of the 1930s. There's usually not much surf here, but it has its moments and the beach is well-used by swimmers and tanning enthusiasts.

As you continue past the intersection of Pacific Coast Highway and Sunset Boulevard, the beach narrows and the shoreline grows sporadically rocky. Topanga State Beach is a mixture of sand and rock. The mouth of Topanga Creek is a

gathering place for surfers. Sedimentary sea cliffs rise close to shore. In one more mile, your route crosses another narrow state beach, Las Tunas.

You'll hike past the neighborhood beaches of Las Flores, La Costa and Big Rock. Beyond Big Rock is the infamous Zonker Harris Accessway, a focal point of the ongoing debate betweeen the California Coastal Commission, which is determined to provide access to the coast, and some Malibu residents who would prefer the public stay out. The original sign read "Zonker Harris Memorial Beach," honoring a character from the Doonesbury comic strip who once had the compulsion to acquire the perfect tan.

Soon you'll arrive at Surfrider Beach (Malibu Lagoon State Beach). When the natives say "Malibu Beach," this is what they mean: the site of beach-blanket movies and Beach Boy songs. Surfrider is a mixture of sand and stone and surfers. Just inland, Malibu Lagoon hosts many different kinds of waterfowl, both resident and migratory. The beach is rock cobble on the ocean side of the lagoon. To the landward side of the lagoon stretches the alluvial flatland deposited by Malibu Creek. The city of Malibu is situated here.

Around Malibu Point, you begin walking across the narrow and sandy beach lined by the exclusive Malibu Colony residences, home to many a movie star. Toward the west end of the colony, the beach narrows considerably and houses are built on stilts, with the waves pounding beneath them.

As you walk along Malibu's beaches, rejoice that you do not see State Highway 60, the Malibu Freeway. In the 1960s, a plan was hatched to build a causeway along Malibu Beach, supported on pilings offshore. A breakwater would have converted the open shore into a bay shore. The wonderful pounding surf would have been reduced to that of a lake; the beach biota completely destroyed.

The beach grows wider and more public at Corral State Beach, located at the mouths of Corral and Solstice Canyons. In the 1960s, a landslide-prone and seismically active Corral Canyon was the proposed site of the Malibu Nuclear Power Plant.

Pushing on, the intrepid walker rounds Latigo Point to Escondido Beach, a small sandy beach, deposited by Escondido Creek. Local divers enjoy the clear waters here. A mile west of Escondido is Paradise Cove Beach, accessible only to hikers and those willing to pay. There's a private fishing pier here and the beautiful beach is a favorite locale of moviemakers.

Rounding a minor coastline bulge, you reach Dume Cove. A footpath is taken, ascending to the top of the Point Dume headlands. A trail allows exploration of the point. In winter, Point Dume is an ideal place to watch for migrating California gray whales.

Malibu Beach
Malibu Beach Trail

Highlights: When Southern California natives say "Malibu Beach" this popular surfing spot is what they mean: the site of beach-blanket movies and Beach Boys songs. The state beach—formerly known as Surfrider—is a mixture of sand and stone. More than 200 bird species have been observed at Malibu Lagoon.

Distance: A mile or so to walk around Malibu Lagoon and down-coast a ways to Malibu Pier. Depending on the tide, you can walk 2-3 miles up-coast from Malibu Lagoon.

Directions: Malibu Lagoon State Beach is located at Pacific Coast Highway and Cross Creek Road in Malibu.

FOR FREDERICK HASTINGS RINDGE, OWNER OF 22 MILES of Southern California coast, life in the Malibu of a century ago was divine. "The enobling stillness makes the mind ascend to heaven," he wrote in his memoir, *Happy Days in Southern California*, published in 1898.

Long before Malibu meant good surfing, a movie star colony and some of the most expensive real estate on earth, "The Malibu" was a shorthand name for Topanga Malibu Sequit, an early 19th-Century rancho. This rancho extended from Topanga Canyon to the southeast to Ventura County on the northwest, from the tideline to the crest of the Santa Monica Mountains.

This beautiful locale attracted the attention of a wealthy Massachusetts businessman, Frederick Rindge, who was looking for an ideal spread "near the ocean, and under the lee of the mountains, with a trout brook, wild trees, good soil and excellent climate, one not too hot in summer."

Rindge bought the ranch and proceeded to divide his time between a townhouse in Los Angeles, from which he directed his business affairs—and his beloved rancho. The New Englander-turned-ranchero gloried in rounding up cattle, inspecting citrus groves and walking his St. Bernard along his many miles of private shoreline.

But Rindge's happy days ended rather abruptly when a 1903

Malibu Beach: Surf City, U.S.A.

fire burned his property. He died just two years later. His widow, May Rindge, decided to keep the rancho intact and to keep the public out of her coastal kingdom. Armed guards patrolled the dominion of the woman the newspapers called "The Queen of Malibu." For more than three decades, she not only stopped tourists and settlers, but blocked the state from completing Pacific Coast Highway. Eventually, however, the whole rancho was subdivided into ocean front lots and 100-acre "ranchos," as well as sites for hotels, yacht clubs and small summer homes.

Across from the lagoon is a stunning California landmark, the Adamson House, a beautiful Spanish-style home, built by Frederick Rindge's daughter Rhoda Adamson. The house, built in 1929, makes lavish use of ceramic "Malibu Tile." The grounds have been restored to their former beauty, with many ornamental trees and shrubs. Fountains and flagstone pathways wind through the landscaped grounds.

Adjoining the Adamson House is the Malibu Lagoon Museum, which contains a collection of artifacts and rare photographs that depict the various eras of "The Malibu," as this section of coastal Southern California was known.

First follow the nature trails around the lagoon.

Down-coast the walker will soon reach the historic 700-foot Malibu Pier, built in 1903. It's a favorite of fishermen and tourists. Sportfishing boats depart from the pier.

Farther down-coast is Zonker Harris Accessway, long the focus of debate between the California Coastal Commission, determined to provide access to the coast, and some Malibu residents who would prefer the public stay out. The original sign read "Zonker Harris Memorial Beach," honoring a character from the Doonesbury comic strip whose primary goal once was to acquire the perfect tan.

Up-coast, you'll pass Malibu Point; here the strong southwest swell refracts against a rock reef and creates the waves that makes Malibu so popular with surfers. Next you walk the narrow and sandy beach lined by the exclusive Malibu Colony residences, home to many a movie star. Toward the west end of The Colony, the beach narrows considerably and houses are built on stilts, with the waves sometimes pounding beneath them.

As you walk along Malibu Beach, rejoice that you do not see State Highway 60, the Malibu Freeway. In the 1960s a plan was hatched to build a causeway along Malibu Beach, supported on pilings offshore. A breakwater would have converted the open shore into a bay shore. The wonderful pounding surf would have been reduced to that of a lake.

The beach is wider and more public at Corral State Beach, located at the mouths of Corral and Solstice Canyons.

Zuma Beach, Point Dume
Zuma-Dume Trail

Highlights: *Zuma Beach is one of Los Angeles County's largest sand beaches and one of the finest white sand strands in California. Zuma lies on the open coast beyond Santa Monica Bay and thus receives heavy breakers crashing in from the north. From sunrise to sunset, board and body surfers try to catch a big one. Every month the color of the ocean and the cliffs seem to take on different shades of green depending on the season and sunlight, providing the Zuma Beach walker with yet another attraction.*

Distance: Zuma Beach to Point Dume is 1 mile round trip; to Paradise Cove is 3 miles round trip

Directions: From Pacific Coast Highway, about 25 miles up-coast from Santa Monica and just down coast from Zuma Beach County Park, turn oceanward on Westward Beach Road and follow it to its end at a (fee) parking lot.

Consult a tide table. Passage is easier at low tide.

D URING THE WHALE-WATCHING SEASON (APPROXI-mately mid-December through March), walkers ascending to the lookout atop Point Dume have a good chance of spotting a migrating California gray whale.

This walk travels along that part of Zuma Beach known as Westward Beach, climbs over the geologically fascinating Point Dume Headlands for sweeping views of the coast, then descends to Paradise Cove, site of a romantic little beach and a fishing pier.

Proceed down-coast along sandy Westward Beach. You'll soon see a distinct path leading up the point. The trail ascends through a plant community of sea fig and sage, coreopsis and prickly pear cactus to a lookout point.

From atop Point Dume, you can look down at Pirate's Cove, two hundred yards of beach tucked away between two rocky outcroppings. In past years, this beach was the scene of much dispute between nude beach advocates, residents and the county sheriff.

As you stand atop the rocky triangle projecting into the Pacific, observe the dense black Zuma volcanics and the much softer white sedimentary beds of the sea cliffs extending both east and west. The volcanics have resisted the crashing sea far better than the sedimentary rock and have protected the land behind from further erosion, thus forming the triangle shape of the point.

After enjoying the view and watching for whales, retrace your steps a short distance and continue on the main trail over the point, which has been set aside as a preserve under the protection of the California Department of Fish and Game. A staircase lets you descend to the beach.

A mile of beach-walking brings you to Paradise Cove, sometimes called Dume Cove. It's a secluded spot, and the scene of much television and motion picture filming. The Sand Castle restaurant and a private pier are located at the cove.

Leo Carrillo State Beach
Leo Carrillo Beach Trail

Highlights: *Leo Carrillo is one of the more interesting and most natural beaches in Los Angeles County. At Sequit Point, the dividing line between Los Angeles and Ventura counties, you'll find good surfing, swimming, snorkeling and a cluster of caves and coves.*

Distance: From Leo Carrillo State Beach to the county line is 3 miles round trip.

Directions: Leo Carrillo State Beach is located just down-coast from where Mulholland Highway intersects Pacific Coast Highway. Park along PCH (free) or in the state beach lot (fee).

THE STATE BEACH IS NAMED AFTER ACTOR ANGELINE Leo Carrillo, famous for his television role as Pancho, the Cisco Kid's sidekick. Los Angeles-born Carrillo, a descendant of a prominent Old California ranching family, was quite active in local recreation and civic matters.

The beach is an ever-popular locale for moviemakers, and after the propmaster installs palm trees the beach doubles for a South Seas locale.

Leo Carrillo State Beach is stabilized to some extent by minor rocky breaks in the shoreline and by extensive kelp beds offshore. Seals sometimes come ashore.

Head up-coast toward Sequit Point. The point bisects the beach, forming a bay to the south. Surfers tackle the south swell, battling the submerged rocks and kelp beds.

As you near the point, you'll pass a path which leads under the highway and connects the beach with the sycamore-shaded campground. The state parks department got a little carried away with pouring asphalt at Leo Carrillo, but it's still a very nice place. Scramble around the rocks of Sequit Point to several rock formations, caves, coves, a rock arch and some interesting tidepools.

North of the point, Leo Carrillo Beach offers good swimming with a sandy bottom. When the beach narrows and the houses multiply, return the way you came.

El Dorado Nature Center
El Dorado Nature Trail

Highlights: *Next to its beach, El Dorado Nature Center is Long Beach's biggest "natural attraction." Established in 1969, this man-made wildlife sanctuary includes two lakes and a stream, tree-lined meadows and low rolling hills. It's a serene habitat for flora and fauna as well as a tranquil retreat for humans.*

Distance: 2-mile loop through El Dorado Nature Center.

Directions: From the San Diego Freeway (405), exit on Studebaker Road and travel north about 2 1/2 miles to Spring Street. Take a right on Spring and proceed 3/4 of a mile to the entrance of El Dorado Park Nature Center. You can park in the lot by the nature center museum for a fee, or for free along Spring Street.

SOUTHERN CALIFORNIANS HAVE LONG LAMENTED THE destruction of the natural world caused by freeway construction. But in one community, freeway building resulted in the formation of a unique nature center.

Back in the mid-1960s, during construction of the San Gabriel River/San Diego Freeway interchange, earth movers were moving millions of cubic yards of earth. Thanks to concerned citizens and conservationists, some of that earth was moved to form 800-acre El Dorado Regional Park and 80-acre El Dorado Nature Center. The park has wide lawns, ball fields and picnic areas. The Nature Center is a surpise—an oasis in the midst of the metropolis.

Surely this land has undergone a strange evolution: from San Gabriel River floodplain to beanfields to freeway interchange to nature preserve. Only in Southern California!

Several ecological zones are represented in the nature preserve, which for the most part, emphasizes native California flora. Walkers can tour oak woodland, grassy meadow, and chaparral communities, which are representative of Southern California plant communities, and can meander among redwoods and a white alder grove—vegetation typical of the northern part of the state.

More than 150 bird species have been counted here,

El Dorado Nature Center, a small museum perched on an island, is a good place to learn about Southern California's plant life and wildlife. This satellite museum of the Natural History Museum of Los Angeles County features a "hands-on" ecology exhibit and a gallery that displays the work of nature artists and photographers.

Kids will particularly enjoy a visit to the nature center. The museum's exhibits, interpretive walks and even the pint-sized drinking fountains were designed with kids in mind.

Two miles of easy trail circle El Dorado. A one-mile nature trail is keyed to a pamphlet available from the museum. Another mile of trail loops around the preserve's two ponds.

Bird-watchers flock to the preserve because more than 150 resident and migratory bird species have been sighted. A bird checklist is available at the museum.

Pick up a nature trail interpretive pamphlet from the museum, then head out across the bridge into the reserve. Enjoy the native plant communities, including a cattail-lined creek and a chaparral-cloaked hillside. And keep an eye out for two nonnatives that have been part of the Southland scene for more than a century and seem like natives—the large, plume-like pampas grass from South America and the ubiquitous eucalyptus. Be sure to get the "big picture" from the Observation Tower, the preserve's highest point.

When you reach a trail junction, you can proceed straight ahead on the "One Mile" nature trail or bear right for a two-mile hike. The second mile of trail meanders past the park's ponds before returning to the Nature Center building.

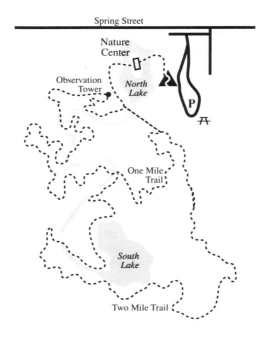

Signal Hill
Signal Hill Trail

Highlights: *Sierra Club outings leaders report that often more than a hundred hikers turn out for evening strides around the hill. Signal Hill is anything but a natural environment, but the great views of harbor and city and the camaraderie of the trail usually add up to a fun trip.*

Distance: 4-mile loop of Signal Hill with 300-foot elevation gain.

Directions: From the San Diego Freeway (405) in Long Beach, take the Cherry Ave. Signal Hill exit. Head south on Cherry one-half mile to Willow. Turn right and after a mile, make a right on Redondo, then right on aptly named Hill Street. Proceed to the base of Signal Hill. Depending on your time and/or inclination, you can park at the base of the hill or closer to the top.

S IGNAL HILL HAS LONG BEEN SYNONYMOUS WITH OIL. Atop this Long Beach prominence a great oil field was discovered in 1921. Alamitos #1, as the discovery well was known, produced 600 barrels a day. Soon Signal Hill was covered with derricks, which produced 250,000 barrels a day.

The hill is a quieter place now, though a number of active wells are still pumping black gold. Because Signal is the only hill for miles around, it has long drawn walkers trying to stay in shape or get a view.

During the 1840s, the hill was the property of rancher John Temple, who called his spread Los Cerritos—"Little Hills." The hill was renamed when the Coast Survey of 1889 used it as a signal point.

Signal Hill and its geologic cousins to the north—Baldwin Hills—were uplifted as a result of activity from the Newport-Inglewood Fault Zone. One result of this fault activity was that oil accumulated beneath various anticlines, or domes of rock.

Signal Hill achieved worldwide recognition for the petroleum and profits it produced, but the hill has never been known as a model oil field. Haphazard development and excessive drilling led to an ugly and dangerous environment.

Signal Hill—the mountain—has been cleaned up some since

239

its heyday, and its slopes now host more houses than oil wells. Still, walkers should use caution, avoid drilling equipment and respect "No Trespassing" signs. There isn't a single path around the hill; rather, you improvise a route on Signal's dirt and paved roads.

To fully enjoy the great clear-day views, bring along binoculars and a city map.

Follow Panorama Drive or the dirt road below it in a counter-clockwise direction. You'll pass oil wells, get a view to the north of the San Diego Freeway, the planes arriving and departing from Long Beach Airport, and many square miles of suburbia. Eucalyptus and palm trees line the up-and-down dirt roads. Lemon grass and California poppies add a little color to the ugly hillsides.

Your route crosses Burnett Street and you join a dirt road on the west side of the hill. Growing on this slope is a zany mixture of flora—banana palms and California fan palms, Canary Island pines, lemonade berry and brittle bush.

Only the hawks(!) circling overhead have a better view than you. The view west takes in the Palos Verdes Peninsula. Catalina Island, thirty miles away, is visible on a clear day.

Looking south and west you can identify the Queen Mary and its three stacks and count a number of man-made oil islands. Dominating the coast is the massive Los Angeles/Long Beach harbor complex and the tall cranes used for loading containerized cargo. Several bridges spanning the harbor are also in view, including the Vincent Thomas Bridge.

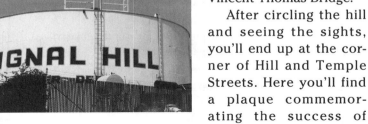

After circling the hill and seeing the sights, you'll end up at the corner of Hill and Temple Streets. Here you'll find a plaque commemorating the success of Southland's oil pioneers and Alamitos #1: "...a success which has, by aiding in the growth and expansion of the petroleum industry, contributed so much to the welfare of mankind."

Cabrillo Beach, White's Point
Cabrillo Beach Trail

Highlights: *This walk begins at Cabrillo Beach, the only real sand beach for miles to the north and south, passes Cabrillo Marine Museum, and ends up at historic White's Point. For the most part, your route is atop the San Pedro and Palos Verdes Bluffs, but there's ample opportunity on this easy family excursion to descend to the sea. Your hiking and tidepool-viewing pleasure will be increased immeasurably if you walk during low tide.*

Distance: From Cabrillo Beach to White's Point is 3 miles round trip.

Directions: Take the Harbor Freeway south to San Pedro and exit on Gaffey Street. Follow Gaffey seaward to 22nd and turn left. Turn right on Pacific Avenue and then left on 36th Street. Fee parking is available either near the museum or at Cabrillo Beach.

ALL BUT FORGOTTEN TODAY, THE ROCKY COVE JUST down coast from White's Point in San Pedro once flourished as a Roaring Twenties health spa and resort. All that remain today are some sea-battered cement ruins and lush overgrown gardens.

White's Point was originally settled at the turn of the century by immigrant Japanese fishermen who harvested the bountiful abalone from the waters off Palos Verdes Peninsula. Tons of abalone were shipped to the Far East and tons more were consumed locally in Los Angeles' Little Tokyo. In a few years the abalone was depleted, but an even greater resource was discovered at White's Point—sulfur springs.

In 1915 construction of a spa began. Eventually the large Royal Palms Hotel was built at water's edge. Palm gardens and a golf course decorated the cliffs above. The sulfur baths were especially popular with the Japanese population of Southern California.

The spa boomed in the 1920s, but the 1933 earthquake closed the springs. The cove became part of Fort McArthur during World War II, the Japanese-American settlers were incarcerated in internment camps, and the resort was soon overwhelmed by crumbling cliffs and the powerful sea.

Cabrillo Marine Museum is well-worth a visit. It has marine displays, aquariums with live fish and good shell collections. One exhibit interprets the history of White's Point. The museum sponsors tidepool walks, grunion watches and is a coordinating point for whale-watching cruises.

March up sandy Cabrillo Beach, which has a monopoly on the grunion, since the sand-seeking fish have few other spawning options along Palos Verde Peninsula. You'll soon pass the San Pedro breakwater and Cabrillo fishing pier.

Just up-coast from Cabrillo Beach is the rocky shoreline of Point Fermin Marine Life Refuge. Limpets, crabs and lobsters are a few of the many creatures found in the bountiful tidepools. After rock-hopping among the tidepools, you must follow a dirt path or the paved road up to the top of the coastal bluffs; it is all but impossible to walk around Point Fermin via the shoreline route. Walk uphill along Bluff Place to a parking lot at the terminus of Pacific Avenue and join a blufftop trail. This path takes you past remains of "Sunken City," a 1930s housing tract built on bluffs that soon collapsed. Palm trees and huge chunks of asphalt are all that remain of the oceanside housing tract.

Soon you'll arrive at Point Fermin Park and its handsome Victorian-style lighthouse, built in 1874 from materials shipped around Cape Horn. Shortly after the bombing of Pearl Harbor, the lighthouse became an observation point.

Two coastal accessways lead down the park's bluffs to the rocky shoreline. As you near White's Point, you'll see a palm garden with fire pits. Royal Palms Hotel was once situated here until overcome by the sea. Storm-twisted palms and overgrown gardens are a reminder of flush times long past. Royal Palms is a state beach popular with surfers.

Ahead at White's Point are some curious cement remains of the resort. Beyond the point stretch the rugged cliffs and cobblestone shores of Palos Verdes Peninsula. Return the same way or if you have the time, walk on. The difficult terrain will ensure that few follow in your footsteps.

Palos Verdes Peninsula
Palos Verdes Peninsula Trail

Highlights: *Exploring this beach is like walking over a surface of broken bowling balls. The route is rocky and progress slow, but that gives you more time to look down at the tidepools and up at the magnificent bluffs.*

Distance: Malaga Cove to Rocky Point is 5 miles round trip; to Point Vincente Lighthouse is 10 miles round trip

Directions: Take Pacific Coast Highway to Palos Verdes Boulevard. Bear right on Palos Verdes Drive. As you near Malaga Cove Plaza, turn right at the first stop sign (Via Corta). Make a right on Via Arroyo, then another right into the parking lot behind the Malaga Cove School. The trailhead is on the ocean side of the parking area where a wide path descends the bluffs above the Flatrock Point tidepools. A footpath leaves from Paseo Del Mar, 1/10 mile past Via Horcada, where the street curves east to join Palos Verdes Drive West.

G EOGRAPHICALLY, THE PALOS VERDES BLUFFS AND beaches resemble the Channel Islands. Geologists say that long ago, before the Ice Age began, the Peninsula was an island, separated from the rest of Los Angeles basin by the sea. However, toward the end of the last glacial period, the eighteen-mile-long Peninsula was connected to the mainland by masses of sediment discharged from the mountains to the north.

The Peninsula is famous for its rocky cliffs, which rise from 50 to 300 feet above the ocean and for its thirteen wave-cut terraces. These terraces, or platforms, resulted from a combination of uplift and sea-level fluctuations caused by the formation and melting of glaciers. Today the waves, as they have for so many thousands of years, are actively eroding the shoreline, cutting yet another terrace onto the land.

While enjoying this walk, you'll pass many beautiful coves, where whaling ships once anchored and delivered their cargo of whale oil. Large iron kettles, used to boil whale blubber, have been found in sea cliff caves. Indians, Spanish rancheros and Yankee smugglers have all added to the Peninsula's romantic history. Modern times have brought white-stuccoed, red-tiled mansions to the Peninsula bluffs, but the beach remains almost pristine. Offshore, divers explore the rocky bottoms for abalone and shellfish. Onshore, walkers enjoy the wave-scalloped bluffs and splendid tidepools.

Check a tide table and walk only at low tide.

From the Malaga Cove School parking lot, descend the wide path to the beach. A sign indicates you're entering a seashore reserve and asks you to treat tidepool residents with respect. To the north are sandy beaches for sedentary sun worshipers. Active rock-hoppers clamber to the south. At several places along this walk you'll notice that the great terraces are cut by steep-walled canyons. The first of these canyon incisions can be observed at Malaga Cove, where Malaga Canyon slices through the north slopes of Palos Verdes Hills, then cuts west to empty at the cove.

The coastline curves out to sea in a southwesterly direction and Flatrock Point comes into view. The jade-colored waters swirl around this anvil-shaped point, creating the best tidepool area along this section of coast. Above the point, the cliffs soar to 300 feet. Cloaked in morning fog, the rocky seascape here is reminiscent of Big Sur.

Rounding Flatrock Point, you pick your way among the rocks, seaweed and the flotsam and jetsam of civilization to Bluff Cove, where sparkling combers explode against the rocks and douse the unwary with their tangy spray. A glance over your right shoulder brings a view of Santa Moncia Bay, the Santa Monica Mountains in gray silhouette and on the far horizon, the Channel Islands.

A mile beyond Bluff Cove, Rocky (also called Palos Verdes) Point juts out like a ship's prow. Caught fast on the rocks at the base of the point is the rusting exoskeleton of the Greek freighter *Dominator*, a victim of the treacherous reef surrounding the Peninsula.

Trek around Rocky Point to Lunada Bay, a good place to observe the terrace surfaces. From here you'll walk under almost perpendicular cliffs that follow horseshoe-shaped Lunada Bay. Shortly you'll round Resort Point, where fisher-

Pt. Vincente lighthouse: Beacon for hardy coast walkers.

men try their luck. As the coastline turns south, Catalina can often be seen glowing on the horizon. Along this stretch of shoreline, numerous stacks, remnants of former cliffs not yet dissolved by he surf, can be seen.

The stretch of coast before the lighthouse has been vigorously scalloped by thousands of years of relentless surf. You'll have to boulder-hop the last mile to Point Vincente. The lighthouse has worked its beacon over the dark waters since 1926. Guided tours of the lighthouse are available by appointment.

Passage is usually impossible around the lighthouse at high tide; if passable, another half-mile of walking brings you to an official beach access (or departure) route at Long Point.

Palos Verdes Hills
Portuguese Bend Trail

Highlights: *The little-known and infrequently traveled trails of the Palos Verdes Peninsula offer the walker a tranquil escape from metropolitan life. During the spring, the hills are colored an emerald green and sprinkled with wildflowers.*

Distance: Del Cerro Park to Badlands Slide Area is 2 1/2 miles round trip with a 400-foot elevation gain.

Directions: From the San Diego Freeway (405) in Torrance, exit on Crenshaw Boulevard and head south. Continue on Crenshaw past Pacific Coast Highway, and into the hills of Rancho Palos Verdes. Park at boulevard's end at the side of the road or at nearby Del Cerro Park. The trail begins at a steel gate which separates the end of Crenshaw Boulevard from the beginning of a dirt fire road.

> "In Palos Verdes one has the impression of entering a paradise designed by the Spanish for the annointed of heaven." —LOUIS BROMFIELD, *Vogue*, 1930

THIS SHORT LOOP TRIP, SUITABLE FOR THE WHOLE family, explores the hills above Portuguese Bend, one of the most geologically interesting (and unstable) areas in Southern California. Earth movement during 1956-57 wrecked approximately 100 homes. The rate of movement was more than an inch a day!

Portuguese Bend takes its name from the Portuguese men who practiced the risky, but lucrative, business of shore whaling. Most of the hardy whalers who worked the waters off Palos Verdes Peninsula from the 1850s to the 1880s were of Portuguese descent. Many a whale was slaughtered, but the Peninsula whaling operation was abandoned; not for lack of gray whales, but because of a shortage of fuel with which to process blubber into oil.

The route I've dubbed Portuguese Bend Trail links various paths and fire roads and offers great clear-day views of the Peninsula and Catalina Island.

Head down the unsigned fire road, which is officially named Crenshaw Extension Trail. Leaving red-roofed million-dollar residences behind, you'll look ahead to a million-dollar view. The green hills, bedecked with lupine in spring, roll to the sea. Geology students will note several marine terraces, while botany students will observe the Peninsula's unique blend of native brush and imported flora gone wild.

A half-mile descent from the trailhead brings you to a water tank and an unsigned three-way intersection. The leftward trail climbs to a fire station. The trail dead-ahead will be your return route on this walk. Continue right with Crenshaw Extension Trail, which soon drops into a wildflower-splashed meadow known as Peacock Flats. It's doubtful you'll see a peacock here, but you might hear the shrill call of the "watchdog of the Peninsula" from other parts of the trail. The aggresssive birds are popular pets around here, but they do many get on the nerves of local residents, some of whom favor banishing them from the area.

Above Peacock Flats, two short trails lead up a hill topped with a dozen pine trees. From the crest of this hill, known as Eagle's Nest, you'll have grand clear-day views of Catalina. The nest is close to the southwestern-most point of the Peninsula, meaning Catalina is but seventeen nautical miles away; you can often identify many of the island's geographical features.

Return to the main trail which heads northwest then makes a long horseshoe bend to the southeast. After descending past a stand of eucalyptus and a water tank, you'll begin crossing the geologically unstable terrain known as Badlands Slide Area.

A water pipe on the left parallels the dirt road at this point. Look sharply left for an unsigned trail that climbs to the east. After a steep and tentative start, the trail widens and ascends at a more moderate pace atop a canyon wall. Sweet-smelling fennel lines the path, which turns north and climbs to the above-mentioned three-way trail junction. Retrace your steps on Crenshaw Extension Trail to the trailhead.

South Coast Botanic Garden
South Coast Trail

Highlights: *The beauty of this romantic garden belies its unlovely past. The site site was once an open pit mine, later a dump; reclamation efforts transformed it into a botanic garden. Today, not only walkers and garden buffs, but horticulturists and reclamation experts travel from near and far to study this innovative project.*

Distance: A mile or so round trip.

Directions: From the Harbor Freeway (110) in Wilmington, exit on on Pacific Coast Highway. Go west 3 miles to Crenshaw Boulevard, then turn south to the South Coast Botanic Garden.

BEGINNING IN THE 1920S, DIATOMACEOUS EARTH (used in abrasives, filtering systems, insulation) was dug from a huge Palos Verdes Peninsula pit. When the diatomite were exhausted, the County of Los Angeles acquired the site for a landfill, burying 3.5 million tons of trash during the 1960s.

After the landfill was filled, a decision was made to create a garden. Numerous horticultural problems had to be overcome: soil settling (which is why the land was unsuitable for building), lack of compost (diotomaceous earth has none), and root-wrecking heat and gases given off by buried vegetable matter.

Major plant collections include roses, succulents, flowering fruit trees and even redwoods. Among the specialized sections are an herb garden, a vegetable garden and an English garden. Besides the usual family/eco arrangements common to botanic gardens, South Coast has some impressive groupings by color—blue, pink and yellow. The garden particularly emphasizes plants from Australia, the Mediterranean and southern Africa—flora that thrive in Southern California's similar climate.

For the walker, a system of trails leads through the garden and over to a manmade lake. The garden's high points offer superb clear-day panoramas of Los Angeles.

Chapter X

TOPANGA ROAD

Santa Monica Mountains

Quote to remember: "*The copper-hued men who roamed these hills not so long ago were very likely better tenants than you and I will be. And when we are gone, as we will go, a few unnoticed centuries will wipe out our bravest scars, our most determined trails.*"

—JOHN RUSSELL MC CARTHY,
Those Waiting Hills, the Santa Monicas, 1924

SANTA MONICA MOUNTAINS

BORDERED BY TWO OF THE BUSIEST FREEWAYS IN THE world—the Ventura and the San Diego—they remain a near-wilderness. Within easy reach of 16 million people, they nevertheless offer solitude and plenty of silent places.

Geography: The Santa Monicas are the only relatively undeveloped mountain range in the U.S. that bisects a major metropolitan area. They stretch all the way from Griffith Park in the heart of Los Angeles to Point Mugu, 50 miles away. The range is 12 miles wide at its broadest point, and it reaches an elevation of a little over 3,000 feet.

One of the few east-west trending ranges in the country, the Santa Monica Mountains can cause a little geographic confusion to the first-time visitor. The Santa Monica Bay and Malibu coastline also runs east-west alongside the mountains, so that the mountain explorer actually looks south to view the ocean and heads west when heading "up the coast."

Natural attractions: The mountains are a Mediterranean ecosystem, the only one in the country under National Park Service protection. Large stretches are open and natural, covered with chaparral and oak trees, bright in spring with wildflowers. Oak woodland and fern glens shade gentle seasonal creeks.

The largest areas of open space are in the western part of the mountains. Point Mugu State Park holds the finest native tall grass prairie and the best sycamore grove in the state. The gorge cut by Malibu Creek is an unforgettable sight.

In the eastern part of the mountains, open space is harder to come by, but those pockets that do exist are all the more valuable because they are so close to the metropolis. Canyons such as Los Liones, Caballero, Rustic and Sullivan are precious resources.

History: Ancestors of the Chumash Indians lived in the mountains as early as 7,000 years ago. Abundant food sources helped the Chumash become the largest Indian tribal group in

California at the time of Juan Cabrillo's arrival in 1542. The Chumash's highly developed culture included oceangoing plank canoes called *tomols* and a system of astronomy that was both mystical and practical.

Spanish missionaries, soldiers and settlers displaced the Chumash. During the 19th Century, the Santa Monicas were controlled by a few large land holdings—including Rancho Topanga-Malibu-Sequit and Rancho Guadalasca—and used primarily for cattle raising. As the land holdings were broken up, ranchers supplemented their modest living by renting space to visiting horsemen and vacationers.

Conservationists proposed Whitestone National Park in the 1930s and Toyon National Park in the 1960s, but it wasn't until Will Rogers, Topanga, Malibu Creek and Point Mugu State Parks were set aside in the late 1960s that the mountains received any substantial government protection. In 1978, the bill creating Santa Monica Mountains National Recreation Area was approved by Congress.

Administration: Some 65,000 acres of public land is preserved within the boundaries of the Santa Monica Mountains National Recreation Area. This represents about one-third of the 200,000 acres covered by the range. The National Recreation Area is not one large area, but a patchwork of state, federal and county land, as well as private property still to be acquired. Particularly effective at securing a wide variety of properties has been the Santa Monica Mountains Conservancy, a state agency.

Sullivan Canyon
Sullivan Canyon Trail

Highlights: *Sullivan Canyon above Brentwood is one of the gems of the eastern portion of the Santa Monica Mountains. Stately oaks and sycamores shade a seasonal creek and a fine trail travels the length of the canyon.*

Distance: 8-mile loop with 1,100-foot elevation gain

Directions: From the San Diego Freeway (405) in west Los Angeles, exit on Sunset Boulevard. and head west 2 1/2 miles to Mandeville Canyon Road. Turn right and after 1/4 mile turn left on Westridge Road, which you'll follow a bit more than a mile to Bayliss Road. Make a left, travel 1/4 mile, make another left on Queensferry Road. and follow this road another 1/4 mile to its end. Park near the end of the road.

SULLIVAN CANYON IS ATTRACTIVE TO ITS OWNER— the Los Angeles County Sanitation District, albeit for other than aesthetic reasons. Sullivan and its neighbor, Rustic Canyon, have long been proposed as landfill sites. Protests by environmentalists have thus far derailed the dump so for now, Sullivan Canyon is a beautiful place to roam.

Sullivan's high and narrow canyon walls display handsome sandstone outcroppings, as well as a blue-gray bedrock known as Santa Monica slate. During winter and spring, the canyon walls are colored with clusters of ceanothus.

Casual walkers will enjoy a nearly flat stroll a mile or three along the canyon floor. More energetic hikers will make a loop trip by by climbing out of the canyon and traveling Sullivan's west ridge. Views from the ridge are quite good.

The trail begins at the end of Bayliss Road, where a frequently-traveled equestrian trail, ascending from the wilds of Brentwood, joins the road. Walk down an asphalt road (closed to vehicles) a hundred yards to a cement flood control apron, then turn right and enter sylvan Sullivan Canyon.

The wide trail meanders near a willowy streambed, beneath the boughs of antiquarian oaks and across carpets of lemon grass. Three miles of tranquil trail brings you to a couple of eucalyptus trees on your left. This is a good turnaround point.

Those hikers wanting to complete this loop trip, will continue up canyon on an old dirt road. After a half-mile ascent, the road forks. The right fork leads to Mulholland Drive, which you can see about a half-mile away. You'll take the left fork and ascend a little farther to an unsigned junction with dirt Fire Road 26. A right turn offers another route to Mulholland Drive, but you'll turn left and begin descending the west ridge of Sullivan Canyon. Occasionally you'll get a glimpse to the east of Sullivan, but the better views are to the west of Rustic Canyon and the bold slopes of Topanga State Park. If it's not foggy, the coastal views are pretty good too.

The only shade on the ridge route occurs about halfway down, where you'll find a small clump of oaks and a little bench. Farther down the ridge, you'll reach a yellow gate and a paved road leading down to the Boy Scouts' Camp Josepho.

A few hundred yards past this turnoff, you'll walk under some telephone lines—your clue to begin looking sharply to your left for the unsigned connector trail that will return you to the bottom of Sullivan Canyon. As the road bears right, you'll head left for a telephone pole, pass directly under the poles two guide wires and join the footpath. The trail, quite steep but in good condition, drops several hundred feet in a quarter-mile and deposits you back on the canyon floor. Turn down-canyon, and travel a half-mile back to the trailhead.

Nearby Mission Canyon was filled with garbage. Activists are working to spare Sullivan and Rustic from a similar fate.

Will Rogers' Inspiration Point
Will Rogers Trail

Highlights: Tour the "Cowboy Philosopher's" home and ranch at Will Rogers State Historic Park. Then enjoy the coast, mountain and metropolis views from Inspiration Point.

Distance: To Inspiration Point is 2 miles round trip with a 300-foot elevation gain

Directions: From Sunset Boulevard in Pacific Palisades, 4 1/2 miles inland from Sunset's junction with Pacific Coast Highway, turn inland on the access road leading to Will Rogers State Historic Park. Leave your car (state park day use fee) near the polo field or near Rogers' house.

WILL ROGERS, OFTEN CALLED THE "COWBOY Philosopher," bought a spread in the Santa Monica Mountains in 1922. He and his family enlarged their weekend cottage to 31 rooms.

The Oklahoma-born Rogers toured the country as a trick roper, punctuating his act with humorous comments on the news of the day. His roping act led the humorist to later fame as a newspaper columnist, radio commentator and movie star.

Today, the ranch and grounds of the Rogers Ranch is maintained as Will Rogers State Historic Park, set aside in 1944. Watch the short film on Rogers' life at the park visitors center and tour the ranch house, still filled with his prized possessions.

Rogers himself designed the riding trails that wind into the hills behind his ranch. The path to Inspiration Point is an easy

From Inspiration Point: Grand views of the metropolis.

walk for the whole family. Walkers who want more than an inspiring view can join other park trails. (See Rustic Canyon and Topanga Canyon descriptions in this guide.)

Join the path near the tennis courts west of park headquarters and begin ascending north into the mountains. Join the main, wide bridle path.)

Rogers Trail ascends a ridge overlooking nearby Rivas Canyon and leads to a junction, where you take the turnoff for Inspiration Point. Not really a point at all, it's actually more of a flat-topped knoll; nevertheless, clear-day views are inspiring: the Santa Monica Bay, the metropolis, the San Gabriel Mountains, and even Catalina Island.

Rustic Canyon
Rustic Canyon Trail

Highlights: *Rustic Canyon is every bit as woodsy and secluded as its name suggests. The surprisingly rugged little enclave is located in the Pacific Palisades section of the Santa Monica Mountains.*

Distance: Loop through Will Rogers State Historic Park and Rustic Canyon is 6 miles round trip with 900-foot elevation gain.

Directions: From Sunset Boulevard in Pacific Palisades, turn north on the access road leading to Will Rogers State Historic Park. There is a state park day use fee. Park near the polo field or Rogers' house. A tour of the "Cowboy Philosopher's" home is well worth your time.

T O THE GREAT CONCERN OF CONSERVATIONISTS, THE greater part of Rustic Canyon is owned by the Los Angeles County Sanitation District. That means—you guessed it—the canyon could become the site of Rustic Sanitary Landfill.

However, the canyon has many conservationist friends who speculate that Rustic and neighboring Sullivan Canyon will be used as bargaining chips in attempts to "trade" for more remote and less ecologically significant potential dumpsites.

For the walker, Sullivan Canyon (see description in this guide) and neighboring Rustic Canyon are an interesting contrast. Sullivan is a gently sloping canyon with a wide flat floor shaded by sycamores. Rustic is wild, narrow, steep, with dramatic rock walls. One way to reach Rustic Canyon is to descend via Sullivan Canyon; another way (this walk) is via Will Rogers Park.

Rustic Canyon has a storied past. A hundred years ago, the Santa Monica Forestry Station was established adjacent to the canyon. The many eucalyptus in and around the canyon are a result of tobacco millionaire/builder of Venice/ forestry pioneer Abbot Kinney's efforts. The eucalyptus, an Australian import, thrived in Southern California but to Kinney's disappointment proved to be a miserable source of timber.

Most of Rustic Canyon remained undeveloped until the early 1920s when it became the woodsy retreat of a group of Los Angeles business-men known as The Uplifters. The group, at first an offshoot of the Los Angeles Athletic Club, was chartered to "uplift art, promote good fellowship and build a closer acquaintance among its members." It was L. Frank Baum, author of the Wizard of Oz books who came up with the name, "The Lofty and Excellent Order of the

A canyon as rustic as its name.

Uplifters." Cabins, clubhouse buildings and an outdoor the-ater were built in the canyon. The club went strong during the 1920s, slowed during the Depression years, and came to an end after World War II.

This walk begins in Will Rogers State Historic Park. You'll follow the trail to Inspiration Point, march a mile or two up the Backbone Trail, then descend into Rustic Canyon and loop back to Will Rogers.

One highlight of Rustic Canyon is Rustic Creek. Most Santa Monica Mountains' watercourses flow only after rains, but Rustic Creek is one of the few which is spring-fed and thus usually flows all year round through the lower reaches of the canyon.

About a mile of the trail through Rustic Canyon is right next to, and even in, Rustic Creek. It's wet going, it's poor trail, and its not for beginning hikers.

From Will Rogers home, on the east side of a wide field, take the paved road leading past a line of eucalyptus trees to a riding ring. Soon you'll intersect a dirt road. Turn left on this road (actually, right is okay too, because the roads join). If you head left, be sure to stay on the main fire road and ignore rightward turns on lesser roads. The fire road ascends to a place just below Inspiration Point, where you'll spot an information kiosk. Continue to Inspiration Point for inspiring clear day views of the city if you wish, but this hike joins a trail to the left of an information kiosk.

Climbing Chicken Ridge, the trail offers great views of downtown, Century City, the sweep of Santa Monica Bay, Catalina Island. (The trail you're following is the beginning of the Backbone Trail, a 65-mile path that when completed will travel the spine of the Santa Monica Mountains from Will Rogers Park to Pt. Mugu State Park.) After a mile's climb along the ridge, the trail crests, then descends another quarter-mile to an unsigned three-way junction. The two leftward trails are high and low route continuations of the Backbone, but you'll turn sharply to the right and begin a steep descent on a connector trail. This manzanita-lined trail wastes no time descending a half-mile over a slippery slope to the bottom of Rustic Canyon. Ahead is a white barn and an unsigned intersection with Rustic Canyon Trail. Left up Rustic Canyon leads to Camp Josepho, the Boy Scout camp. You bear right, down-canyon.

Rustic Canyon Trail stays at the canyon bottom, crossing and re-crossing the creek. You'll pass the ruins of some homes that have suffered the ravages of fire and flood. Rustic Canyon flora includes the usual riparian growth plus some stray exotics such as cactus, aloe, jade, and periwinkle. German ivy, a pretty but invasive plant with little yellow flowers, has really taken over in some spots.

You'll pass a small dam. The trail narrows, the canyon walls close in. Nearing the state park, you'll follow an elaborate trail, fashioned with enough wooden trestles to support a freight train, then cross a white bridge over a culvert, and spy the parking lot and Rogers' house where you began this hike.

Temescal Canyon
Temescal Canyon Trail

Highlights: *This steep hike gradually climbs via Temescal Fire Road to scenic overlooks among the highest summits (over 2,000 feet) in the Santa Monicas. From the overlooks, you can see Santa Ynez, Temescal and Rustic Canyons, as well as the Los Angeles Basin and the great blue Pacific.*

Distance: From the canyon floor to Ridge Overlook is 5 1/2 miles round trip with 700-foot gain; to Rogers Road is 12 1/2 miles round trip with 1,600-foot gain.

Directions: From Sunset Boulevard in Pacific Palisades, turn north on Temescal Canyon Road. Proceed for 1/2 mile and park in the open area, just before the Presbyterian Conference Grounds. Walkers must sign in and out at the gate. Respect the quiet and privacy of the grounds.

A S YOU SWEAT IT OUT CROSSING THE EXPOSED RIDGE above Temescal Canyon, you might be amused to learn that "temescal" is what the Chumash Indians called their village sweathouse. The Chumash took as many as two ceremonial sweat baths a day, in what anthropologists speculate might have been a religious ritual. A fire burned in the center of the sweathouse. When the Chumash began to perspire, they scraped the sweat off with special sticks, then rushed out and leaped into a cold stream.

Head up-canyon on the paved road, passing a number of meeting halls and residences. The route, shaded by coast live oak, next follows a washed out road along Temescal Creek.

The trail climbs through a narrow gorge of the canyon and, 1 1/2 miles from the trailhead, crosses over to the west (left) side of the canyon. You might want to stop and cool off at a small waterfall. At the canyon crossing stands an old burned bridge, which fell victim to the 1978 Mandeville Fire that blackened the upper reaches of Temescal Canyon. Scramble up the steep slope to the other side of the canyon and begin switchbacking up the mountainside. The fire road levels out atop a northwest-trending ridge. The view to the southwest

259

down at the housing developments isn't too inspiring, but the view of the rough unaltered northern part of Temescal Canyon is. Proceed along the ridge; you'll see some rock outcroppings. A short side trip off the fire road will bring you to Skull Rock, where you can climb inside the wind-formed (aeolian) caves to cool off or picnic.

Return the same way or continue on the fire road.

Joining the fire road from the left are Split Rock Road and a mile farther north, Trailer Canyon Road. A microwave tower, atop what locals have dubbed "Radio Peak," stands halfway between the two points.

One-and-a-half miles of mostly level walking beyond the Trailer Canyon intersection brings you to Rogers Road. Near the intersection is Temescal Peak (2,126 feet), highest peak in Topanga State Park. If you wish, scramble up a short and steep firebreak to the top for a fine view.

Rogers Road, a segment of the Backbone Trail, leads six miles rightward to Will Rogers State Historic Park and leftward to intersections with both loops of the Eagle Springs Trail, which in turn leads to Topanga State Park headquarters.

The above extensions suggest a car shuttle or a very long day of hiking. Otherwise, return the same way via Temescal Canyon Fire Road to the trailhead.

Los Liones Canyon
Los Liones Canyon Trail

Highlights: *Rugged Los Liones Canyon is but a mile from Sunset Boulevard, but very much apart from the Westside city scene. "The Overlook" offers grand views of West Los Angeles and Santa Monica Bay.*

Distance: Los Liones Drive to The Overlook is 6 miles round trip with 1,500-foot gain. From Paseo Miramar to The Overlook is 5 miles round trip with 1,200 foot gain.

Directions: (To Los Liones Drive trailhead) From Pacific Coast Highway in Pacific Palisades, turn inland on Sunset Boulevard 1/4 mile. Turn left on Los Liones Drive and follow it to road's end and a small parking area. Don't park in the adjacent church lot. (To Paseo Miramar) From Sunset Boulevard, proceeding inland, the next left after Los Liones Drive is Paseo Miramar. Follow this winding road through a residential area to its end at the vehicle gate across East Topanga Fire Road. Park safely and considerately on Paseo Miramar.

MOST WALKERS AND PICNICKERS ENTER TOPANGA State Park from the main entrance off Topanga Canyon Boulevard and figure it's the only way into the park. Few realize that there are about a half-dozen ways to reach the park by road, a dozen ways by trail.

The state park, sometimes billed as "the largest state park within a city limit in the U.S." has entrances on the San Fernando Valley side where an unpaved portion of Mulholland Highway crosses the park, and it has a couple of entrances on the Pacific Palisades side as well.

One of these Palisades paths is Los Liones Trail, which travels through Los Liones Canyon to East Topanga Fire Road. East Topanga Fire Road does not, as its name might suggest lead east-west; rather, it travels more or less north-south but does so on the east side of Topanga State Park.

This walk leads to a viewpoint sometimes called Parker Mesa Overlook, sometimes called Topanga Overlook, but most often simply called The Overlook. Views of West Los Angeles and the sweep of Santa Monica Bay are superb.

Sunset (the descending day star not the winding boulevard) views are often inspiring.

Two trails help you reach the inspiring view. Los Liones Canyon Trail climbs through its namesake canyon to East Topanga Fire Road which in turn leads to Topanga Overlook. Or the hiker may head directly for The Overlook via the fire road.

From The Overlook, the ambitious walker could trek into the main part of Topanga State Park.

(From Los Liones Canyon) March past the vehicle gate and follow the trail into the canyon. After a quarter-mile, the trail begins to climb in earnest, switchbacking through the chaparral.

After leveling out for a stretch, the path then switchbacks even more earnestly through thickets of ceanothus. Los Liones Trail intersects East Topanga Fire Road about 1/4 mile from the road's beginning at Paseo Miramar.

Turn left (northwest) on the fire road and continue your ascent. For a short while the road travels a cool, north slope and you get good over-the-right shoulder views of neighboring Santa Ynez Canyon, a canyon that's wild and dramatic in its upper reaches (in the state park) and atrociously subdivided in its lower reaches outside park boundaries.

A two-mile ascent along the fire road brings you to a junction with a trail leading south along a bald ridge. Join this trail, which travels a half-mile to The Overlook.

Enjoy clear-day panoramas of Westside L.A., Santa Monica Bay, Palos Verdes and Catalina Island.

The Heart of Topanga

Eagle Rock Loop Trail
(Backbone Trail)

Highlights: *This walk explores quiet and imperturbable Topanga Canyon, surrounded by suburban sprawl but retaining its rural character. In the heart of the state park, the walker will discover Eagle Rock, Eagle Spring and get topographically oriented to Topanga. The energetic will enjoy the one-way journey from Topanga to Will Rogers State Historic Park.*

Distance: To Eagle Rock via Eagle Rock/Eagle Springs Loop is 6 1/2 miles round trip with 800-foot gain; to Will Rogers SHP via Eagle Rock, Fire Road 30, Rogers Rd. is 10 1/2 miles one way with a 1,800-foot loss

Directions: From Topanga Canyon Boulevard, turn east on Entrada Road; that's to the right if you're coming from Pacific Coast Highway. Follow Entrada Road by turning left at every opportunity until you arrive at Topanga State Park. The trailhead is at the end of the parking lot. Expect a park day use fee.

To Will Rogers State Historic Park trailhead: If you're taking the longer hike and want to be met (or leave your car) at Will Rogers State Historic Park, here are the directions to that destination: From Sunset Boulevard in Pacific Palisades, turn north at the park entrance. The road leads up to Rogers' estate, now a state historic park that interprets the cowboy/comedian/philosopher's life. Near Will Rogers' home, a signed trail climbs to Inspiration Point. Rogers Trail intersects it 1/10th mile past the Inspiration Point Junction.

THE TOPANGA STATE PARK TO WILL ROGERS STATE Historic Park section of the Backbone Trail has been finished for quite some time and has proved very popular. The lower reaches of the trail tour the wild side of Topanga Canyon while the ridgetop sections offer far-reaching inland and ocean views.

Until the 1880s, there was little permanent habitation in the canyon. Early settlers tended vineyards, orchards, and cattle ranches. In the 1920s, the canyon became a popular weekend destination for Los Angeles residents. Summer cabins were built along Topanga Creek and in subdivisions in the surrounding hills. For one dollar round trip fare, tourists could board a Packard auto stage in Santa Monica and be driven up Pacific Coast Highway and Topanga Canyon Road to the Topanga Post Office and other, more scenic spots.

Most Topanga trails are good fire roads. A longer one-way option takes you along brushy ridges to Will Rogers State Historic Park. On a blustery winter day, city and canyon views are superb.

From the Topanga State Park parking lot, follow the distinct trail eastward to a signed junction, where you'll begin hiking on Eagle Springs Road. You'll pass through an oak woodland and through chaparral country. The trail slowly and steadily gains about 800 feet in elevation on the way to Eagle Rock. When you reach a junction, bear left on the north loop of Eagle Springs Road to Eagle Rock. A short detour will bring you to the top of the rock.

To complete the loop, bear sharply right (southwest) at the next junction, following the fire road as it winds down to Eagle Spring. Past the spring, you return to Eagle Spring Road and retrace your steps back to the trailhead.

Three-mile long Musch Ranch Trail, which passes from hot chaparral to shady oak woodland, crosses a bridge and passes the pond, is another fine way to return to the trailhead.

To Will Rogers State Historic Park: Follow the loop trip directions to the northeast end of Eagle Rock/Eagle Spring Loop, where you bear right on Fire Road 30. In 1/2 mile you reach the intersection with Rogers Road. Turn left and follow the dirt road (really a trail) for 3 1/2 miles, where the road ends and meets Rogers Trail. Here a level area and solitary oak suggest a lunch stop. On clear days enjoy the spectacular views in every direction: To the left is Rustic Canyon and the crest of the mountains near Mulholland Drive. To the right, Rivas Canyon descends toward the sea.

Stay on Rogers Trail, which marches up and down several steep hills, for about two more miles, until it enters Will Rogers Park near Inspiration Point.

Santa Ynez Canyon
Santa Ynez Trail

Highlights: *Ferns, falls, and dramatic sandstone cliffs are some of the delights of a ramble through Santa Ynez Canyon in Topanga State Park.*

Distance: Trippet Ranch to Santa Ynez Canyon Falls is 6 miles round trip with 1,000-foot elevation gain; From Palisades Highlands to the falls is 2 1/2 miles round trip with 200-foot gain.

Directions: From Topanga Canyon Boulevard, turn east on Entrada Road; that's to the right if you're coming from Pacific Coast Highway and to the left if you're coming from the Ventura Freeway (101). Follow Entrada Road by turning left at every opportunity until you arrive at Topanga State Park.

If you're not feeling energetic, you can easily reach Santa Ynez Canyon via the Palisades Highland trailhead. From Sunset Boulevard in Pacific Palisades, a short distance inland from Pacific Coast Highway, turn north on Palisades Drive. As you enter the Palisades Highlands community, turn left on Verenda De La Montura. Park near the signed trailhead.

SANTA YNEZ CANYON—AND ITS SEASONAL WATER-falls—can be reached from two trailheads; one is located at the edge of the tony Palisades Highlands development, the other is found in the heart of Topanga State Park. The canyon is pleasant year-around, but particularly inviting after a rainstorm.

From the main part of the state park, this walk descends a ridge into Santa Ynez Canyon, then heads upstream to a 15-foot waterfall. Remember that the uphill part of this journey comes last; pace yourself accordingly.

(From Topanga State Park): From the parking lot, you may proceed up the wide main trail or join the park's nature trail (a prettier way to go) and ascend past some oaks. Both the nature trail and the main trail out of the parking lot lead a short quarter-mile to Fire Road 30A. Turn left on the dirt fire road and travel a short distance to signed Santa Ynez Trail.

Start your descent into Santa Ynez Canyon.

High on the canyon wall, you'll get good views of the canyon and of the ocean beyond. A half-mile descent brings you to an outcropping of reddish sandstone. The main route of Santa Ynez Trail stays atop a ridgeline, but you'll notice a few steep side trails that lead to the right down to the canyon floor.

Soap plant, a spring bloomer with small, white, star-like flowers is abundant along the trail. This member of the lily family was a most useful plant to early residents of the Santa Monica Mountains. Indians cooked the bulbs to concoct a glue for their arrows. They also made a lather of the crushed bulbs and threw it into creeks to stun fish. Settlers stuffed mattresses with the plant's fiber.

Enjoy the views of tilted sandstone and the great bowl of Santa Ynez Canyon. As the trail nears the canyon floor it descends more precipitously. Once on the canyon bottom, turn left (down-canyon) and enter a lush environment shaded by oak and sycamore. The trail meanders with a seasonal creek to a signed junction. You'll turn left and head up-canyon on a path that crosses the creek several times. The fern-lined pools and the handsome sandstone ledges create an idyllic scene, marred only by the graffiti certain cretins have spray-painted on the boulders.

About 3/4 mile of travel brings you to the base of the waterfall. Beyond the fall are more cascades, but continuing farther is recommended only for experienced rock-climbers; most hikers make a U-turn here and head for home.

(From Palisades Highlands): This walk departs from what I call the Designer Trailhead. Here Santa Ynez Creek, lined by orange/beige artificial walls, spills over a cement creekbed. Creekside trees have been enclosed in planters, and stream-crossings are accomplished by means of cylindrical-shaped cement "stepping-stones." Once beyond this trail travesty, the path takes you into a canyon that's really quite lovely. Coast live oaks, sycamore and bay laurel line the trickling seasonal creek. Half-a-mile along, the trail passes a pipe gate and forks. A sign points the way to Santa Ynez Falls, 3/4 mile farther up the canyon.

Getting Off on Mulholland
Garapito, Bay Tree Trails

Highlights: *For the walker, storied Mulholland Drive offers a great "back door" approach to the mountains, though some of the very best hiking begins from the very worst stretches of the road. The seven miles of dirt road between the San Diego Freeway and Topanga Canyon Boulevard are a little bit of Baja—dusty and bone-jarring. But the drive is worth it, because between Mulholland Drive and Pacific Palisades, on the back side of Topanga State Park, are wild tributaries of Rustic and Garapito Canyons.*

Distance: 7 1/2 miles round trip with 900-foot elevation gain.

Directions: From the San Diego Freeway (405), a few miles south of its junction with the Ventura Freeway (101), exit on Mulholland Drive and proceed 5 1/2 miles west to a yellow-gate fire road on your left. Landmarks along the way: an old missile tracking station is 2 1/2 miles before (east of) the trailhead; Caballero Trail (a fire road) is a quarter mile east of the trailhead on your right.

From the Valley, another way to go: Exit the Ventura Freeway in Woodland Hills on Topanga Canyon Boulevard, head south to Mulholland Drive, turn left and continue 3 3/4 miles to the trailhead on your right.

The dirt portion of Mulholland is best negotiated in a vehicle with high ground clearance.

MULHOLLAND DRIVE HAS LONG BEEN A ROAD TO remember. "Fifty-five miles of scenic splendor" its boosters called the road when construction began in 1924.

L.A.'s mountain highway has been featured in dozens of movie chase scenes. During the 1950s and 1960s, it was a place to race and a place to park; some of the city's best-known "make-out" spots were Mulholland's scenic turnouts.

But Mulholland is more than a link to the city's history; it appeals to today's traveler as well. It offers a chance to explore the crests and canyons of the Santa Monica Mountains from Universal City west to Leo Carrillo State

Beach on the Ventura County line. The Santa Monica Mountains Conservancy has promoted the concept of a scenic parkway—the original idea for Mulholland Drive—that would literally and symbolically link the far-flung parks and reserves in the Santa Monica Mountains.

The paths off Mulholland described below appeal to the walker who wants to get away from it all. Bay Tree Trail follows a creek bed for much of its length; it's subject to the whims of winter rains and a seasonal creek, and consequently is the kind of trail that's difficult to maintain.

Allow yourself plenty of time for this walk, which experienced walkers will enjoy much more than novices. You'll want to linger in the canyon bottoms and you'll find that it will take you much longer to climb out than to climb into the canyon.

Follow dirt Temescal Fire Road on a gentle half mile descent to a place where power lines cross the road and look for signed Garapito Canyon Trail on your right. (At this trail junction, you'll notice Bent Arrow Trail leading east while Temescal Fire Road swings south; you'll be returning to this junction via one or the other of these routes.)

Garapito Canyon Trail descends through dense thickets of chaparral—ceanothus mostly, along with some mountain mahogany. Tunneling through the tall brush, the trail switchbacks down to the sycamore-shaded canyon bottom, crossing two forks of narrow Garapito Creek.

From the canyon bottom, the trail then ascends out of its namesake canyon. You regain all the elevation you lost during your descent, plus a couple hundred feet more, and arrive in 1 1/2 miles at a junction with Eagle Springs Loop Road. To your right is Eagle Rock (a pleasant side trip if you so desire.)

Turn left on the dirt road. A half-mile's travel brings you past a bump on the ridge known, somewhat unimaginatively I would say, as Peak 2104, high point around here. Another half-mile walk brings you to The Hub, Topanga State Park's major trail junction.

Feeling a bit leg-weary? Take the Temescal Fire Road north back to the trailhead.

Otherwise, you'll take fairly level Temescal Fire Road south

William Mullholland's highway allowed visitors to explore the Santa Monica Mountains.

a half mile to another junction. The fire road continues south, bound for Temescal Gateway Park and Sunset Boulevard in Pacific Palisades, but you head left on the signed Backbone Trail (also known as Rogers Road/Trail because it leads to Will Rogers State Historic Park). You proceed only a short quarter-mile, keeping a sharp lookout left for unsigned Bay Tree Trail.

Bay Tree Trail plunges down a rugged canyon wall. During late fall and winter, watch for the green leaves and bright red berries of the toyon, or Christmas berry.

The trail delivers the promised bay trees and much more. Enjoy the pungent smell of the bay laurel and relax in their shade. You'll pass a little trickle of a spring where coyotes like to drink.

Once you reach the canyon bottom, the somewhat faint trail travels down-canyon half a mile to an unsigned junction with Rustic Canyon Trail. (Continuing another half-mile down-canyon brings you to a fork; the trail turns south, but another, trail-less branch of Rustic Canyon beckons to the north. Here, the determined hiker will find Blue Gorge and may boulder-hop up-canyon to a narrows filled with ferns, bay trees, maples and even a couple of tiny seasonal waterfalls.)

For your route back, however, head up-canyon. The washed-out path crosses the creek many times. While the creek itself isn't much to behold, it provides evidence in support of the adage "still waters run deep." The creek has little surface water but evidently much underground because it supports a healthy tangle of creekside vegetation.

The ascent out of the canyon, relatively mellow for three-quarters of a mile, gets wicked about the time you sight Mulholland Drive above, and the last half-mile of climbing on eroded trail isn't much fun.

Once on Mulholland, you can turn left and walk along the dirt drive 1 1/4 miles back to the trailhead. A more enjoyable return route is via Bent Arrow Trail. Join it 50 yards down Mulholland Drive on the south side of the road.

The path contours half a mile southwestward to a junction with Temescal Fire Road. Retracing the first steps of this walk, you ascend half a mile back to Mulholland Drive and the trail-head.

San Fernando Valley to the Sea
Lemming Trail

Highlights: *Caballero Canyon in the San Fernando Valley is your departure point for a tramp across the Santa Monica Mountains to the sea. Families and less-crazy adventurers will enjoy the canyon itself.*

Distance: 12 miles one way with 2,000-foot elevation gain; a pleasant 4-mile round trip walk through Caballero Canyon is a gentler alternative.

Directions: This is a one-way walk so a car shuttle or a helpful non-hiking friend to assist with the transportation logistics is necessary. Leave one car at Will Rogers State Beach (fee) or along Pacific Coast Highway (free) near the intersection of the Coast Highway and Temescal Canyon Road. Next proceed up-coast on PCH to Topanga Canyon Road (27) and drive inland through the canyon to Ventura Boulevard. Turn right (east) and head into Tarzana. Turn right on Reseda Boulevard and follow this road to its end. (A quick route to the Lemming trailhead is to exit the Ventura Freeway (101) on Reseda Boulevard and drive east to its end.)

YOU WON'T FIND ANY LEMMINGS ALONG THE Southern California coast; the furry, short-tailed, mice-like creatures inhabit Arctic, not Mediterranean climes. The Lemming Trail takes its name not from the rodent's presence in the Santa Monica Mountains, but from its proclivity to rush headlong into the sea.

A crisp, cool winter or spring day is a great time to make like a lemming and hike from the San Fernando Valley to the sea. The Lemming Trail offers a grand tour of the Santa Monica Mountains, from Tarzana to Topanga to Temscal to the Pacific on a network of trails and fire roads and be treated to some superb coastal vistas.

Though the Lemming Trail was named for a small rodent, be assured that this is no Mickey Mouse hike. Be prepared for a very long and strenuous day.

Caballero Canyon is the starting point for this long journey, but is also a pleasant destination in its own right. It provides a back-door entrance to Topanga State Park.

For years conservationists have resisted developments in Caballero Canyon and a proposed extension of Reseda Boulevard. The canyon has been the scene of some lively protests. Don't be surprised if the trailhead is a bit awkward to reach because of ongoing construction projects.

Descend to the dirt road (Fire Road 28) that meanders up the bottom of Caballero Canyon. The sycamore-dotted canyon bottom hosts an intermittent stream. After a mile, the fire road veers left and climbs to a locked gate on Mulholland Drive.

Turn right onto Mulholland and after walking a half-mile, look leftward for the Bent Arrow Trail, which will take you into Topanga State Park. Follow this trail, which at first parallels Mulholland, for 1/2 mile as it contours around a steep slope and reaches Temescal Fire Road (Fire Road 30). Turn left and begin a moderate descent. After a mile-and-a-half, you'll pass junctions with fire roads on your right leading to Eagle Rock and Eagle Spring. Continue straight ahead past these junctions on the sharp ridge-line separating Santa Ynez and Temescal Canyons. You'll pass the junction with Rogers Road which leads to Will Rogers State Historic Park. Near the intersection of Rogers Road and Temescal Fire Road is

From the Valley to the sea via Lemming Trail.

Temescal Peak (2,126 feet), highest peak in Topanga State Park. If you wish, scramble up a short and steep firebreak to the top for a fine view.

After one-and-a-half miles of mostly level walking beyond the Rogers Road intersection, you'll pass Trailer Canyon Road and a mile farther south, Split Rock Road. A microwave tower, atop what locals have dubbed "Radio Peak," stands halfway between the points.

As you descend along the ridge, you'll see some rock outcroppings. A short side trip off the fire road will bring you to Skull Rock, where you can climb inside the wind-formed (aeolian) caves to cool off or picnic. From the ridgetop, the view to the southwest down at the housing developments isn't too inspiring, but the view of the rough unaltered northern part of Temescal Canyon is superb.

Temescal Fire Road narrows and switchbacks down into Temescal Canyon. You might want to stop and cool off at the small waterfall here at the Temescal Creek crossing at the bottom of the canyon. Your route crosses over to the east side of the canyon and descends the canyon bottom on a trail shaded by oaks, willows, and sycamores.

You'll join a paved road and walk through the Presbyterian Conference Center, then join paved Temescal Canyon Road— or improvise a parallel route down canyon through a small park managed by the Santa Monica Mountains Conservancy.

After crossing Sunset Boulevard, you'll walk an easy mile through Temescal Canyon City Park to Pacific Coast Highway. Across Coast Highway is Will Rogers State Beach. Local mountaineering tradition dictates that you emulate the lemming and rush into the sea.

Cold Creek Canyon Preserve
Cold Creek Trail

Highlights: *Cold Creek Canyon is one of the secret treasures of the Santa Monica Mountains. A year-round stream and a protected north-facing canyon nurture a rich variety of ferns and flowering plants in the 600-acre preserve.*

Distance: 5 miles round trip with 900-foot elevation gain.

Directions: From the Ventura Freeway (101) in Calabasas, exit on Las Virgenes Road. Head south to Mulholland Highway, turn east and continue to Stunt Road. Turn right and drive 3.38 miles (watch the road paddles for mileage indicators) to the signed Cold Creek Canyon Preserve entrance on your left. Park carefully in one of the turnouts near the entrance. Display the required permit on the dashboard.

To visit Cold Creek Canyon Preserve, open every day of the year, you must call the Mountains Restoration Trust at least three or four days in advance of your visit and request a free permit, which will be mailed to you. Be sure to inquire about docent-led tours of the preserve.

COLD CREEK CANYON WAS ONCE PART OF A RANCH, homesteaded in the early years of this century. It later served as a ranch/retreat for the Murphy family who donated their ranch to the Nature Conservancy in 1970, stipulating that Cold Creek be forever preserved in its natural state.

The natural world of Cold Creek Canyon is diverse. Lining Cold Creek are ferns, flowers and cattails. Winter rains swell the creek, creating a dozen small waterfalls.

A hundred species of birds have been sighted within the preserve, including golden eagles. Hikers may encounter a squirrel, raccoon, deer or bobcat.

Wildflower-lovers will find much to admire. Early bloomers (February to April) include the white blossoms of the milkmaid. Later in spring, look for the bright yellow canyon sunflower and the yellow-orange spotted Humboldt lily.

Remember that this is an upside-down walk; the elevation gain occurs during your return. Save some energy.

274

Head through the gate and down the trail. Pause for a moment at an information board and sign the visitors register.

One of the first shrubs you'll encounter along the trail is red shank, a floral cousin to the far more prolific chamise. You'll recognize it by its characteristic peeling bark. It's a late bloomer—August is its prime time.

An old pickup truck mired in the middle of the trail suggests that the path used to be a road. Occasional breaks in the brush offer views of Calabasas Peak dead-ahead, and a sandstone formation to the right known as Fossil Ridge.

As the path, shaded by oak and bay, nears the canyon bottom, the vegetation becomes more lush. Woodwardia and bracken ferns thrive along Cold Creek. The towering sandstone walls that form Cold Creek absorb rainfall, then slowly release water throughout the year.

A bit more than a mile from the trailhead is the remains of an old house. Sandstone boulders formed the walls of the structure. Quite an ingenious use of materials at hand.

Beyond the rock house, the trail drops steeply into a marshy world of ferns and Humboldt lilies. You'll cross Cold Creek on a wooden footbridge and spot a fern-surrounded waterfall. The trail leads uphill for a time, then returns to the creek.

The trail forks. The right fork heads a short distance up-creek to a small waterfall, while the left dead-ends at the preserve's lower gate on Stunt Road.

Gourmet Way to Saddle Peak
Backbone Trail

Highlights: *New, superb stretch of the Backbone Trail crosses the boulder-strewn crest of the mountains east of Malibu Creek State Park. Hike Saddle Peak, then dine at Saddle Peak Lodge.*

Distance: 3 1/2 miles one-way with 1,500 foot elevation loss.

Directions: From the Ventura Freeway (101) in Agoura, exit on Las Virgenes Road, which passes Mulholland Highway and Malibu Creek State Park, and continues as Malibu Canyon Road. Turn left (east) on Piuma Road and continue a mile to the intersection with Cold Canyon Road. At this junction, you'll find Saddle Peak Lodge, located at 419 Cold Canyon Rd. (213) 655-9770.

(For the sake of your orientation, you can continue a quarter mile on Piuma Road to the lower trailhead; your exit point for this hike.)

From the intersection of Piuma and Cold Canyon Road, follow the latter road north to Mulholland Highway and turn right, driving 3/4 of a mile and turning right on Stunt Road. Continue 2 3/4 more winding miles to a turnout on the left, where there's parking. The signed trailhead is across the road.

DOES TRAIL FOOD TO YOU CONJURE UP IMAGES OF dried-up baloney sandwiches, squished and melted candy bars, trail mix that would choke a horse?

Do the hastily assembled lunches you pack in your day pack give you hiker's heartburn?

A "yes" to the above questions means you're likely ready for a treat at trail's end—a meal that's as memorable as a good hike. Such a treat can be found on Saddle Peak, which offers a trail that begins with grand views of the Santa Monica Mountains and ends at Saddle Peak Lodge, an adventure in dining.

A rustic, very male atmosphere prevails at the lodge; the "Iron John" interior includes a large hearth, heavy wooden chairs and tables and lots of animal heads mounted on the walls.

Brunch is served at 11 and 2, Saturday and Sunday. The restaurant is also open for dinner Wed-Sun, 5 p.m. to midnight. Hikers be warned that the lodge insists on a dress code: no jeans, sneakers or shorts. This probably means you need to carry a change of clothes in your day pack.

Even without a meal at the lodge, Saddle Peak is well worth exploring. The peak—actually two peaks with a "saddle" in between, is one of the highest points in the central part of the mountains. Handsome sandstone formations, views of Malibu Creek watershed and botanically intriguing Dark Canyon are three highlights of a hike down the western slope of Saddle Peak.

"Down" is the operative word here. From the trailhead on Stunt Road, it's quite a descent to the trailhead on Piuma Road near the Saddle Peak Lodge. This day hike definitely suggests a one-way (downhill) trek with a car shuttle. A one-way walk is all the more judicious if you stuff yourself at the lodge; the prospect of a steep climb back up Saddle Peak is enough to give you indigestion.

The path heads southwest a short ways and soon reaches a junction with the true Backbone Trail. You head right (west) and drop into an oak woodland.

Large boulders frame over-the-shoulder views of Cold Creek Canyon to the northeast and Calabasas Peak to the north. After winding among the boulders for a time, the path serves up another dramatic view, this one to the west: Malibu Creek State Park and the dramatic canyon cut by its namesake creek.

Beyond this viewpoint the trail begins an earnest descent over the western slope of Saddle Peak. Down the chaparral-cloaked slope you plunge, switch-backing through ceanothus and manzanita to the cool, moist, sycamore- and alder-shaded Dark Canyon. On the canyon bottom thrive ferns, Humboldt lily and tangles of wild grape.

The trail ascends out of Dark Canyon to the Piuma Road trailhead. It's a quarter-mile walk along Piuma Road to the Saddle Peak Lodge.

Malibu Creek State Park
Malibu Creek Trail

Highlights: *The trail along Malibu Creek explores the heart of the State Park. It's an easy, nearly level walk that visits a dramatic rock gorge and little Century Lake.*

Distance: From the parking area to Rock Pool is 3 1/2 miles round trip with 150-foot gain; to Century Lake is 4 1/2 miles round trip with 200-foot gain

Directions: From Pacific Coast Highway, turn inland on Malibu Canyon Road and proceed 6 1/2 miles to the park entrance, one-fourth mile south of Mulholland Highway. If you're coming from the San Fernando Valley, exit the Ventura Freeway (101) on Las Virgenes Road and continue four miles to the park entrance. There is a state park day use fee.

BEFORE LAND FOR MALIBU CREEK STATE PARK WAS acquired in 1974, it was divided into three parcels belonging to Bob Hope, Ronald Reagan and 20th Century Fox. Although the park is still used for movie-making, it's primarily a haven for day hikers and picnickers.

From the parking area, follow the wide fire road. You'll cross the all-but-dry creek. The road soon forks into a high road and a low road. Go right and walk along the oak-shaded high road, which makes a long, lazy left arc as it follows the north bank of Malibu Creek. You'll reach an intersection and turn left on a short road that crosses a bridge over Malibu Creek.

You'll spot the Gorge Trail and follow it upstream a short distance to the gorge, one of the most dramatic sights in the Santa Monica Mountains. Malibu Creek makes a hairpin turn through 400-foot volcanic rock cliffs and cascades into aptly named Rock Pool. The *Swiss Family Robinson* television series and some Tarzan movies were filmed here.

Return to the trailhead or retrace your steps back to the high road and bear left toward Century Lake. As the road ascends you'll be treated to a fine view of Las Virgenes Valley. Cresting the hill, you'll look down on Century Lake. Near the lake are hills of porous lava and topsy-turvy sedimentary rock

layers that tell of the violent geologic upheaval that formed
Malibu Canyon. The man-made lake was scooped out by members of Crag's Country Club, a group of wealthy, turn-of-the-
century businessmen who had a nearby lodge.

You can call it a day here, or continue on the fire road past
Century Lake. You'll pass the location of the now- removed set
for the "M*A*S*H" television series. The prominent Goat
Buttes that tower above Malibu Creek were featured in the
opening shot of each episode.

"The Gorge," Malibu Creek

Trail to the Chief
Reagan Ranch Trail

Highlights: *Reagan's Ranch, now part of Malibu Creek State Park, is a delight for hikers, who can enjoy the ranch's rolling meadowland and grand old oaks, and even probe the origins of the former president's conservative political philosophy.*

Distance: 4-mile loop through Malibu Creek State Park; 300-foot gain.

Directions: From Santa Monica, take Pacific Coast Highway upcoast to Malibu Canyon Road, turn inland and proceed to Mulholland Highway. Turn left and drive 3 miles to the ranch entrance at the corner of Mulholland and Cornell Road. Or from the Ventura Freeway (101) in Agoura, exit on Kanan Road and head south. Make a left on Cornell Road and follow it to its intersection with Mulholland Highway. The trailhead is on the southeast corner. Park carefully alongside Cornell Road.

B EFORE RONALD REAGAN PURCHASED WHAT WAS TO become the most well-known ranch in the world—Rancho del Cielo in the Santa Ynez Mountains above Santa Barbara—he owned another spread in the Santa Monica Mountains.

During the 1950s when Reagan hosted TV's *Death Valley Days*, he desired a more rural retreat than his home in Pacific Palisades. He bought the 305-acre ranch in the hills of Malibu as a place to raise thoroughbred horses. Land rose greatly in value, and taxes likewise; the tax increases really piqued Reagan and influenced his political philosophy. From this point on, he would be hostile toward government programs that required more and more tax dollars to fund.

Reagan's Ranch boosted his political career: it was the locale of many a barbecue and gathering attended by the well-heeled politicos who would support his gubernatorial campaign. When Reagan was elected governor in 1966, he moved to Sacramento, and sold his ranch to a movie company. Today the ranch makes up the northwest corner of Malibu Creek State Park. When the property was acquired, the ranch house was in such grim condition that it had to be destroyed. The Reagan barn still stands and is now used for offices and storage by state park employees.

Trails loop through the Reagan Ranch and connect with the main part of the state park. One path, which I've dubbed Reagan Ranch Trail, uses a combination of trails—Yearling, Deer Leg, Lookout, Crag's Road and Cage Canyon—to explore Reagan country and the heart of the park.

Winter, after rains put a little green in the grassy meadows, and spring, when lupine, larkspur and poppies pop out all over, are the best seasons for a visit.

Enter the park on Yearling Road. The dirt road leads a quarter-mile past a row of stately eucalyptus and soon arrives at the old Reagan barn. Continue on the road which passes a corral and heads across a meadow. Soon you'll pass the first of a couple of side trails leading rightward into a grove of oaks and linking up with Deer Leg Trail. Continue straight ahead on the meadow trail.

During spring, wildflowers color the field, a 3/4-mile long grassy strip. At the east end of the meadow, the trail dips in and out of a canyon, tunnels through some high chaparral and ascends an oak-crowned ridge. Atop the ridge is a great view of Malibu Creek and the main features of the state park. Also on the ridgetop is an unsigned trail junction. You'll take the left-leading trail and begin descending southeast on well-named Lookout Trail. The trail drops to Crag's Road, the state park's major trail, near Century Lake.

Crag's Road leads east-west with Malibu Creek and connects to trails leading to the site of the old "M*A*S*H" set, the Backbone Trail and the park visitors center. More immediately, when you make a right on the road, you pass close to Century Lake. Near the lake are hills of porous lava and topsy-turvy sedimentary rock layers that tell of the violent geologic upheaval that formed Malibu Canyon. The man-made lake was scooped out by members of Crag's Country Club, a group of wealthy, turn-of-the-century businessmen who had a nearby lodge.

Walk up Crag's Road about 200 hundred yards and join

unsigned Cage Canyon Trail on your right. The trail makes a short and rapid ascent of the oak- and sycamore-filled canyon and soon brings you to an unsigned intersection with Deer Leg Trail. Here you bear left and begin traveling under a canopy of oaks. You'll get occasional glimpses of the rolling grassland of the Reagan Ranch below.

One attractive oak grove shades a barbecue area where the Reagans once entertained. This grove is a good place for a picnic or rest stop.

Soon you'll bear leftward at a trail junction and begin ascending the cool north slope of a hillside above the ranch. Leaving the oaks behind, the trail climbs a brushy hillside to an overlook. Enjoy the view of exclusive Malibu Lake and Paramount Ranch. The trail intersects a fire road, which you take to the right on a steep descent to the meadow near park headquarters. The road vanishes here, so walk fifty yards across the meadow to Yearling Road, which leads back to the trailhead.

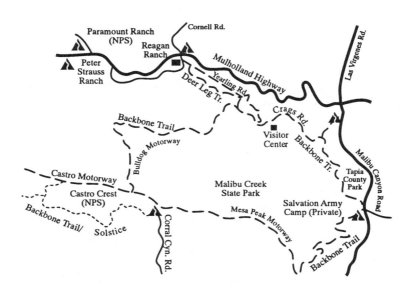

Paramount Ranch
Coyote Trail, Stream Terrace Trail

Highlights: *At Paramount Ranch, a western town and rugged scenery that has attracted generations of moviemakers offers some nice walks.*

Distance: The nature trails are each a half-mile long; a couple of park trails are linked in a 5K walk/run route.

Directions: From the Ventura Freeway (101) in Agoura, exit on Kanan Road. Drive south 3/4 mile, forking left onto Cornell Road, then proceeding 2 1/2 miles to Paramount Ranch.

EVEN IN 1921 BURBANK WAS TOO BUSY A PLACE FOR filming Westerns on location so Paramount Studios purchased a 4,000 acre spread in the then-remote Agoura area. Paramount Ranch had many a desirable location: mountains, meadows, creeks, canyons, oak and walnut groves. One dramatic mountain—Sugarloaf Peak—is said to have inspired the famous Paramount logo.

Besides innumerable Westerns, such 1930's classics as *The Adventures of Marco Polo* and *Tom Sawyer* were filmed here.

Paramount sold the ranch in 1946 but a smaller part of it, including Western Town, continued to be used for filming. The ranch was particularly popular during the 1950s heyday of the TV western when *The Cisco Kid, Bat Masterson, Have Gun Will Travel* and many more horse operas were filmed here.

The National Park Service purchased the ranch in 1979. Today, filmmakers continue to use the Western town and the surrounding hills for features, television series and commercials.

Recently the park more than doubled in size with the acquisition of the Historic Oaks portion of the old ranch by the Santa Monica Mountains Conservancy. Located adjacent to the existing Paramount Ranch property, this locale, too, was popular with moviemakers. And it was long cherished by the public as well, who knew it as the site of the Renaissance Pleasure Faire.

For the walker, Paramount Ranch offers a stroll through Western Town, a loop around what used to be a sports car race track, and a couple of miles of hiking trail.

Coyote Canyon Nature Trail begins behind Western Town, heads up Medea Creek and meanders among some handsome oaks. Halfway along the trail, there's a good hilltop view back at Western Town and of Goat Buttes towering above nearby Malibu Creek State Park. Sometimes an interpretive brochure is available at the trailhead.

You can join Stream Terrace Trail south of the parking lot by the old racetrack. The path ascends a hill for vistas of Western Town, Malibu Lake and Sugarloaf Peak.

Runners will note the ranch's marked 5-K route that links the race track and a couple paths.

A walk through the Wild West at Paramount Ranch.

Peter Strauss Ranch
Peter Strauss Loop Trail

Highlights: *The Lake Enchanto resort where thousands of Angelenos flocked in the 1930s and 1940s is now a quiet retreat on the banks of Triunfo Creek.*

Distance: 1 mile round trip

Directions: From the Ventura Freeway (101) in Agoura, exit on Kanan Road, proceeding south 2 3/4 miles to Troutdale Road and turn left. At Mulholland Highway, turn left again, cross the bridge over Triunfo Creek and turn into the Peter Strauss Ranch parking area. After parking, walk back to Mulholland, cross the bridge over Triunfo Creek, then join the signed trail behind the ranch house. (If the creek is low enough, you can just hop across it to the trailhead.)

T HE LARGEST SWIMMING POOL WEST OF THE Rockies." That was once the boast of Lake Enchanto, a resort and amusement park popular in the 1930s and 40s. Sometimes 5,000 Southlanders a weekend would come to swim, fish, picnic and enjoy the amusement rides. A Big Band-style radio program was broadcast live, while L.A. notables and Hollywood stars danced the night away.

During the 1960s a plan was hatched to develop a theme park—Cornell World Famous Places—that would replicate Egyptian pyramids and Mt. Fuji. Meanwhile, Lake Enchanto itself disappeared when the dam backing up Triunfo Creek washed away in a flood. These plans never materialized, the property was sold for back taxes, and finally ended up in the hands of actor-producer Peter Strauss, who purchased the former resort in 1977. After Strauss restored and improved the property, it was acquired by the Santa Monica Mountains Conservancy, who deeded it to the National Park Service.

The trail begins near a eucalyptus grove and a former aviary, switchbacks up the hillside behind the ranch house, then loops back down the slope. After the hike, kids will enjoy playing with tadpoles in Triunfo Creek.

Castro Crest,
Corral Canyon
Backbone Trail

Highlights: *You can stalk the Santa Susana tarweed—and some genuinely pretty flowering plants—on a nice loop trail along the Castro Crest area of the Santa Monica Mountains.*

Distance: A 6-mile loop along Castro Crest and through upper Solstice Canyon with 1,000-foot elevation gain.

Directions: From Pacific Coast Highway, about 2 miles up-coast from Malibu Canyon Road, turn inland on Corral Canyon Road. Proceed 5 1/2 miles to road's end at a large dirt parking lot.

I T'S A HUMBLE ENOUGH PLANT, A LOW MASS OF WOODY stems and dull green herbage, clinging to life among the rocks. To most of us, the Santa Susana tarweed is a plant only a botanist could love—or even find.

From its discovery about 80 years ago until the late 1970s, the tarweed was believed to exist only atop isolated sandstone outcroppings in its namesake Santa Susana Mountains. In 1977, the Santa Susana tarweed was discovered high on the Castro Crest area of the Santa Monica Mountains, and later atop Calabasas Peak and in Charmlee County Park.

Hemizonia minthornii may seem even more homely than it is because it comes from a beautiful botanic family—the Sunflower Family, in fact. Other members of the family—goldfields, golden yarrow, California everlasting and tidytips are real lookers and even such family members as shrubby butterweed and milk thistle have their moments in the sun.

Well, the Santa Susana tarweed isn't that ugly; in autumn it dons a cloak of yellow flowers. Its botanical name, *minthornii* honors—perhaps a poor choice of words—botanist Theodore Wilson Minthorn and his sister Maud who collected in Southern California early this century.

Geologically minded walkers will also enjoy tramping along Castro Crest. Towering above the parking area is the gray sandstone/mudstone Sespe Formation, formed 40 to 25 million years ago. Down in Upper Solstice Canyon is the Coal Canyon Formation, of marine deposition, laid down 60-50 million years ago. Many mollusks are visible in the long rock slabs.

Even those walkers without interest in botany or earth science will enjoy this outing. It samples both high and low segments of the Backbone Trail, provides great views and a good aerobic workout.

From the parking area, head past the locked gate up the wide dirt road, Castro Motorway. (You're walking the Backbone Trail, a path that when completed will travel 65 miles along the spine of the Santa Monica Mountains.) After a short climb, you'll enjoy a fine view of Mt. Baldy and the San Gabriel Mountains and of the Santa Susana Mountains—home of the elusive tarweed. A great place to look for it is about 3/4-mile from the trailhead on the north side of the dirt road near the junction of Castro Motorway with Bulldog Motorway.

Bulldog Motorway on your right leads to Malibu Creek State Park and its many miles of trail, but you continue climbing another 3/4 mile to a junction with Newton Canyon Motorway, which you'll join by bearing left. (Castro Motorway continues west toward a forest of antennae atop Castro Peak.) Newton Motorway descends to a junction at a saddle. You could go straight (south) here and drop into Upper Solstice Canyon; this would cut off about two miles from the six-mile round trip distance of this hike.

Bear right on the stretch of Backbone Trail called Castro Trail and head west for a mile to paved Latigo Canyon Road. Walk along the road for a short while and join Newton Motorway on your left, which passes by a private residence then descends to the saddle discussed above and the connector trail leading back toward Castro Motorway. Continue east, meandering along the monkeyflower- and paintbrush-sprinkled banks of Solstice Creek. Watch for a lovely meadow dotted with Johnny-jump-ups and California poppies. The trail turns north with the creekbed then climbs west for a time up a chaparral-covered slope back to the trailhead on Corral Canyon Road.

Solstice Canyon Park
Solstice Canyon Trail

Highlights: *Solstice Canyon Park preserves a tranquil canyon and offers some fine walks and a chance to see the Mathew Keller house, oldest in the Santa Monica Mountains. From the park's upper slopes, you might even sight gray whales migrating past Point Dume.*

Distance: 6-mile loop through Solstice Canyon Park with 600-foot elevation gain.

Directions: From Pacific Coast Highway, about 17 miles upcoast from Santa Monica and 3 1/2 miles upcoast from Malibu Canyon Road, turn inland on Corral Canyon Road. At the first bend in the road, you'll leave the road and proceed straight to the very small Solstice Canyon parking lot. Beyond the parking lot, the park access road is usually closed; however, on weekends, visitors are permitted to drive in and park in a second, larger lot, located just up the road.

T O MODERN CITY DWELLERS, SOLSTICE MAY SEEM TO be nothing more than a scientific abstraction—the time when the sun is farthest south or north of the equator. To some of the earliest occupants of Southern California, the Chumash, however, the winter solstice was a very important occasion. It was a time when the cosmic balance was very delicate. The discovery of summer and winter solstice observation caves and rock art sites, have convinced anthropologists that the Chumash possessed a system of astronomy that had both mystical meaning and practical application. To those of us who buy all our food in the supermarket, winter solstice is just a date on the calendar, but to the Chumash, who needed to know about when berries would ripen, when the steelhead would run up Malibu Creek, when game would migrate, the day was an important one.

Solstice Canyon Park opened on summer solstice, 1988. The Santa Monica Mountains Conservancy purchased the land from the Roberts family. The park is administered by the Mountains Conservancy Foundation, the operations arm of the Conservancy.

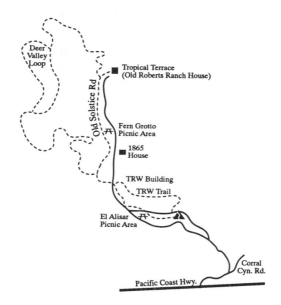

The Foundation transformed the 550-acre Roberts Ranch into a park. Ranch roads were converted to foot trails, and invasive plants were eliminated.

Destroyed by a 1982 fire, the Roberts family home was an extrordinary ranch-style residence that was highly praised by many home and architectural publications. The house incorporated Solstice Canyon's creek, waterfalls and trees into its unique design.

Another Solstice Canyon house—the Mathew Keller House—was built in 1865 and is the oldest house in Malibu, perhaps in the Santa Monica Mountains. When restoration is complete, the house will become a museum and visitor center.

Solstice Canyon's third structure of note is really a strange one. It resembles a kind of futuristic farm house with a silo attached and defies architectural categorization. Bauhaus, maybe. Or perhaps Grain Elevator Modern. From 1961 to 1973 Space Tech Labs, a subsidiary of TRW, used the building to conduct tests to determine the magnetic sensitivity of satellite instrumentation. The TRW buildings are now headquarters for the Santa Monica Mountains Conservancy.

Several trails explore Solstice Canyon. TRW Loop Trail leads to the canyon bottom, where the hiker can pick up Old Solstice Road (closed to vehicular traffic) and saunter through the canyon. Sostomo Trail climbs the park's east and south-facing ridges and offers fine coastal views.

Saunter up the park road to a small house, which is headquarters for the Mountains Conservancy Foundation. Near the house, join signed TRW Trail, which switchbacks up toward the headquarters of the Santa Monica Mountains Conservancy.

TRW Trail crosses a paved road, ascends west, then drops south into Solstice Canyon. You'll turn right on Old Solstice Road. In a few minutes you'll pass the 1865 Mathew Keller House and in a few more minutes—Fern Grotto. The road travels under the shade of oak and sycamore to its end at the remains of the old Roberts Ranch House. Palms, agave, bamboo, bird of paradise and many more tropical plants thrive in the Roberts' garden-gone-wild. A waterfall, fountain and an old dam are some of the other special features found in this paradisiacal setting known as Tropical Terrace.

Just below Tropical Terrace is signed, Sostomo Trail, which ascends a chaparral-cloaked slope that still bears evidence of the 1982 fire. The trail dips in and out of a streambed, begins climbing, and offers a great view of Solstice Canyon all the way to the ocean.

At a junction, the trail splits, with the right fork leading to Sostomo Overlook, while you head left toward Deer Valley. The trail crosses an open slope then tops a ridge for a great view of Point Dume. The trail briefly joins a dirt road, then resumes as a path and descends a coastal scrub-covered slope to the bottom of Solstice Canyon. A right turn on Old Solstice Road leads past El Alisar Picnic Area and returns you to the trailhead.

Zuma Canyon
Zuma Loop Trail

Highlights: *Most rugged and pristine canyon in the Santa Monica Mountains. Deep V-shaped gorge sculpted by mountain stream.*

Distance: Around mouth of Zuma Canyon is 2 1/2 miles round trip; trekking through the canyon and returning via Zuma Ridge Trail is 9 miles round trip with 1,700-foot elevation gain.

Directions: From Pacific Coast Highway in Malibu, head up-coast one mile past an intersection with Kanan-Dume Road and turn right on Bonsall Drive (this turn is just before the turnoff for Zuma Beach). Drive a mile (the last hundred yards on dirt road) to road's end at a National Park Service parking lot. At the trailhead, you'll find a drinking fountain on one side of the gate, a horsey guzzler on the other.

W HEN YOU TURN INLAND OFF PACIFIC COAST Highway onto Bonsall Drive and enter Zuma Canyon, the canyon looks like many others in the mountains; huge haciendas perched on precipitous slopes, accompanied by lots of lots for sale.

But the road ends and only footpaths enter Zuma Canyon. And therein lies the difference between Zuma and other canyons; no paved road violates its sanctity.

Malibu and Topanga, Temescal and Santa Ynez—perhaps these canyons and others in the Santa Monica Mountains looked like Zuma a century ago: a creek cascading over magnificent sandstone boulders, a jungle of willow and lush streamside flora, fern-fringed pools and towering rock walls.

Zuma Canyon, a National Park Service property, finally opened to public use in 1989 after much negotiation with private property holders. It's one of the gems, if not the scenic gem, of the Santa Monica Mountains National Recreation Area.

Hikers can partake of Zuma Canyon's grandeur via two routes: By following a trail from the mouth of the canyon, or by a dirt road that drops into the canyon's midsection.

For an easy family walk join Zuma Canyon Loop Trail, which leads up the west side of the canyon, then explores the canyon mouth. After a little over a mile, the trail ends. Kids will enjoy emulating the considerable frog population and splashing in the creek.

Hardy hikers will relish the challenge of the gorge. Two miles of trail-less creek-crossing and boulder-hopping is required in order to reach a dirt road that crosses the canyon. A return to the trailhead via Zuma Ridge Trail (a dirt road) offers another perspective of Zuma Canyon.

Except for times of flooding, Zuma Canyon is accessible all year, but each season has its advantages and disadvantages. During winter and spring the water level is apt to be high, making it a wet and wild journey through the canyon. Fall is pretty nice, especially if a little water has lingered in the creek. A summer trek, with high temperatures, is something of an ordeal. The high rock walls of the canyon, combined with a cloud cover, creates a steam bath situation ("It's not the heat, it's the humidity..." hikers complain.)

A hike through Zuma Canyon's rugged middle section requires sturdy shoes. Allow for at least two hours—and maybe three—to cover the canyon's two trail-less miles. And during winter and spring, plan to get wet.

Follow the wide path into the oak- and sycamore-dotted mouth of the canyon. The trail soon splits: the quickest way into Zuma Canyon is on the path straight ahead; however, for a bird's eye view of the canyon, go left and soon you'll arrive at a second trail junction.

Signed Ridge Access Trail continues straight uphill (connecting to Zuma Ridge Trail; it will be part of your return route if you choose the strenuous option of this hike). Join signed Zuma Loop Trail and begin ascending, soon arriving at yet another junction, this time with Rim Trail. Continue on the loop trail.

After descending through a sycamore-filled ravine, the loop trail brings you back to the canyon floor, where you turn left, up the canyon. The trail crosses the creek, passes a stand of eucalyptus and dead ends. You can return to the trailhead by retracing your steps back down the canyon floor and following Zuma Canyon Trail through the lush creekside vegetation.

Hikers continuing through Zuma Canyon will begin boulder-hopping up-canyon. The canyon walls soon close in on you. Way up ahead, you'll see towering Saddle Rock, a Santa Monica Mountains landmark.

When you see the power lines (very high) overhead, it means you have but a half-mile of travel to reach the dirt road that will take you out of Zuma Canyon. Turn left on the dirt road and begin a winding and somewhat steep ascent of the canyon's west wall.

High atop the canyon wall, you'll intersect Zuma Ridge Trail (another dirt road) and turn left. Your shadeless descent will take you past numerous junctions with lesser roads servicing the electrical transmission towers, but you will ignore them and continue on the main road.

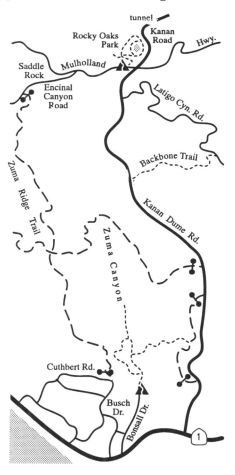

In truth, Zuma Ridge Trail offers better views of Triunfo Canyon on your right than Zuma Canyon on your left. Ahead of you, at your feet, lies Zuma Beach and the so-called Malibu Riviera.

Zuma Ridge Trail ends at a big-enough-to-stop-a-loco-motive steel gate at the end of Busch Drive. Follow the dirt road below some water tanks, then pass through a fence and join Canyon Access Trail for the short descent to the floor of Zuma Canyon. Turn right on Zuma Canyon Trail and return to the trailhead.

Rocky Oaks Park
Rocky Oaks Trail

Highlights: *Rocky Oaks packs a lot of park into a little area: an oak woodland, a grassland, brushy hills, a pond, and near-perfect picnic ground. A little loop trail links the sights.*

Distance: 1 mile round trip

Directions: From the Ventura Freeway (101) in Agoura, exit on Kanan Road and drive south. Turn right (west) onto Mulholland Drive, then right into the park.

UNTIL THE LATE 1970S, ROCKY OAKS PARK WAS A working cattle ranch. The grassland (pasture) and pond (for cattle) are remnants of that era.

Rocky Oaks, acquired by the National Park Service in 1981, is one of those little places perfect for a picnic or a little leg-stretcher of a walk.

From the parking area, a signed path leads to the oak-shaded picnic area; another path heads for directly for the pond. Rainfall determines the depth—indeed, the existence of—the pond. These two paths intersect, and ascend a brushy hillside to an overlook, which offers views of the park and surrounding mountains.

Charmlee by the Sea
Ocean Vista Trail

Highlights: *Charmlee, a county park perched in the Santa Monica Mountains above Malibu, often has outstanding spring wilflower displays. Most of the park is a large open meadow; the flower display, given timely rainfall, can be quite good. Lupine, paintbrush, larkspur, mariposa lily, penstemon and California peony bust out all over.*

Distance: 3-mile loop through Charmlee Natural Area County Park

Directions: From Pacific Coast Highway, about 12 miles upcoast from the community of Malibu, head into the mountains on Encinal Canyon Road 4 1/2 miles to Charmlee Natural Area County Park.

B EFORE YOU HIT THE TRAIL, STOP AT CHARMLEE'S small nature center and inquire about what's blooming where. Also pick up a copy of a brochure that interprets the park's Fire Ecology Trail. This nature trail interprets the important role of fire in Southern California's chaparral communities.

In addition to fine flora, good views are another reason to

"Caterpillar phacelia" Charmlee is a great wildflower-watching spot.

visit Charmlee. The Santa Monica Mountains spread east to west, with the Simi Hills and Santa Susana Mountains rising to the north. Down-coast you can see Zuma Beach and Point Dume and up-coast Sequit Point in Leo Carrillo State Park. Offshore, Catalina Island and two of the Channel Islands—Anacapa and Santa Cruz—can sometimes be seen.

Beginning in the early 1800s this Malibu meadowland was part of Rancho Topanga-Malibu-Sequit and was used to pasture cattle. For a century-and-a-half, various ranchers held the property. The last of these private landholders—Charmain and Leonard Swartz—combined their first names to concot the euphonious Charmlee. Los Angeles County acquired the Charmlee property in the late 1960s and opened the 460-acre park in 1981.

For the walker, Charmlee is one of the few parks, perhaps even the only park, that actually seems to have a surplus of trails. Quite a few paths and old ranch roads wind through the park, which is shaped like a big grassy bowl.

Because the park is mostly one big meadow fringed with oak trees, it's easy to see where you're going and improvise your own circle tour of Charmlee. Bring a kite and a picnic to this undiscovered park and take it easy.

Saunter through the park's picnic area on a dirt road, which travels under the shade of coast live oaks. The trail crests a low rise, offers a couple of side trails to the left to explore, and soon arrives at a more distinct junction with a fire road leading downhill along the eastern edge of the meadow. This is a good route to take because it leads to fine ocean views.

Follow the road as it skirts the eastern edge of the meadow and heads south. Several ocean overlooks are encountered but the official Ocean Overlook is a rocky outcropping positioned on the far southern edge of the park. Contemplate the coast, then head west to the old ranch reservoir. A few hundred yards away is an oak grove, one of the park's many picturesque picnic spots.

You may follow any of several trails back to the trailhead or join Fire Ecology Trail for a close-up look at how Southern California's Mediterranean flora rises from the ashes.

Nicholas Flat
Nicholas Flat Trail

Highlights: *Leo Carrillo State Beach has always been a pleasant place to catch a wave or some rays. Now, after the state added a large chunk of Santa Monica Mountains parkland to the state beach, Leo Carrillo is a pleasing place to take a hike.*

Distance: Leo Carrillo State Beach to Nicholas Flat is 7 miles round trip with 1,600-foot elevation gain.

Directions: From the west end of the Santa Monica Freeway in Santa Monica, head up-coast on Pacific Coast Highway about 25 miles to Leo Carrillo State Beach. (Free parking along Coast Highway, and fee parking in the park's day use area.) Signed Nicholas Flat trailhead is located a short distance past the park entry kiosk, opposite the day use parking area.

NICHOLAS FLAT TRAIL DEPARTS FROM PACIFIC COAST Highway and climbs inland up steep, scrub-covered slopes to a wide meadow and a small pond. From its high points, the trail offers good views of the Malibu coast.

Nicholas Flat Trail can also be savored for one more reason: In Southern California, very few trails connect the mountains with the sea. About eighty-five percent of all Californians live within 30 miles of the coast; in the Southland, most of the extensive coastal trail system that existed a hundred years ago has been covered with pavement or suburbs. Nowadays, to find a lot of trails that lead from Coast Highway into the mountains, you'd have to travel to the Big Sur region or the parklands north of San Francisco.

Get an early start on the Nicholas Flat Trail. Until you arrive at oak-dotted Nicholas Flat itself, there's not much shade en route. The trail crosses slopes that are quite colorful.

If the state park hasn't mowed its "lawn" lately, the first fifty yards of Nicholas Flat Trail will be a bit indistinct. Immediately after its tentative beginning, the trail junctions. The right branch circles the hill, climbs above Willow Creek, and after a mile, rejoins the main Nicholas Flat Trail. Enjoy this interesting option on your return from Nicholas Flat.

Take the left branch, which immediately begins a moderate to steep ascent of the grassy slopes above the park campground. The trail switchbacks through a coastal scrub community up to a saddle on the ridgeline. Here you'll meet the alternate branch of Nicholas Flat Trail. From the saddle, a short side trail leads south to a hilltop, where there's a fine coastal view. From the viewpoint, you can see Point Dume and the Malibu coastline. During the winter, it's a good place to bring your binoculars and scout the Pacific horizon for migrating whales.

The pond at Nicholas Flat.

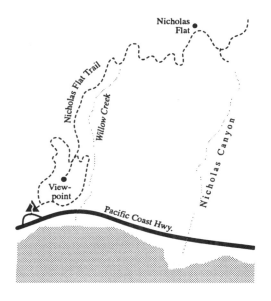

Following the ridgeline, Nicholas Flat Trail climbs inland over chaparral-covered slopes. Keep glancing over your right shoulder at the increasingly grand coastal views, and over your left at the open slopes browsed by the park's nimble deer.

After a good deal of climbing, the trail levels atop the ridgeline and you get your first glimpse of grassy, inviting Nicholas Flat. The trail descends past a line of fire-blackened, but unbowed, old oaks and joins an old ranch road that skirts the Nicholas Flat meadows. Picnickers may unpack lunch beneath the shady oaks or out in the sunny meadow. The trail angles southeast across the meadow to a small pond. The man-made pond, used by cattle during the region's ranching days, is backed by some handsome boulders.

Return the way you came until you reach the junction located 3/4 mile from the trailhead. Bear left at the fork and enjoy this alternate trail as it descends into the canyon cut by Willow Creek, contours around an ocean-facing slope, and returns you to the trailhead.

Circle X Ranch
Mishe Mokwa Trail

Highlights: *Sandstone Peak, highest peak in the Santa Monica Mountains, is one of the highlights of a visit to Circle X Ranch, a park located on the border of Los Angeles and Ventura counties. The park has more than 30 miles of trail and a much-needed public campground.*

Distance: 5-mile circle tour of Circle X Ranch with 1,100-foot elevation gain.

Directions: Drive up-coast on Pacific Coast Highway past the outer reaches of Malibu, a mile past the Los Angeles County line. Turn inland on Yerba Buena Road and proceed five miles to Circle X Ranch. You'll pass the park's tiny headquarters building and continue one more mile to the signed trailhead on your left. There's plenty of parking.

THE STATE COASTAL CONSERVANCY AWARDED FUNDS to the Santa Monica Mountains Conservancy to purchase the 1,655-acre Circle X Ranch from the Boy Scouts of America. The National Park Service now administers the park.

Half a century ago, the land belonged to a number of gentlemen ranchers, including movie actor Donald Crisp, who starred in *How Green Was My Valley.*

Members of the Exchange Club purchased the nucleus of the park in 1949 for $25,000 and gave it to the Boy Scouts. The emblem for the Exchange Club was a circled X—hence the name of the ranch.

About two decades ago, the Scouts, in an attempt to honor Circle X benefactor Herbert Allen, petitioned the United States Department of the Interior to rename Sandstone Peak. The request for "Mount Allen" was denied because of a long-standing policy that prohibited naming geographical features after living persons. Nevertheless, the Scouts held an "unofficial" dedication ceremony in 1969 to honor their leader.

Sandstone Peak—or Mount Allen, if you prefer—offers outstanding views from its 3,111-foot summit. If the five-mile up-and-back hike to the peak isn't sufficiently taxing, park rangers can suggest some terrific extensions.

From the signed trailhead, walk up the fire road. A short quarter-mile of travel brings you to a signed junction with Mishe Mokwa Trail. Leave the fire road here and join the trail, which climbs and contours over the brushy slopes of Boney Mountain. Late spring blooms include black sage, golden yarrow and wooly blue curls. Look for the orange-red, waxy petals of the rare lance-leaved dudleya.

Breaks in the brush offer good views to the right of historic Triunfo Pass, which was used by the Chumash to travel from inland to coastal areas. The "drive-in movie screen" you see atop Triunfo Peak is really an old microwave relay station.

Mishe Mokwa Trail levels for a time and tunnels beneath the boughs of handsome red shanks. Growing beneath the drought-resistant chaparral plants found along the trail are some ferns. The opportunistic ferns take advantage of the shade offered by the chaparral and tap what is for the Santa Monica Mountains a relatively munificent water table located just below the surface. It's unlikely that the hiker will often find yuccas and ferns grow-ing in close proximity on the same slope.

The trail descends into Carlisle Canyon. Across the canyon are some striking red volcanic formations, among them well-named Balanced Rock. The path, shaded by oak, and laurel, drops into the canyon at another aptly named rock formation—Split Rock.

Split Rock is the locale of a trail camp, shaded by oak and sycamore. An all-year creek and a spring add to the camp's charm. It's a fine place for a picnic.

Hikers have had a long tradition of walking through the split in Split Rock.

From Split Rock bear right past an old outhouse—"the historic four-holer" as it is known—and begin your ascent out of Carlisle Canyon on an old ranch road. From the road's high point, you'll look straight ahead up at a pyramid-like volcanic rock formation the Boy Scouts call Egyptian Rock. To the northwest is Point Mugu State Park. You are walking on the Backbone Trail, which when completed will stretch 65 miles from Will Rogers State Historic Park to Point Mugu State Park.

The fire road turns south and you'll pass a trail camp located amid some cottonwoods. Past the camp, the fire road angles east. Look sharply to the right for a short, unsigned trail that leads to Inspiration Point. Mount Baldy and Catalina Island are among the inspiring sights pointed out by a geographical locater monument.

Continue east on the fire road and you'll soon pass the signed intersection with Boney Peak Trail. This trail descends precipitously to park headquarters. If for some reason you're in a hurry to get down, this bone-jarring route is for you.

Continue ascending on the fire road. After a few switchbacks look for a steep trail on the right. Follow this trail to the top of Sandstone Peak. "Sandstone" is certainly a misnomer; the peak is one of the largest masses of volcanic rock in the Santa Monica Mountains. Sign the summit register and enjoy the

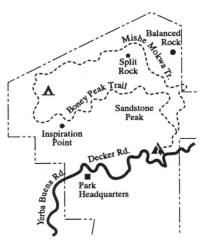

commanding, clear-day views: the Topatopa Mountains where condors once roosted, the Oxnard Plain, the Channel Islands, and the wide blue Pacific.

After you've enjoyed the view, you'll descend a bit more than a mile on the fire road back to the trailhead.

Where Monarchs Reign: Sycamore Canyon

Sycamore Canyon Trail

Highlights: *During October and November, Sycamore Canyon offers the twin delights of falling autumn leaves and fluttering butterflies. A trail follows the canyon on a gentle northern traverse across Point Mugu State Park, the largest preserved area in the Santa Monica Mountains.*

Distance: Big Sycamore Canyon to Deer Camp Junction is 6 1/2 miles round trip with a 200-foot gain; Return via Overlook Trail is 10 miles round trip with 700-foot gain.

Directions: Drive up-coast on Highway 1, 32 miles from Santa Monica, to Big Sycamore Canyon Campground in Point Mugu State Park. Outside the campground entrance is an area where you may park. Walk past the campground entrance through the campground to a locked gate. The trail begins on the other side of the gate.

E VERY FALL, MILLIONS OF MONARCH BUTTERFLIES migrate south to the forests of Mexico's Transvolcanic Range and to the damp coastal woodlands of Central and Southern California. The monarch's awe-inspiring migration and formation of what entomologists call over-wintering colonies are two of nature's most colorful autumn events.

All monarch butterflies west of the Rockies head for California in the fall; one of the best places in Southern California to observe the arriving monarchs is Big Sycamore Canyon in

Point Mugu State Park.

The monarch's evolutionary success lies not only in its unique ability to migrate to warmer climes, but in its mastery of chemical warfare. The butterfly feeds on milkweed—the favored poison of assasins during the Roman Empire. This milkweed diet makes the monarch toxic to birds; after munching a monarch or two and becoming sick, they learn to leave the butterflies alone.

The butterflies advertise their poisonous nature with their conspicuous coloring. They have brownish-red wings with black veins. The outer edge of the wings are dark brown with white and yellow spots. While one might assume the monarch's startling coloration would make them easy prey for predators, just the opposite is true; bright colors in nature are often a warning that a creature is toxic or distasteful.

Sycamore Canyon Trail takes you through a peaceful wooded canyon, where a multitude of monarchs dwell, and past some magnificent sycamores. The sycamores that shade the canyon bearing their name are incomparable. The lower branches, stout and crooked, are a delight for tree-climbers. Hawks and owls roost in the upper branches.

Take the trail up-canyon, following the creek. Winter rains cause the creek to rise, and sometimes keeping your feet dry while crossing is difficult. Underground water keeps much of the creekside vegetation green year around—so this is fine hike in any season.

One-half mile from the campground you'll spot Overlook Trail, which switchbacks to the west up a ridge and then heads north toward the native tall grass prairie in La Jolla

304

Valley. Make note of this trail, an optional return route.

A second half-mile of nearly level canyon walking brings you to another major hiking trail that branches right—the Serrano Canyon Trail.

Another easy mile of walking beneath the sycamores brings you to a picnic table shaded by a grove of large oak trees. The oaks might be a good turnaround spot for a family with small children. The total round trip distance would be a little over 4 miles.

Continuing up the canyon you'll pass beneath more of the giant sycamores and soon arrive at Wood Canyon Junction, the hub for six trails that lead to all corners of the park. Bear left on signed Wood Canyon Trail and in a short while you'll reach Deer Camp Junction. Drinking water and picnic tables suggest a lunch stop. Oak trees predominate over the sycamores along Wood Canyon Creek; however, the romantic prefer the sycamores, some of which have large clumps of mistletoe in the upper branches.

You can call it a day here and return the way you came. As you hike down the canyon back to the campground, the large and cranky bluejay population will scold you, but don't let them stop you from enjoying one of California's finest sycamore savannas.

To return via Overlook Trail: Continue past the junction with Wood Canyon Trail and Deer Camp Junction on Wood Canyon Trail, which becomes Pumphouse Road. You'll climb over the divide between Sycamore Canyon and La Jolla Valley. Upon reaching a junction, you'll head south on the Overlook Trail, staying on the La Jolla Canyon side of the ridge. True to its name, Overlook Trail offers good views of grassy mountainsides, Boney Peak and Big Sycamore Canyon.

You'll pass an intersection with Scenic Trail, then descend from the ridge back to the floor of Big Sycamore Canyon. Bear right and follow the fire road 1/2 mile back to the trailhead.

THE SYCAMORES, SYCAMORE GROVE.
LOS ANGELES, CAL.

City Walks

For the walker who prefers

sidewalks to footpaths

or who wants urban without

going out on the

urban edge, the city has

much to offer.

A BEGINNING DOZEN CITY WALKS MIGHT INCLUDE such streets as Broadway downtown, Melrose Avenue, Fairfax Avenue, Westwood Boulevard, Montana Avenue and Main Street in Santa Monica. For a walk through a graceful past, try the Civic Center in Pasadena; for a walk on the zany side, head for the Venice Beach boardwalk. Add ethnic explorations of El Pueblo de Los Angeles Historic Park, Koreatown and Little Tokyo. And don't forget that tourist must-see/ once-in-a-native's-lifetime visit to Hollywood's Walk of Fame, and a stroll over the sidewalk's stars.

One of the author's favorite city walks is Sunset Boulevard to the Sea; that's right, 26 miles from downtown to ocean's edge in Pacific Palisades. This marathon (literally) walk is a feast for the senses, a barrage of images and cultures from Echo Park to Hollywood to Westwood to Will Rogers Beach.

Guided walks help you learn more about the history, diverse cultures, art and architecture of particular sections of the metropolis. If you'd rather go it alone, some communities offer maps and brochures to encourage on-foot visitation.

Guided Walks

The Los Angles Conservancy not only preserves landmark buildings, it interprets their cultural significance with a series of guided walking tours.

Conservancy tours include: Art Deco, Biltmore Hotel, Broadway Theaters, Bullocks Wilshire Building, Little Tokyo, Marble Masterpieces, Pershing Square Landmarks, Seventh Street, Spring Streeet, Terra Cotta and Union Station.

Most tours begin at 10 a.m. and last about two hours. Tours are free to Conservancy members, and at modest cost for the general public. For recorded tour information, call 213-623-TOUR. For reservations call 213-623-CITY.

Hollywood, particularly the glamour of old Hollywood, is hard to find on your own, which is why two walking tours offered by the nonprofit Hollywood Heritage organization are a good way to go. A Hollywood Boulevard walk departs from the famed Capitol Records building and includes stops at Grauman's (now Mann's) Theater.

Self-Guided Walks

Some Los Angeles-area communities welcome visitors afoot and encourage self-guided walking tours with friendly advice, maps and interpretive pamphlets.

An excellent walking tour of downtown is outlined in the American Automobile Association's *California/Nevada TourBook.*

A Guide to Beverly Hills, published by the Beverly Hills Visitors Bureau includes a superb self-guided walking tour of the city's 20-block "Golden Triangle." Walkers get a glimpse into the city's rich history and diverse architecture. Walkers stroll past the world-famous shops and exclusive art galleries of Rodeo Drive, as well as through the lovely Beverly Gardens.

The walk begins and ends at the Beverly Hills Visitors Bureau, 239 S. Beverly Drive. (213) 271-8174

Glendale: The Urban Hikeway, a brochure offered by the city of Glendale, details three walks. The Financial/Fremont Park Route (3 miles) guides you through residential strets, then into the heart of downtown. The two-mile long Brand Shopping Route explores Brand Boulevard and the Glendale Galleria. The Historic/Civic Route (2 1/2 miles) leads past many historical buildings and today's Civic Center. Call: (818) 548-2140.

Ten Tours of Pasadena offers the walker an up-close look at a terrific concentration and diversity of landmark buildings and special neighborhoods. Experience the Craftsman Bohemia era of the lower Arroyo Seco, the Victorians along Orange Grove Avenue, as well as some of the greatest works by Greene and Greene. Thanks to the tour brochure's good maps, the walks (1-2 miles each) can be combined for a great all-day adventure. For more information and a brochure, contact the Urban Conservation League at City Hall: (818) 577-4206

An Historic Walking Tour of Downtown Long Beach points out the remaining historic buildings along Pine Avenue and Ocean Boulevard. View the Mediterranean Revival Ocean Center Building, the Spanish Revival Breakers Hotel, the Art Deco Bradley Building and more.

Call the Long Beach Area Convention and Visitors Council: (310) 436-3645.

The Walker's
Index

Celebrating the Scenic, the Sublime and the Ridiculous

Points of Interest Visited by

Walk Los Angeles: Adventures on the Urban Edge

Best Observation Point for Watching Migrating California Gray Whales:
Pt. Dume above Zuma Beach

Highest Peak Within Los Angeles City Limits:
Mt. Lukens (5,074 feet)

Largest State Park Within the City Limits of Any American City:
Topanga State Park (9,000 acres), within L.A. city limits

The Rewards of Public Office (Los Angeles County Supervisors With Parks Renamed for Them):
Otterbein County Park now (Pete) Schabarum Regional County Park; Puddingstone Reservoir now Frank G. Bonelli Regional County Park; Baldwin Hills State Recreation Area now Kenneth Hahn State Recreation Area

Location of L.A.'s First TV Transmitter:
Mt. Lee, better known as the location of the Hollywood sign

Best Historical Walk:
Mt. Lowe Railway Trail, San Gabriel Mountains

Most Inappropriate Place Name:
Sandstone Peak (it's granite) in the Santa Monica Mountains

Second-most Inappropriate Place Name:
Crystal Lake (it's usually green with algae)

First National Forest Set Aside in California:
The San Gabriel Timberland Reserve (now Angeles National Forest), established in 1892

Worst Los Angeles Wildfire in Terms of Loss of Life: 36 workmen perished in a 1933 brushfire in the Mineral Wells area of Griffith Park

Walkers At Fault: Best view of Santa Susana Fault: O'Melveny Park; Best View of Whittier Fault: Schabarum County Park; Best View of Newport-Inglewood Fault: Signal Hill

World's Largest Collection of Native Ceanothus (California Lilac): Rancho Santa Ana Botanic Garden, Claremont

Names shortened from their 18th-Century usage: Mount San Antonio: Old Baldy. De Valle Santa Catalina de Bonia de los Encinos: The Valley. Pueblo de la Reina de Los Angeles: L.A.

First Park in America Lost to Freeway Construction: Arroyo Seco Park to Pasadena Freeway, 1941
First Park in America Made Possible By Freeway Construction: El Dorado Park, Long Beach by San Gabriel River Freeway, mid-1960s

Best Sunset-Viewing: Mt. Hollywood in Griffith Park; Sunset Peak in San Gabriel Mountains

Most Visited National Forest in the United States: Angeles

Only City in U.S. Bisected by a Mountain Range: Los Angeles, by the Santa Monica Mountains

Largest Los Angeles City Park: Griffith, 4,100 acres (five times the size of New York's Central Park) Second largest: O'Melveny, 714 acres

Best Fishing: West Fork, San Gabriel River

We'll Be Dead Before It's Done Award: To the Santa Monica Mountains' Backbone Trail; after more than 25 years, only two-thirds of this 65-mile-long trail has been completed

Best Place to Observe Migrating Monarch Butterflies: Big Sycamore Canyon, Pt. Mugu State Park

Most Visited Park:
Griffith with approximately 10 million visitors per year
Least Visited Park:
Cold Creek Canyon Preserve with approximately 1,000 visitors per year

Republican Strongholds:
(President Ronald) Reagan Ranch, (Senator Frank) Flint Peak, (Governor) George Deukmejian Wilderness Park

Spanish or English, but not both, please:
Montecito Hills (Little Hills Hills); Rio Hondo River (Deep River River); Arroyo Seco Canyon (Dry Canyon Canyon)

Average Number of Days Pollution Exceeds the Federal Standard for Air Quality:
Verdugo Mountains, 40; Puente Hills, 37; Arroyo Seco, 80; Malibu Beach, 0

Best Eats Along the Trail:
Saddle Peak Lodge, off Saddle Peak Trail in Santa Monica Mountains (But grubby hikers beware—there's a dress code)

Parks Honoring Movie Cowboys:
William S. Hart County Park in Newhall, (Ronald) Reagan Ranch—part of Malibu Creek State Park—in Santa Monica Mountains, Wilacre (Will Acres) Park in Hollywood Hills, Will Rogers State Historic Park in Santa Monica Mountains, Leo Carrillo State Park in Santa Monica Mountains

Best Waterfall:
San Antonio Falls, a three-tiered, 60-foot cascade tumbling from the shoulder of Mt. Baldy

They Must Know We're Coming Award: Group award to the many national forest, state park, city and county park ranger stations and visitor information centers that are closed on the weekends—the time when ninety-five percent of us go for a walk.

Information Sources

Angeles National Forest
(headquarters)
701 N. Santa Anita Ave
Arcadia, CA 91006
(818) 574-5200

Arroyo Seco Ranger District:
Oak Grove Park
Flintridge, CA 91011
(818) 790-1151

Crystal Lake Visitor Center
(818) 910-1149
Mt Baldy District
(818) 335-1251

San Gabriel Canyon Information
Station
(818) 969-1012
Tujunga District
(818) 899-1900

Arroyo Seco Park, LA City
(213) 485-5555

Bonelli Regional Park
120 Via Verde
San Dimas, CA 91773
(714) 599 8411

Brand Park
1601 W. Mountain St
Glendale
(818) 548-2000

Cabrillo Marine Museum,
San Pedro
(310) 548-7562

Charmlee Natural Area LADPR
2577 S Encinal Canyon Road
Malibu
(213) 457-7247

Chatsworth Park North, LA City
22300 Chatsworth Street
Chatsworth
(818) 341-6595

Cheeseboro Canyon, NPS
Cheseboro Road
Agoura
(818) 597-9192

Circle X Ranch, NPS
2896 Yerba Buena Road
Malibu
(818 597-9192

Cold Creek Canyon Preserve, MRT
Stunt Road between Schueren and
Mulholland
Calabasas
(213) 456-5627

Descanso Gardens
1418 Descanso Drive
La Canada, CA 91011
(818) 952-4400

Devil Canyon, SMMC
N of 118 Fwy at Topanga Cyn Blvd
Chatsworth
1-800-533-PARK (7275)

Eaton Canyon Nature Center
1750 N. Altadena Drive
Pasadena, CA 91107
(818) 398-5420

El Dorado Park Nature Center
7550 E. Spring Street
Long Beach, CA 90815
(213) 421-9431 x 3415

Elysian Park, LA City
929 Academy Road
Los Angeles
(213) 485-5555

Franklin Canyon Ranch, NPS
Beverly Drive to Franklyn
Canyon Drive
Beverly Hills
(818) 597-9192

Fryman Canyon Park, SMMC
Mullholland Drive at Allenwood Road
Studio City
1-800-533-PARK (7275)

George Deukmejian Wilderness Area
5142 Dunsmore Ave
La Cresecenta
(818) 548-2000

Griffith Park, LA CITY
4730 Crystal Springs Dr
Los Angeles CA 90027
(213) 665-5188

Kenneth Hahn State Recreation
Area (LA County)
4100 S La Cienaga Blvd.
Los Angeles, CA 90056
(213) 291-0199 (park)
(213 586-6543 (district office and
information)

Los Angeles State and County
Arboretum,
301 North Baldwin Avenue
Arcadia, CA 91006
(818) 821-3222

Malibu Creek State Park, CDPR
Las Virgines Road S. of
Mullholland Hwy.
Calabasas
(818) 706-1310

Malibu Lagoon State Beach, CDPR
23200 Pacific Coast Highway
Malibu
(213) 456-8432

Marshall Canyon Regional Park
(714) 599-8411

Monrovia Canyon Park
(818) 359-9446

Mountain Parks Information Number
1-800-533-PARK

O'Melveny Park, LA City
17300 Sesnon Blvd
Granada Hills
(818) 368-5019

Paramount Ranch, NPS
2813 Cornell Road
Agoura
(818) 597-9192

Peter Strauss Ranch (Lake Enchanto)
NPS
30000 Mulholland Hwy.
Agoura
(818) 597-9192

Placerita Canyon County Park
Placerita Nature Center
19152 Placerita Canyon Road
Newhall, CA 91321
(805) 259-7721

Point Mugu State Park CDPR
9000 West Pacific Coast Highway
(818) 706-1310/(805) 987-3303

Porter Ranch LA City
W. end of Rinaldi St. at Tampa Blvd.,
Northridge
(818) 989-8189

Rancho Santa Ana Botanic Garden
1500 North College Avenue
Claremont, CA 91711
(714) 625-8767

Rocky Oaks NPS
Mulholland hwy, west of Kanan Road
Agoura
(818) 597-9192

Runyan Canyon Park, LA City
Franklin Avenue
Los Angeles
(213) 485-5572

San Dimas Canyon County Park
1628 North Sycamore Canyon Road
San Dimas, CA 91773
(714) 599-7512

Santa Monica Mountains National
Recreation Area
30401 Agoura Road, Suite 100
Agoura CA 91301
(818) 597-9192

Schabarum County Park
17250 East Colima Road
Rowland Heights, CA 91748
(818) 854-5560

Serrania Park, LA City
20865 Wells Drive
Woodland Hills
(818) 992-0980

South Coast Botanic Garden
26300 Crenshaw Boulevard
Palos Verdes Peninsula, CA 90274
(310) 544-6815

Topanga State Park CDPR
20829 Entrada Road
Topanga, CA 90290
(213) 455-2465

Theodore Payne Foundation
10459 Tuxford
Sun Valley, CA 91352
(818) 768-1802

Wilacre Park SMMC
3431 Fryman Road at Laurel
Canyon Blvd.
Studio City
1-800-533-PARK
Rangers Office: (818) 506-8788

William S. Hart Park
24151 North San Fernando Road
Newhall CA 91321
(805) 259 0855

Will Rogers State Historic Park CDPR
14253 Sunset Blvd
Pacific Palisades, CA 90272
(213) 454-8212

NPS=National Park Service
LA City=Los Angeles City Recreation
and Parks Department
SMMC=Santa Monica Mountains
Conservancy
CDPR=California Department of Parks
and Recreation
MRT=Mountains Restoration Trust
Note: Addresses with zip codes can
be used for correspondence.

Index

AWARD-WINNING NATURE WRITER and long time *Los Angeles Times* Hiking columnist JOHN MCKINNEY is the author of a half dozen nature guides for Olympus Press, including *Day Hiker's Guide to Southern California.*